Real Grammar

Understand English. Clear and simple.

Carl Eldridge

National Library of Australia Cataloguing-in-Publication entry:

Creator: Eldridge, Carl, author.

Title: Real Grammar / Carl Eldridge.

ISBN: 9781925497670 (paperback)
                  9781925497724 (eBook)

Subjects: English language--Grammar--Study and teaching.

Dewey Number: 425

Published by Carl Eldridge and InHouse Publishing

www.realgrammar.com

www.inhousepublishing.com.au

Acknowledgements

I'd like to thank my wife, Satoko. Your love and support while writing this book has been amazing.

I am very grateful for the support of my family. Thank you Pam Eldridge, Ken Eldridge, Marie Petersen and Sue O'Connor.

A special thank you to Rodney Huddleston whose deep understanding of the workings of the English language has been an incredible insight.

Thank you to Ocean Reeve, Caroline Mackay and the team at InHouse Publishing.

Thank you to others who have given feedback during the various stages of writing this book, especially: Shane Marsan, Midori Marsan, George Gillet, Yuuki Nishihara, Joe Guthrie and Michael Carey.

Contents

iv

introduction

If you are the kind of person who needs to understand and needs to know *why*, this book is for you!

We understand grammar by looking at the core concepts of the language. We look at how the different parts of a sentence are combined to say what we want to say. *Real Grammar* describes the core meaning of each part simply, and this simple knowledge can then be used in a variety of situations. I know you don't want long explanations, so these concepts are presented with diagrams, examples and practice activities.

In this book, we break English grammar down into seven sections:
- basic parts of speech: word order, adding time and place, basic verbs, why some verbs end in *s*, how nouns are used (talking about one or more, *a/an*, *the* etc.).
- how we use different verb forms (*eat*, *ate*, *eating*, *eaten*).
- the core meanings of *will/would*, *can/could*, *shall/should*, *may/might* and *must* and why and how they are used in different situations.
- different ways of talking about the future and the past.
- saying what people think and say ("He said..." "She said...").
- adding information: *in*, *on*, *at*, *to*, *for*, *by*, *with* etc., adjectives, adverbs, comparing, other ways of adding information.
- adding information with another subject and verb (and object etc.).

Real Grammar explores the structure of the English language to help us understand it. We look at why we use different parts of speech and how English works from the core out. Understanding these core concepts gives us the freedom to express ourselves with clarity and confidence.

I wish you all the best with your studies,

Carl

P.S. You don't need to know grammar terminology to speak English well. (Most native speakers don't know it!) This book is designed to allow you to study grammar without complex terminology, allowing you to focus your studies on language you will actually use.
Grammar terminology has been included in small print in the top right corner of pages so you can cross-reference with other resources.

how to use this book

This book is designed to be read from start to end. It explains many concepts of English grammar that are all connected. Each section builds upon what has previously been covered.

Students may want to focus on specific areas of grammar. The book has been divided into seven parts which contain related concepts. Students are encouraged to study whole parts that include the specific areas of grammar they want to focus on. This gives them a deep understanding of important core concepts that relate to the specific grammar point they want to learn about. Any specific grammar points that students are having trouble with can be looked up in the index and studied directly along with related concepts.

timelines

The *verb forms*, *options and possibilities* and *future and past* sections are about time. In this book timelines are used to visually tell us what the verbs are referring to.

This is a our basic timeline:

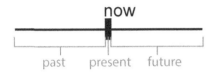

The time we are talking about is framed with a rounded rectangle.

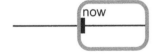

This book describes English as having two tenses, consistent with linguistic theory. The rounded rectangle allows us to see the clear differences between the two English tenses and how they are used.

descriptive grammar

This book provides a descriptive grammar for students studying English. **Descriptive** grammar means that we **describe** the language that English speakers use in order to understand it better. Traditional grammar books take a prescriptive approach and prescribe rules and exceptions for students to memorize and follow.

"Prescriptivists want to tell you how you **ought** to speak and write, while descriptivists want to tell you how people actually **do** speak and write." - Rodney Huddleston and Geoffrey K. Pullum (2002), *The Cambridge Grammar of the English Language*, Cambridge University Press.

Real Grammar explains how people actually **do** use English. We explore concepts to understand **how** and **why** different parts of speech are used. *Real Grammar* is for those who want to learn how people **really** use the English language.

1

Constructing basic sentences
SVO word order, place and time

word order

Different languages arrange their words in different orders. English has a strict word order. This is the order English uses.

Subject	Verb	Object	
I	eat.		I eat.
I	work.		I work.
We	run.		We run.
I	like	chocolate.	I like chocolate.
We	have	breakfast.	We have breakfast.
I	play	soccer.	I play soccer.

Practice

Put these words in the correct order.

Example:
drink coffee I → I drink coffee.

We golf play → _____.
fish I eat → _____.
like cheese I → _____.

English uses Subject-Verb-Object (SVO) word order.
Here are some different word orders used in different languages.

Word order	English equivalent	Proportion of languages	Example languages
SOV	"She him loves"	45%	Latin, Japanese, Afrikaans
SVO	**"She loves him"**	42%	**English**, Mandarin, Russian
VSO	"Loves she him"	9%	Biblical Hebrew, Irish
VOS	"Loves him she"	3%	Malagasy, Baure
OVS	"Him loves she"	1%	Apalai, Hixkarvana
OSV	"Him she loves"	<1%	Warao

source: Wikipedia
Frequency distribution of word order in languages surveyed by Russell S. Tomlin in 1980s.

do

We use *do* in questions and answers. We put *do* first to show it is a question.

do	Subject	Verb	Object		Answer
Do	you	eat?		Do you eat?	Yes, I do.
Do	you	work?		Do you work?	No, I don't
Do	they	run?		Do they run?	Yes, they do.
Do	you	like	swimming?	Do you like swimming?	No, I don't.
Do	they	have	breakfast?	Do they have breakfast?	Yes, they do.
Do	you	play	soccer?	Do you play soccer?	No, I don't.

Practice
Make these sentences questions. Use 'you'. Write answers.

Example:

I drink coffee. (yes) ➜ Do you drink coffee? Yes, I do.

I like seafood. (no) ➜ _____? _____,_____.

I drive. (yes) ➜ _____? _____,_____.

I do karate. (no) ➜ _____? _____,_____.

don't

We make these sentences negative by adding *don't* (do not).

Subject	don't (do not)	Verb	Object	
I	**don't**	eat.		I don't eat.
I	**don't**	work.		I don't work.
We	**don't**	run.		We don't run.
I	**don't**	like	swimming.	I don't like swimming.
We	**don't**	have	breakfast.	We don't have breakfast.
I	**don't**	play	soccer.	I don't play soccer.

Practice
Make these sentences negative.

Example:

I drink coffee. ➜ I don't drink coffee.

I like seafood. ➜ _____.

I drive. ➜ _____.

I do karate. ➜ _____.

adding a place

As humans, vision is our strongest sense. Our brains are wired to visualize *where* things are. When speaking English, we visualize where things are in the English way.

We use *at*, *in* and *on* to say *where* something is or happens.

At a point in space.   **At an event.**

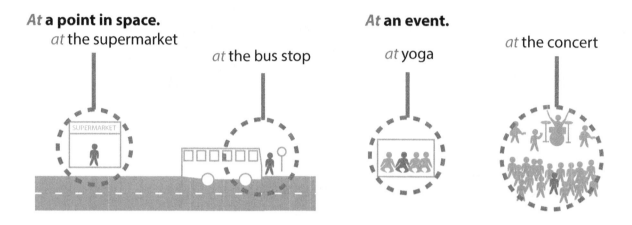

In a boundary: Where the area starts and ends IS important.

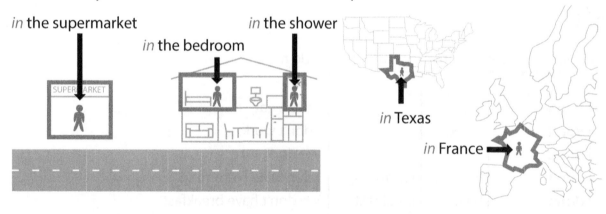

On a surface: Where the area starts and ends IS NOT important.

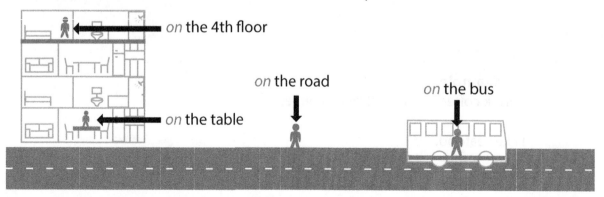

Subject	Verb	Object	Place	
I	work		**at the supermarket**	I work at the supermarket.
I	am		**at the bus stop.**	I'm at the bus stop.
I	am		**at yoga.**	I'm at yoga.
I	am		**at the concert.**	I'm at the concert.
I	am		**in the supermarket**	I'm in the supermarket.
I	play	guitar	**in the bedroom.**	I play guitar in the bedroom.
I	wash	my hair	**in the shower.**	I wash my hair in the shower.
I	live		**in Texas.**	I live in Texas.
They	like	wine	**in France**	They like wine in France.
I	am		**on the 4th floor.**	I'm on the 4th floor.
Dinner	is		**on the table.**	Dinner is on the table.
The bus	is		**on the road.**	The bus is on the road.
I	read	books	**on the bus.**	I read books on the bus.

See how we add a place to these sentences we previously studied. (See page 2.)

Subject	Verb	Object	Place	
I	eat		**at work.**	I eat at work.
I	work		**on a boat.**	I work on a boat.
We	run		**in the park.**	We run in the park.
I	like	swimming	**in the sea.**	I like swimming in the sea.
We	have	breakfast	**at home.**	We have breakfast at home.
I	play	soccer	**at school.**	I play soccer at school.

Practice

Which would you use in the following situations? Complete the sentences using *at* or *in*.

1. Owen and Charlotte plan to meet at the shopping mall. Owen arrives and calls Charlotte.
   Owen: I've just arrived. Where are you?
   Charlotte: I'm __ the supermarket.
2. Owen is at home and decides to call Charlotte.
   Owen: Where are you?
   Charlotte: I'm __ the supermarket.

Practice

Complete the sentences using *in*, *on* and *at*.

1. I live __ Chicago.
2. I live __ an apartment.
3. I live __ the 6th floor.
4. I live __ room 608.
5. I'm __ Mexico.
6. I'm __ the beach.
7. I'm __ the sand.

adding a time

We can't see time, so we visualize *when* the same way as we visualize *where*.

We use *at*, *in* and *on* to say *when* something is or happens.

At a point in time.   **At an event in time.**

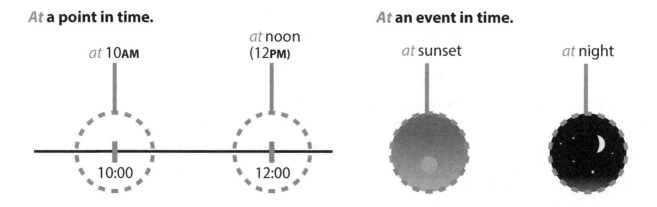

In: When the period of time starts and ends IS important.

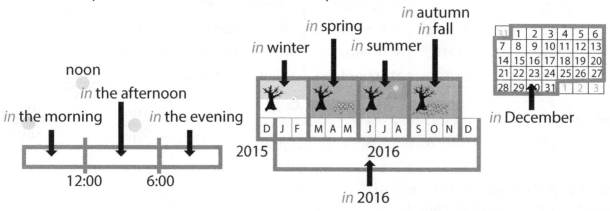

On: When the period of time starts and ends IS NOT important.

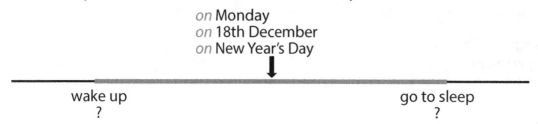

We think of a day as being the time from when we wake up to the time we go to sleep. Exactly when a person wakes up and goes to sleep is not important.

Subject	Verb	Object	Time	
I	start	work	**at 10AM.**	I start work at 10AM.
I	have	lunch	**at noon.**	I have lunch at noon.
I	walk	the dog	**at sunset.**	I walk the dog at sunset.
I	sleep		**at night.**	I sleep at night.
I	have	breakfast	**in the morning.**	I have breakfast in the morning.
I	play	guitar	**in the afternoon.**	I play guitar in the afternoon.
I	wash	my hair	**in the evening.**	I wash my hair in the evening.
I	ski		**in winter.**	I ski in winter.
They	travel		**in spring.**	They travel in spring.
We	swim		**in summer.**	We swim in summer.
We	hike		**in fall.**	We hike in fall.
Christmas	is		**in December.**	Christmas is in December.
I	finish	high school	**in 2025.**	I finish high school in 2025.
I	study	English	**on Monday.**	I study English on Monday.
We	celebrate	the new year	**on December 31st.**	We celebrate the new year on DEC 31.
We	sleep		**on New Year's Day.**	We sleep on New Year's Day.

See how we add a time to these sentences we previously studied. (See page 2.)

Subject	Verb	Object	Time	
I	eat		**at 6PM.**	I eat at 6PM.
I	work		**on Wednesdays.**	I work on Wednesdays.
We	run		**in the morning.**	We run in the morning.
I	like	swimming	**in summer.**	I like swimming in summer.
We	have	breakfast	**at 7:30.**	We have breakfast at 7:30.
I	play	soccer	**on Sundays.**	I play soccer on Sundays.

Practice
Complete the sentences using *in, on* and *at.*

1. I start work ___ 9AM.
2. I finish work early ___ Fridays.
3. I finish ___ 4PM.
4. I have a holiday ___ January.
5. I go back to work ___ January 18th.
6. I play golf ___ Sundays.

To speak English like a native English speaker you need to think like a native English speaker.
Start by visualizing space and time the same way as a native English speaker.
Visualize *where* and *when* with *in, on* and *at.*

adding a place and time

We can add a time and a place if we want. We can put the place first…

Sub.	Verb	Object	Place	Time	
I	eat		**at work**	**at 6PM.**	I eat at work at 6PM.
I	work		**on a boat**	**on Wednesdays.**	I work on a boat on Wednesdays.
We	live		**in Japan**	**in the 21st Century.**	We live in Japan in the 21st Century.
I	like	swimming	**in the sea**	**in summer.**	I like swimming in the sea in summer.
We	have	breakfast	**at home**	**at 7:30.**	We have breakfast at home at 7:30.
I	play	soccer	**at the park**	**on Sundays.**	I play soccer at the park on Sundays.

…or the time first.

Sub.	Verb	Object	Time	Place	
I	eat		**at 6PM**	**at work.**	I eat at 6PM at work.
I	work		**on Wednesdays**	**on a boat.**	I work on Wednesdays on a boat.
We	live		**in the 21st century**	**in Japan.**	We live in the 21st century in Japan.
I	like	swimming	**in summer**	**in the sea.**	I like swimming in summer in the sea.
We	have	breakfast	**at 7:30**	**at home.**	We have breakfast at 7:30 at home.
I	play	soccer	**on Sundays**	**at the park.**	I play soccer on Sundays at the park.

We can add more information about places.

Sub.	Verb	Object	Place	Place	
I	eat		**at the café**	**at work.**	I eat at the café at work.
I	work		**on a boat**	**on the river.**	I work on a boat on the river.
We	live		**in Tokyo**	**in Japan.**	We live in Tokyo in Japan.
I	like	swimming	**in the sea**	**in Hawaii.**	I like swimming in the sea in Hawaii.
We	have	breakfast	**at home**	**on the balcony.**	We have breakfast at home on the balcony.
I	play	soccer	**on the field**	**at the park.**	I play soccer on the field at the park.

We can add more information about time.

S.	Verb	Object	Time	Time	
I	eat		**at 6PM**	**on Sundays.**	I eat at 6PM on Sundays.
I	work		**on Wednesdays**	**in June.**	I work on Wednesdays in June.
We	live		**in the 21st century**	**in the 2010s.**	We live in the 21st century in the 2010s.
I	like	swimming	**at night**	**in summer.**	I like swimming at night in summer.
We	have	breakfast	**at 7**	**in the morning.**	We have breakfast at 7 in the morning.
I	play	soccer	**on Sundays**	**at 6:30.**	I play soccer on Sundays at 6:30.

> Add as much information as you like. Important or more specific information comes first. Additional information comes later. This often depends on the situation.

where and when

We use *where* to ask about **places**.

Where	do	Sub.	Verb	Object	Place
Where	do	you	work?		
		I	work		on a boat
Where	do	they	live?		
		They	live		in Japan.
Where	do	you	like	swimming?	
		I	like	swimming	in the sea.
Where	do	they	have	breakfast?	
		They	have	breakfast	at home
Where	do	you	play	soccer?	
		I	play	soccer	at the park.

Where do you work?
I work **on a boat**.
Where do they live?
They live **in Japan**.
Where do you like swimming?
I like swimming **in the sea**.
Where do they have breakfast?
They have breakfast **at home**.
Where do you play soccer?
I play soccer **at the park**.

We don't need to say the words in gray. They have already been said so we can leave them out.

We use *when* to ask about **times**.

When	do	Sub.	Verb	Object	Place
When	do	you	eat?		
		I	eat		at 6PM.
When	do	you	work?		
		I	work		on Wednesdays.
When	do	you	like	swimming?	
		I	like	swimming	in summer.
When	do	they	have	breakfast?	
		They	have	breakfast	at 7:30.
When	do	you	play	soccer?	
		I	play	soccer	on Sundays.

When do you eat?
I eat **at 6PM**.
When do you work?
I work **on Wednesdays**
When do you like swimming?
I like swimming **in summer**.
When do they have breakfast?
They have breakfast **at 7:30**.
When do you play soccer?
I play soccer **on Sundays**.

We sometimes don't say *at* when we say a time. In this situation it is obvious that it is a time.

Practice

Write questions for the answers.

Example: <u>*When do you play soccer?*</u>
  I play soccer on Sundays.

1. _____
   I swim **at the beach**.
2. _____
   They have dinner **at 7PM**.
3. _____
   I read books **on the bus**.

4. _____
   I live **in Canada**.
5. _____
   I finish work **at 5:30**.
6. _____
   We travel **in spring**.

yesterday, today, tomorrow

Today is the day it is now.
Yesterday was the day before today.
Tomorrow is the day after today.

Sunday	Monday	Tuesday	Wednesday	Thursday	Friday	Saturday	Sunday	Monday
					yesterday	**now** today	tomorrow	

We use *last*, *this* and *next* for years months and weeks.

January	February	March	April	May	June	July	August	September
			last month	**now** this month	next month			

Yesterday, *today*, *tomorrow*, *last*, *this* and *next* describe time in relation to now.
In, *on* and *at* are used when we say what day, month or year we are referring to.

The game is **tomorrow**.
The game is *on* Wednesday.

The final is **next month**.
The final is *in* April.

We use:

yesterday	today	tomorrow
last year	this year	next year
last month	this month	next month
last week	this week	next week

2

Basic verbs

meanings, third person *s*

be

We use *be* (*am*, *is* and *are*) to refer to something we are describing.

Subject	Verb (*be*)	Description	
I	**am**	a woman.	I'm a woman.
I	**am**	a man.	I'm a man.
I	**am**	Italian.	I'm Italian.
I	**am**	Japanese.	I'm Japanese.
I	**am**	hungry.	I'm hungry.
I	**am**	happy.	I'm happy.

We can describe **where** someone or something is.

  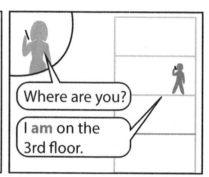

Subject	Verb (*be*)	Place	
I	**am**	at the airport.	I'm at the airport.
I	**am**	in New York.	I'm in New York.
I	**am**	on the 3rd floor.	I'm on the 3rd floor.

We can describe **when** something is.

Subject	Verb (*be*)	Time	
The meeting	**is**	at 10:30.	The meeting is at 10:30.
New Year's day	**is**	in January.	New Year's day is in January.
The lesson	**is**	on Monday.	The lesson is on Monday.

We usually use *I'm* instead of *I am*. It's shorter and easier.

have

We use *have* to refer to a part of something, or something additional.

Subject	Verb (*have*)	Object
I	**have**	a cat
I	**have**	brown hair.
I	**have**	an older brother.
I	**have**	a headache.

I have a cat

I have brown hair.

I have an older brother.

I have a headache.

Compare *be* and *have*.

Practice
Complete the sentences using *am* and *have*. Use the short form of *am* ('m).

Example:
I _'m_ Tom.

1. I _____ Tom.
2. I _____ Scottish.
3. I _____ brown hair.
4. I _____ blue eyes.
5. I _____ a nice smile.
6. I _____ tall.
7. I _____ a police officer.

What am I?

1. I _____ big.
2. I _____ big ears.
3. I _____ heavy.
4. I _____ four legs.
5. I _____ a tail.
6. I _____ gray.
7. I _____ an elephant.

?

be (am, are, is)

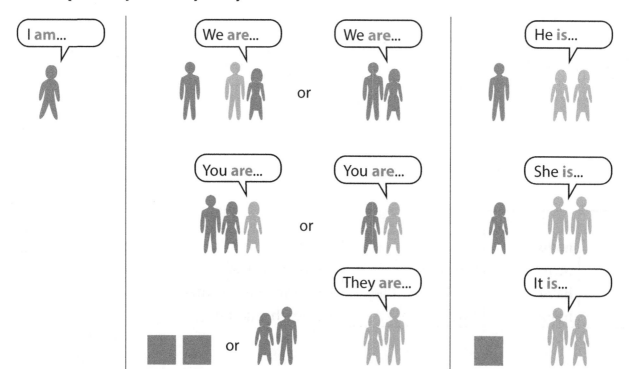

We use *am* to talk about ourselves (I **am**...).
We use *are* to talk about two or more people or things, or the person we are talking to (You **are**...).
We use *is* to talk about one other person or thing (not ourselves or the person we are talking to).
In English we always need to know if we are talking about **one thing** or **more than one thing**.

Subject	Verb (*be*)	Description	
I	**am**	a man.	I'm a man.
You	**are**	a woman.	You're a woman.
We	**are**	Italian.	We're Italian.
They	**are**	Japanese.	They're Japanese.
She	**is**	a doctor.	She's a doctor.
He	**is**	a student.	He's a student.
It	**is**	hot.	It's hot.

Practice
Complete the sentences using *am*, *are* or *is*. Use the short forms ('m, 're and 's).

1. She_____ American.
2. He_____ English.
3. I_____ Korean.
4. It_____ a bird.

5. You_____ Canadian.
6. They_____ bus drivers.
7. We_____ taxi drivers.
8. I_____ happy.

We often add *do* when we make questions. These questions ask about the **verbs**.

Subject	Verb	Object	Place/Time
I	**work.**		
I	**live**		in Japan.
They	**play**	soccer.	

→
→
→

do	Subject	Verb	Object	Place/Time
Do	you	**work?**		
Do	you	**live**		in Japan?
Do	they	**play**	soccer?	

Questions with *be* are not about the verbs. They ask about the **descriptions**, **places** or **times**.

Subject	*be*	Description	Place/Time
I	am	**hungry.**	
We	are		**in Japan.**
The game	is		**on Sunday.**

→
→
→

be	Subject	Description	Place/Time
Are	you	**hungry?**	
Are	we		**in Japan?**
Is	the game		**on Sunday?**

Practice
Complete the questions using *do, am, are* or *is*.

1. _____ she American?
2. _____ you run?
3. _____ you like chicken?
4. _____ you at work?

5. _____ they hungry?
6. _____ they like hamburgers?
7. _____ he young?
8. _____ I awake?

We add *not* after *be* to make negatives. There may be more than one way to shorten it.

Subject	Verb (*be not*)	Description
I	**am not**	a man.
You	**are not**	a woman.
We	**are not**	Italian.
They	**are not**	Japanese.
She	**is not**	a doctor.
He	**is not**	a student.
It	**is not**	hot.

	I'm not a man.
You aren't a woman.	You're not a woman.
We aren't Italian.	We're not Italian.
They aren't Japanese.	They're not Japanese.
She isn't a doctor.	She's not a doctor.
He isn't a student.	He's not a student.
It isn't hot.	It's not hot.

The full words (*am not*, *are not* and *is not*) are often used in writing and for emphasis when speaking. We almost always use the short forms (*'m not*, *aren't/'re not*, *isn't/'s not*).

Practice
Complete the sentences using the short forms *'m not, aren't* or *'re not, isn't* or *'s not*.

1. She_____ American.
2. He_____ English.
3. I_____ Korean.
4. It_____ a bird.

5. You_____ Canadian.
6. They_____ bus drivers.
7. We_____ taxi drivers.
8. I_____ happy.

adding *s* to verbs

We add *s* to verbs when we are talking about ONE other person or thing (*he*, *she* or *it*).

Subject	Verb	Object/Place			Subject	Verb	Object/Place	
I	eat.		→		He	**eats.**		He eats.
You	work.		→		It	**works.**		It works.
We	live	in Europe.	→		She	**lives**	in Europe.	She lives in Europe.
They	like	swimming.	→		He	**likes**	swimming.	He likes swimming.
We	have	breakfast.	→		He	**has**	breakfast.	He has breakfast.
They	play	music.	→		It	**plays**	music.	It plays music.

Have becomes *has*.

We have breakfast. → he **has** breakfast.

We add *es* to verbs that end in *-o*, *-ch*, *-x*, *-sh* and *–ss* to make the extra *s* sound in the word clear.

I do karate. → He **does** karate.
You go to school . → She **goes** to school.
We watch TV. → He **watches** TV.
They fix cars. → She **fixes** cars.
I push buttons. → He **pushes** buttons.
I miss you. → She **misses** you.

Practice

Complete the sentences.

1.　　　　I like fish. → He _____.
2.　We mix cement. → She _____.
3.　　He drinks milk. → We _____.
4.　They play tennis. → She _____.
5.　　You have a car. → I _____.
6.　I have black hair. → He _____.
7.　　We go to work. → She _____.

We use *does* in questions and answers.

does	Subject	Verb	Object/Place
Does	he	eat?	
Does	it	work?	
Does	she	live	in Europe?
Does	he	like	swimming?
Does	she	have	breakfast?
Does	it	play	music?

Does he eat?
Does it work?
Does she live in Europe?
Does he like swimming?
Does she have breakfast?
Does it play music?

Answer
Yes, he does.
No, it doesn't.
Yes, she does.
No, he doesn't
No, she doesn't.
Yes, it does.

We can make these sentences negative by adding *doesn't* (does not).

Subject	doesn't	Verb	Object/Place
He	**doesn't**	eat.	
It	**doesn't**	work.	
She	**doesn't**	live	in Europe.
He	**doesn't**	like	swimming.
She	**doesn't**	have	breakfast.
It	**doesn't**	play	music.

He doesn't eat.
It doesn't work.
She doesn't live in Europe.
He doesn't like swimming.
She doesn't have breakfast.
It doesn't play music.

These sentences have **TWO** verbs. Only the *first* verb gets the *s*. Using *does* instead of *do* (*doesn't* instead of *don't*) provides the essential information. The other verbs stay in the basic form.

Practice

Make these sentences questions.

Example:
I drink coffee. ➔ (She) **Does** she drink coffee?

I like seafood. ➔ (He)_____?
I shower. ➔ (He)_____?
I do karate. ➔ (She)_____?

Make these sentences negative.

Example:
I drink coffee. ➔ He **doesn't** drink coffee.

I like seafood. ➔ She _____.
I shower. ➔ We _____.
I do karate. ➔ He _____.

Complete the sentences with the correct form of the words in brackets.

Example: He __*doesn't like*__ (not like) fish.

1. _____ she _____ (eat) beef?
2. He _____ (eat) beef.
3. We _____ (not play) golf.
4. _____you _____ (play) golf?
5. _____ he _____ (play) golf?
6. _____ you _____ (live) in Brazil?

7. _____ she _____ (live) in Brazil?
8. _____ they _____ (live) in Brazil?
9. She _____ (not smoke).
10. He _____ (not drink).
11. They _____(not live) in Miami.
12. He _____(like) tennis.

who and what

We use *who* to ask about a **person**. We use *what* to ask about a **thing**.

We ask about the **subject**.

wh-	Subject	Verb	Object/Place/Time
Who		lives	in Washington?
	I	live	in Washington.
	I	do.	
What		is	in the bag?
	Clothes	are	in the bag.

We ask about the **object**.

wh-	do	Subject	Verb	Object
Who	**does**	she	help?	
		She	helps	the poor.
What	**do**	you	eat?	
		We	eat	vegetables.

We say what kind of thing we want to know about.

what	(kind of thing)		Subject	Verb	Object
What	**sports**	do	you	play?	
			I	play	soccer.
What	**food**	do	you	like?	
			I	like	chocolate.
What	**time**	is	it?*		
			It	is	4:10.

*When we ask about **now** we say 'What time is it?'
When we ask about another time we use *what time*, *what day*, *what month*, *what year* or *when*.
We say 'What time is the meeting?' or 'When is the meeting?'

Practice

Make questions.

Example: Who *lives in Washington* ?
         I do. (I live in Washington.)

1. What _____?
    I like soccer and tennis.
2. Who _____?
    Victoria does. (Victoria plays tennis on Saturdays.)
3. What _____?
    I like rock, blues and pop music.
4. What _____?
    I like Italian food.
5. Who _____?
    Me! (I want chocolate ice-cream.)
6. What _____?
    I have breakfast at 6:20.
7. What _____?
    I read mysteries.

go

We use *go* to talk about movement from one place to another place. Things move to a destination. The destination can be a place, event, thing or person.

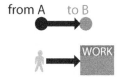

I go **to work** at 6PM.

Subject	Verb (*go*)	Destination	Time	
I	go	**to work**	at 6PM.	I go to work at 6PM.
You	go	**to karate**	on Wednesdays.	You go to karate on Wednesdays.
We	go	**to Japan**	every winter.	We go to Japan every winter.
They	go	**to the sea**	in summer.	They go to the sea in summer.
She	goes	**home**	at 7:30.	She goes home at 7:30.
He	goes	**to the doctor**	once a year.	He goes to the doctor once a year.

We use *to* with destinations we can easily point out or circle.

I go **to work**.   I go **to LA**.   I go **to California**.   I go **to America**.

We don't use *to* with *home* or with other words like *overseas* and *abroad*, as they are not destinations we can clearly define. We can't point to *home*, *overseas* or *abroad* on a map.

Where is home?

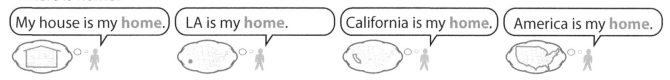

My house is my **home**.   LA is my **home**.   California is my **home**.   America is my **home**.

I go **home** at 7:30.
This could mean: to my house, my city, my state, my country, etc. depending on the situation.

I'm **home**!
This is often said when people arrive home. (the idea: it doesn't matter where it is; it could be a country, house, etc. - a place I feel is home)

A: Where are you?
B: I'm **at home**.
This refers to someones house. We need to make it clear we are talking about a point in space, so we use *at* to express home as a point.

get

We use *get* to talk about changes. *Get* can be used in lots of situations.

NOT have (object) | **have (object)**

get (object)

She **doesn't have** a hat. | She **gets** a hat. | She **has** a hat.

Subject	Verb (*get*)	Object	Place/Time
I	**get**	breakfast	at the café.
You	**get**	milk	from a cow.
He	**gets**	coffee	every morning.
She	**gets**	groceries	at the supermarket.

Keeping things simple is good. *Get* is a simple verb that can be used instead of other verbs, such as: *receive*, *buy*, or *obtain*.

NOT be (description) | **be (description)**

get (description)

It **isn't** hot. | It **gets** hot. | It **is** hot.

Subject	Verb (*get*)	Description	Place/Time
It	**gets**	hot	in summer
You	**get**	older	every year.
She	**gets**	hungry	at lunch time.
He	**gets**	sleepy	in the afternoon.

In this situation, *get* can be used instead of *become*.

NOT be (at a place) | **be (at a place)**

go (to a place) **get (to a place)**

SCHOOL

We **aren't** at school. | We **go** to school. | We **get** to school. | We **are** at school.

Subject	Verb (*get*)	Place	Time
I	**get**	to work	at 8:30.
We	**get**	to school	at 8:50.
She	**gets**	home	at 7PM.
He	**gets**	to bed	at midnight.

In this situation, *get to (place)* can be used instead of *arrive at (place)*.

3

One or more

articles, plural and singular, countable and uncountable nouns

a/an

In English we always need to know if we are talking about one thing or more than one thing. We use *a* and *an* to talk about **one** thing. There are many of these things in the world.

What's that? | It's **a** cat.

What's this? | It's **an** umbrella.

We use *an* before a vowel sound (a, e, i, o, u).

Subject	Verb	Object
I	have	**an uncle.**
She	has	**a bicycle.**
He	has	**an apple.**

I have an uncle.
She has a bicycle.
He has an apple.

Subject	Verb	Description
I	am	**a woman.**
He	is	**a child.**
She	is	**an engineer.**

I'm a woman.
He's a child.
She's an engineer.

Subject	Verb	Object/Place
A man	lives	in that house.
A student	studies.	
A pilot	flies	planes.

A man lives in that house.
A student studies. (What a typical student does.)
A pilot flies planes. (What a typical pilot does.)

It's **a banana**.

It's **a pear**.

It's **an apple**.

It's **an orange**.

Practice

Complete the sentences using *a* or *an*.

1. Is that ____ pear?
2. No, it's ____ apple.
3. We don't have ____ air conditioner.
4. Do you have ____ TV?

5. She's ____ doctor.
6. I'm ____ waiter.
7. He eats ____ egg every day.
8. You're ____ interesting person.

adding *s* to nouns

We add *s* when we are talking about more than one thing.

Most words end in -s, but we sometimes use different words (person/people, woman/women).

Subject	Verb	Object
I	have	**six uncles.**
She	has	**two bicycles.**
We	like	**apples.**

I have six uncles.
She has two bicycles.
We like apples. (Generally, not one specific apple.)

Subject	Verb	Description
We	are	**women.**
You	are	**children.**
They	are	**engineers.**

We are women.
You are children.
They are engineers.

Subject	Verb	Object/Place
Three people	live	in that house.
Students	study.	
Pilots	fly	planes.

Three people live in that house.
Students study. (Generally, what students do.)
Pilots fly planes. (Generally, what pilots do.)

They're **bananas.**

They're **pears.**

They're **apples.**

They're **oranges.**

Practice

Complete the sentences. Use *a* or *an* or add an *s*.

1. I have two _____ (sister).
2. Can I have _____ (hot dog) please.
3. They're _____ (pilot).
4. I play _____ (video game).
5. I eat three _____(banana) every morning.
6. _____ (mechanic) fixes cars.
7. _____ (bus driver) drive buses.
8. A lot of _____ (man) like sport.

23

things we sometimes don't count

There are some things we easily count. We use *a* or *an* or add an *s*.

Here is an apple.
We use *a* or *an* for **one** thing.

Here are two apples.
We add an *s* for **more than one** thing.

However, we can't always count apple. Once it is cut it is hard to imagine how many apples. We simply say it is apple (without *an* or *s*). If we want to count it we can easily count the slices.

Here is some apple.
We don't use *an* or *s*.
(Here are four **slices** of apple.)

There are some things we usually can't count. When we imagine wine there are many things we can imagine. Wine comes in many sizes so we can't usually count it. We say generally what it is.

This is wine.
(a glass of wine)

This is wine.
(a bottle of wine)

This is wine.
(a barrel of wine)

We count glasses, bottles or barrels.

However, in some situations we can count wine.

A beer and **a red wine**, please.

We have **two red wines**: a Merlot and a Shiraz.

We can count it. We know they want **one glass** of red wine because of the situation.

We can count the wines. There are **two kinds** we can choose from.

We count things when we imagine one or more of the thing we are talking about. We don't count things when we imagine parts of something.

I like **bananas**.
I imagine taking whole bananas and eating them. I eat bananas.

These are **bananas**.   This is **a banana**.

I like **watermelon**.
I imagine taking slices of watermelon and eating them. I don't eat whole watermelons.

This is **a watermelon**.   This is **watermelon**.
(a slice of watermelon)

I like **chickens**.
I imagine whole chickens. I like the birds.

These are **chickens**.
(three chickens)

I like **chicken**.
I like part of the chicken: the part I eat!

This is **chicken**.
(two pieces of chicken)

Practice
Circle the best words. There may be more than one answer.

What is in the fridge?
1. (eggs)(egg)
2. (milks)(milk)
3. (juices)(juice)
4. (grapes)(grape)
5. (strawberries)(strawberry)
6. (cheeses)(cheese) and
7. (lambs)(lamb)

Practice
Circle the best words to complete the sentences. There may be more than one answer.

1. We have (a sofa)(sofa) in our living room.
2. I read (books)(book).
3. Do you need (a medicine)(medicine)?
4. There (are sands)(is sand) in my shoe.
5. Rainbow Beach has colored (sand)(sands).
6. I like (avocados)(avocado) on toast.
7. I buy (avocados)(avocado) at the market.
8. I have some (cakes)(cake) with my tea.
9. I like (beans)(bean).
10. I like (pumpkins)(pumpkin).

things we don't count

There are some words we use to talk about groups of things.

a table and chairs

a sofa

a coffee table

This is **furniture**.

group	things in this group
luggage	bags, suitcases, boxes etc.
equipment	balls, bats, gloves, helmets etc.
silverware	knives, forks, spoons
garbage	things we want to throw away
music	songs, rhythms, melodies, etc.

The word *furniture* talks about these things generally belonging to the same group.

When we want to count these things, we say: a piece of furniture, two pieces of furniture.
We can also count them as separate items: a sofa, two tables.

There are some things we can't see or hear. We think of them as complex things that are made up of many small parts, so we talk about them generally too.

group	things in this group
information	many facts
knowledge	many things a person knows
news	many details of recent events

Some things come in pairs. We count them as pairs.

These are pants
(a pair of pants)
Pants have **two** legs.

These are shoes
(a pair of shoes)
There are **two** shoes.

These are chopsticks
(a pair of chopsticks)
There are **two** chopsticks.

Practice

Circle the best words to complete the sentences.

1. I have some (headphones)(headphone).
2. Scientists do (researches)(research).
3. I need more (informations)(information).
4. She wears (earrings)(earring).
5. He wears (jeweleries)(jewelery).
6. The (electricities are)(electricity is) on.
7. Do you have any (newses)(news)?
8. Take out the (trashes)(trash).
9. I'm thirsty. Where (are my glasses)(is my glass)?
10. I can't see! Where (are my glasses)(is my glass)?

some and any

We use *some* and *any* when the amount is not important. It may be something we can or can't count.

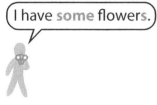

(three flowers)

(a glass of water)

We use *any* in questions and negative sentences.

I have **some** apples. (more than one apple)
I **don't** have **any** apples. (zero apples)
Do you have **any** apples? (zero or some?)

She has **some** bread. (a slice or a loaf etc.)
She doesn't have **any** bread. (none)
Does she have **any** bread? (none or some?)

here and there

We use *here* to refer to where we are. We use *there* to refer to somewhere else. The person we are talking to knows the place we are talking about.

They know because we point to it.

They know because we say where it is.

We often start sentences with *there is* or *there are* and say where it is later in the sentence.

There's a spoon **in the drawer**.
There isn't a restaurant **in the hotel**.
Is there an ATM **near here**?

There are some trees **in the park**.
There aren't any snakes **in my yard**.
Are there any ATMs **near here**?

We also use *there is* or *there are* to simply say things exist. Exactly where is not important.

There's a solution.
There isn't a problem.
Is there anything else?

There are some things to talk about.
There aren't any stupid questions.
Are there any questions?

Practice

Complete the sentences using *a, an, some* or *any*.

1. Do you have _____ sisters?
2. I have _____ car.
3. Is there _____ restroom near here?
4. Are there _____ restrooms near here?
5. There's _____ computer on the desk.
6. There are _____ pens in the drawer.
7. We don't have _____ children.
8. There's _____ ice in the glass.

the

When we use *the* the listener knows which person or thing we are referring to.

We use *the* for things that are common knowledge. (Everybody knows which apple is big.)

This is **an apple**.   This is **an apple**.   This is **an apple**.   This is **an apple**.   This is **an apple**.

This is **the big apple**.

We also use *the* for more than one person or thing.

These are **pears**.   These are **pears**.   These are **pears**.   These are **pears**.   These are **pears**.

These are **the big pears**.

(**the** two big pears)

We use *the* when the listener knows which one we are talking about.

Tara wants **a baseball**.   Tara wants **the baseball**.

The listener often knows which person or thing we are referring to because we talked about it before.

I play in **a band**. There is **an American**, **an Australian** and me.

The Australian plays **the drums**.

a band - we don't know which band.
an American - we don't know which American.
an Australian - we don't know which Australian.

The Australian - the one in the band.
The drums - one of many instruments - we know which one.

We don't use *a* or *the* with names, such as names of people or names of sports.

I play tennis. (Tennis is the name of the sport.)
I play **the** guitar. (We use *the* because the listener knows which instrument I am talking about.)

We often use *the* when we are talking about places. The listener knows what kind of place it is, but which one doesn't matter.
We use *a* when the listener doesn't know which one. They often ask in these situations.

Subject	Verb	Place
I	am	**at the bank.**
She	is	**at the supermarket.**
We	are	**at the beach.**

Which bank is not important. The speaker wants them to picture a standard bank.

Subject	Verb	Place/Event
I	am	**at a restaurant.**
She	is	**at a bar.**
We	are	**at a party.**

Restaurants are all different. The listener doesn't know which one.

Practice

Complete the conversations using *a*, *an* or *the*.

1. A: I have _____ new job.
   B: Great! What's _____ job?
   A: I'm _____ office worker.
   B: Where's _____ office?
   A: It's in _____ city.

2. A: Do you play _____ piano?
   B: I have _____ piano but I don't play it.

3. Can you turn off _____ TV please?
4. I go to _____ park in _____ morning.
5. I work on _____ boat.
6. I swim in _____ sea.
7. _____ restaurant opens at 6.
8. Can I have _____ drink, please?
9. My company has _____ boat and _____ hotel. I work on _____ boat. Anne works in _____ hotel.

names

We often call people and things by their name.

Subject	Verb	Object/Description	
I	am	**Luke.**	name: Luke
Kate	drinks	tea.	name: Kate

We often use *the* in names. There are different ways we name people and things:

name only	*the*(which one)(thing)	*the* (thing) of (origin)	(title) (name)
Amelia Brooks Thomas Ferguson			Ms. Brooks Mr. Ferguson Mt. Everest Lake Victoria
	the Pacific Ocean the Nile River* the Red Sea the Sahara Desert	the Sea of Japan the Gulf of Thailand the Bay of Kotor	
Breakfast Creek Ha Long Bay Niagara Falls			
London Bridge	the Eiffel Tower the Brooklyn Bridge the United Kingdom	the Tower of Babel the Statue of Liberty	
Wall Street			
We often include what it is in its name (bay etc.).	*Which one* is a name, often from a description.	*Origin* is a place or description.	*Titles* are used for people in formal situations.

We often write the things in columns 2 and 3 without *the* on maps and as headings for brochures, books etc. Fewer words makes these things easy to read. *People may also say 'the River Nile'. Saying 'the Nile River' (as written in the table) is more common in modern American English—rivers are usually named this way.

There are lots of ways we can name things. We accept names we hear and use them as others do.

Practice

Complete the paragraph below using *the* when needed. Leave some spaces blank.

I love traveling. I want to travel the world. I want to see: (example)_____ Big Ben, (example) *the* Leaning Tower of Pisa...

(1)_____ Great Sphinx, (2)_____ Angel Falls, (3)_____ Great Wall of China, (4)_____ Machu Picchu, (5)_____ Grand Canyon, (6)_____Mt Fuji, (7)_____ Uluru, (8)_____ Stonehenge, (9)_____ Forbidden City and (10)_____ Empire State Building.

4

Other basic words

pronouns and conjunctions

's

We add *'s* to names to describe who **has** the thing we are talking about.

Joshua **has** a cat.   Ruby **has** brown hair.   Ruby **has** a brother.   Joshua **has** a headache.
Simon is Joshua**'s** cat.   Ruby**'s** hair is brown.   Joshua is Ruby**'s** brother.   Joshua**'s** headache is bad.

Simon   Joshua   Ruby   Joshua   Ruby   Joshua

Subject	Verb	Object/Description	
Simon	is	**Joshua's** cat.	Simon is Joshua's cat.
Joshua	likes	**Ruby's** hair.	Joshua likes Ruby's hair.
Joshua	is	**Ruby's** brother.	Joshua is Ruby's brother.
Ruby's brother	has	a cat.	Ruby's brother has a cat.
Joshua's headache	is	bad.	Joshua's headache is bad.

I have **Joshua's** cat.

We say who owns something.

Ruby has a cat. She doesn't own the cat.
It is Joshua's cat. Joshua owns the cat.
Ruby has **Joshua's** cat.

We ask questions with *whose*.

Whose brother has a cat?
Ruby's brother has a cat.

Practice
Look at the picture of the family and complete the sentences.

Example: Joshua is _Ruby's_ brother.

1. Mike is _____ husband.
2. Kelly is _____ wife.
3. _____ brother is Joshua.
4. _____ sister is Ruby.
5. Joshua and Ruby's mother is _____.
6. _____ is Ruby and Joshua's father.
7. _____ and _____ are Mike and Kelly's children.

Joshua   Mike   Kelly   Ruby

her, his, its, my, our, their, your

We use these words when we refer to people and things and what they have. We know which person or thing we are referring to, so we don't say their name again, we use one of these simpler words.

This is John. **His** house is in the city. (his = John's)

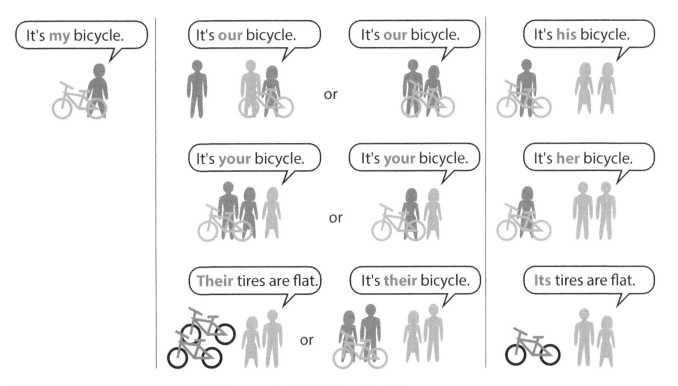

Subject	Verb	Object/Description
John	is	**my** father.
Your favorite sport	is	basketball.
The Earth	is	**our** home.
Their mother	plays	the piano.
Her name	is	Rebecca.
Roger	likes	**his** hair.
Its brakes	don't work.	

John is my father.
Your favorite sport is basketball.
The Earth is our home.
Their mother plays the piano.
Her name is Rebecca.
Roger likes his hair.
Its brakes don't work.

Practice

Complete the sentences. Use *her*, *his*, *its*, *my*, *our*, *their* or *your*.

His (he) name is Angelo.

1. She is _____ (I) sister.
2. Fred is _____ (she) husband.
3. Emily and Johnny are ____ (they) children.
4. We all like music. _____ (we) favorite singer is Taylor Swift.
5. Is this _____ (you) cat?
6. What is _____ (it) name?

33

hers, his, its, mine, ours, theirs, yours

When we know what object we are referring to, we use one of these words and don't say the object.

This is John. The house is **his**. (his = John's)
This is my breakfast. **Yours** is on the table. (yours = your breakfast)

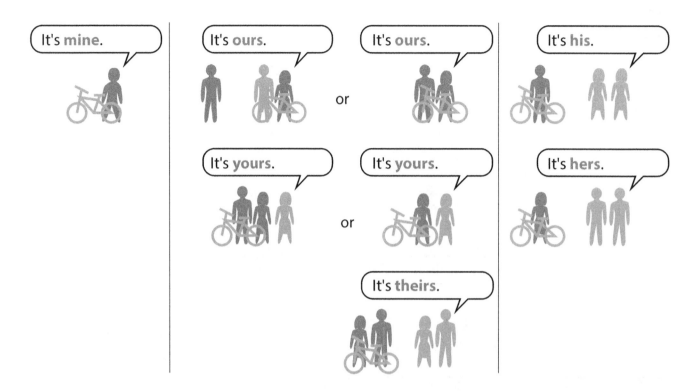

Subject	Verb	Object/Description	
This bag	is	**mine.**	The bag is mine.
Those shoes	are	**his**	Those shoes are his.
The letters	are	**hers.**	The letters are hers.
The towels	are	**theirs.**	The towels are theirs.
The money	is	**yours.**	The money is yours.

Practice

Complete the sentences. Use *hers*, *his*, *mine*, *ours*, *theirs* or *yours*.

1. Whose bag is that? It's _____ (her bag).
2. Your house is tidier than _____ (my house).
3. Here are our dinners. _____(Your dinner) is on the white plate.
4. My clothes are dirty but _____ (their clothes) are clean.
5. Is this my drink? No, it's _____ (his drink).
6. Whose jackets are these? They're _____ (our jackets).

34

one

It = **the** banana.
(the banana the person has)

one = **a** banana
(one of many bananas)

We use *this* and *that* to clearly point out which **one** we are talking about.
We are talking about **one** of many.

We use *these* and *those* to clearly point out which **ones** we are talking about.
We are talking about **more than one** of many.

Practice

Complete the sentences. Use *one*, *ones* or *it*.

1. Where is my key? I can't find ____.
2. The tomatoes are growing well. Look at that ____. ____'s huge!
3. A: Is there an ATM near here?
    B: Yes, there's ____ in the convenience store.
4. These dresses are nice. How much is this ____?
5. These pants are nice. How much are these ____?
6. Those grapes look good. Can I have ____?
7. A: Excuse me, can I use your phone?
    B: Sorry, I don't have ____.

simplifying sentences

When we have already talked about a person or thing, we use a simple word to refer to the same person or thing again.

The example sentences below can be completed with any word from the same row.

	(name)		or	or	or				example sentences
Subject	Tina	I	we	you	they	she	he	it	_They_ (am/<u>are</u>/is) from America.
Object	Tina	me	us	you	them	her	him	it	Stephen likes ___.
Whose (thing)	Tina's	my	our	your	their	her	his	its	This is _____ bag.
Whose	Tina's	mine	ours	yours	theirs	hers	his	its	This bag is _____.

Practice

Complete the sentences. Use the simple words in the table above.

My name is Isabella.
1. _I live_____ (Isabella lives) in Florida.
2. _____ (Isabella has) one brother and one sister.
3. _____ (Isabella's) brother's name is William.
4. _____ (Isabella's) sister's name is Ava.

Ava likes sport.
5. _____ (Ava's) favorite sport is soccer.
6. _____ (Ava) is very good at _____ (soccer).
7. _____ (Isabella likes) _____ (soccer) too.
8. _____ (Ava and Isabella) play _____ (soccer) together on Saturdays.
9. These are _____ (Ava's and Isabella's) soccer balls.
10. This one is _____ (Ava's).
11. This one is _____ (Isabella's).

36

and

We use *and* to add something else to our sentences.

We use *and* to add another noun in the subject.

Subject	Verb	Object
Isabella	plays	soccer.
Ava	plays	soccer.

→

Subject	Verb	Object
Isabella **and** Ava	play	soccer.

We use *plays* when we talk about one other person (not ourselves or the person we are talking to).
We use *play* because we are talking about two people. (See page 16.)

We use *and* to add another noun in the object, time, place etc.

Subject	Verb	Object
Ava	plays	soccer.
Ava	plays	tennis.

→

Subject	Verb	Object
Ava	plays	soccer **and** tennis.

We use *and* to add another verb.

Subject	Verb	Object
Ava	plays	soccer.
Ava	watches	soccer.

→

Subject	Verb	Object
Ava	plays **and** watches	soccer.

We can have two verbs with two objects.

Subject	Verb	Object
Ava	plays	soccer.
Ava	watches	hockey.

→

Subject	Verb	Object	*and*	Verb	Object
Ava	plays	soccer	**and**	watches	hockey.

We can connect two sentences that are about the same topic. The subject and object are different. The verb may be different too.

Subject	Verb	Object
Ava	plays	soccer.
Isabella	watches	hockey.

→

Subject	Verb	Object	*and*	Subject	Verb	Object
Ava	plays	soccer	**and**	Isabella	watches	hockey.

These sentences can be connected with *and* because they are about the same topic: sport.

Practice

Combine the sentences using *and*. Make the sentence as simple as you can.

Example: Mia eats steak. I eat steak. *Mia and I eat steak*_____.

1. Abigail writes music. Abigail records music. _____.
2. Abigail plays the keyboard. I play the drums. _____.
3. Noah studies French. Noah studies English. _____.
4. Jackson trains on Mondays. Jackson trains on Wednesdays. _____.
5. I work on Fridays. I go to a restaurant on Saturdays. _____.

or

We use *or* when we talk about options.

Would you like a ham **and** cheese sandwich?
Yes, please.

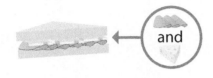

The sandwich has two fillings: ham and cheese.

Would you like a ham **or** cheese sandwich?
A ham sandwich please.

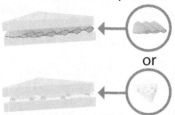

There are two options: ham or cheese. Choose.

We often use *or* with questions. We are giving people a choice.

do	Subject	Verb	Object	Place/Time
Do	you	play	soccer **or** tennis?	
Does	Anthony	jog		in the park **or** at the beach?
Does	Ethan	have	breakfast	at 6AM **or** 7AM?
Do	you	swim **or** cycle?		

We use *or* when we are unsure.

Subject	Verb	Object
Isabella **or** Ava	plays	soccer.

(I'm not sure which person.)

Subject	Verb	Object
Ava	plays	soccer **or** tennis.

(I'm not sure which sport.)

We use *or* when we sometimes choose option (a) and sometimes choose option (b).

Subject	Verb	time/place
I	jog **or** relax	in the park.

(I sometimes jog in the park. I sometimes relax in the park.)

We often use *or* with negatives.

I don't like ham **and** cheese.
(I don't like the combination:
ham and cheese together.)

I don't like ham **or** cheese.
(I don't like either option:
I don't like ham, I don't like cheese.)

We use *or* with negatives to say that the subject doesn't do either of these things.

Subject	(*not*) Verb	Object	Place/Time
I	don't play	soccer **or** tennis.	
Anthony	doesn't jog		in the park **or** at the beach.
Ethan	doesn't have	breakfast	at 6AM **or** 7AM.
I	don't swim **or** cycle.		

Practice

Complete the sentences using *and* or *or*.

Example: Do you prefer tea _*or*_ coffee?

1. I like dancing _____ singing.
2. I don't watch TV _____ read books.
3. I don't like running _____ swimming.
4. I don't know what to get for dinner... pasta __ rice.
5. Can I have a hamburger _____ fries, please?
6. Do you play tennis _____ baseball?
7. I have two brothers _____ a sister.

but

We use *but* to say things are different. We often use *but* to show one statement is positive and the other is negative.

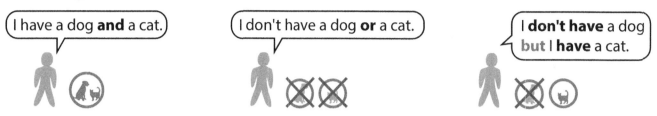

I have a dog **and** a cat.

I don't have a dog **or** a cat.

I **don't have** a dog **but** I **have** a cat.

We join two sentences with *but*.

Subject	(*not*) Verb	Object	Place/Time	*but*	Subject	Verb	Object	Place/Time
Isabella	**doesn't play**	soccer		**but**	she	**reads**	books.	
My dad	**doesn't like**	jogging	in the park	**but**	he	**likes**	swimming.	
I	**don't have**	breakfast	at 6AM	**but**	I	**have**	breakfast	at 7AM.
Isabella	**doesn't call**	Stephen		**but**	she	**calls**	William.	

Either statement can be first.

Subject	Verb	Object	Place/Time	*but*	Subject	(*not*) Verb	Object	Place/Time
Isabella	**reads**	books		**but**	she	**doesn't play**	soccer.	
My dad	**likes**	swimming		**but**	he	**doesn't like**	jogging	in the park.
I	**have**	breakfast	at 7AM	**but**	I	**don't have**	breakfast	at 6AM.
Isabella	**calls**	William		**but**	she	**doesn't call**	Stephen.	

We can leave out information if it has already been said.

Subject	Verb	Object	Place/Time	*but*	Subject	(*not*) Verb	Object	Place/Time
Isabella	**reads**	books		**but**	I	**don't** read	books.	
My dad	**likes**	swimming		**but**	My mom	**doesn't** like	swimming.	
I	**have**	breakfast	at 7AM	**but**	Ethan	**doesn't** have	breakfast	at 7AM.
Isabella	**calls**	William		**but**	she	**doesn't call**	Stephen.	

In some situations, either *and* or *but* can be used.

Use *but* to say that things are **different**. We don't always need to use it with *not*.

Subject	Verb	Object	Place/Time	but	Subject	Verb	Object	Place/Time
Ava	plays	soccer		**but**	Isabella	reads	books.	
I	like	jogging	in the park	**but**	my dad	likes	swimming.	
Ethan	has	breakfast	at 6AM	**but**	I	have	breakfast	at 7AM.
Stephen	emails	Isabella		**but**	Isabella	calls	William.	

Ava plays soccer **but** Isabella reads books. They do **different** things.
I like jogging in the park **but** my dad likes swimming. We like **different** things.
Ethan has breakfast at 6AM **but** I have breakfast at 7AM. We have breakfast at **different** times.
Stephen emails Isabella **but** Isabella calls William. They contact each other in **different** ways.

We can also use *and* to add another statement with a *subject*, *verb* and *object*. It fits in the same sentence because it is about the **same** (or similar) topic.

Subject	Verb	Object	Place/Time	and	Subject	Verb	Object	Place/Time
Ava	plays	soccer		**and**	Isabella	reads	books.	
I	like	jogging	in the park	**and**	my dad	likes	swimming.	
Ethan	has	breakfast	at 6AM	**and**	I	have	breakfast	at 7AM.
Stephen	emails	Isabella		**and**	Isabella	calls	William.	

Ava plays soccer **and** Isabella reads books. The **same** topic: free time activities.
I like jogging in the park **and** my dad likes swimming. The **same** topic: what we like doing.
Ethan has breakfast at 6AM **and** I have breakfast at 7AM. The **same** topic: breakfast.
Stephen emails Isabella **and** Isabella calls William. The **same** topic: contacting friends.

Practice

Complete the sentences using *and* or *but*.

Example: I like swimming _*but*_ I don't like running.

1. I study English _____ I practice speaking it with my friends.
2. I can drive _____ I don't have a car.
3. Madison plays tennis _____ Chloe doesn't.
4. We live near the lake _____ we love it.
5. This restaurant is good _____ expensive.
6. I live in the city _____ I enjoy it.
7. I live in the city _____ I want to move to the country.

5

Review of basic building blocks
pronouns and conjunctions

review of basic building blocks

order

English sentences usually have a subject-verb-object word order.

Subject	Verb	Object
I	eat	fish.

We use *not* in negative sentences.

Subject	*do not*	Verb	Object
I	**don't**	eat	fish.

We change the order when we make questions. We put verbs like *do* and *be (am/are/is)* first.

do	Subject	Verb	Object
Do	you	eat	fish?

We add a place or time to the end of a sentence. We often use *at*, *in* and *on*.

 at   **in**   **on**

Subject	Verb	Object	Place/Time
I	eat	fish	at home.
I	eat	fish	at 7PM.
I	eat	fish	in the office.
I	eat	fish	in summer.
I	eat	fish	on a boat.
I	eat	fish	on Sundays.

---

verbs

be	**have** 	**go**	**get**
I **am** in Moscow.	I **have** a box.	I **go** to school.	I **get** tea at the cafe.
You **are** in Moscow.	You **have** a box.	You **go** to school.	You **get** tea at the cafe.
We **are** in Moscow.	We **have** a box.	We **go** to school.	We **get** tea at the cafe.
They **are** in Moscow.	They **have** a box.	They **go** to school.	They **get** tea at the cafe.
He **is** in Moscow.	He **has** a box.	He **goes** to school.	He **gets** tea at the cafe.
She **is** in Moscow.	She **has** a box.	She **goes** to school.	She **gets** tea at the cafe.
It **is** in Moscow.	It **has** a box.	It **goes** to school.	It **gets** tea at the cafe.

nouns

There are some things we count.

an apple

two apples

There are some things we don't count.

some **apple**

When we use *the*, the listener knows which one or ones.

We use simple words when the listener knows which person or thing we are talking about.

	(name)		or	or	or				example sentences
Subject	Tina	I	we	you	they	she	he	it	*They* (am/<u>are</u>/is) from America.
Object	Tina	me	us	you	them	her	him	it	Stephen likes ___.

We use similar words to say who or what something belongs to.

Whose (thing)	Tina's	my	our	your	their	her	his	its	This is _____ bag.
Whose	Tina's	mine	ours	yours	theirs	hers	his	its	This bag is _____.

Tina's from America.	Stephen likes **Tina**.	This is **Tina's** bag.	This bag is **Tina's**.
I'm from America	Stephen likes **me**.	This is **my** bag.	This bag is **mine**.
We're from America.	Stephen likes **us**.	This is **our** bag.	This bag is **ours**.
You're from America.	Stephen likes **you**.	This is **your** bag.	This bag is **yours**.
They're from America.	Stephen likes **them**.	This is **their** bag.	This bag is **theirs**.
She's from America.	Stephen likes **her**.	This is **her** bag.	This bag is **hers**.
He's from America.	Stephen likes **him**.	This is **his** bag.	This bag is **his**.
It's from America.	Stephen likes **it**.	This is **its** bag.	This bag is **its**.

We use *one* or *ones* when we don't need to say the noun.

A: Which apple would you like?
B: Can I have a big **one**, please?

A: Which apples would you like?
B: Can I have two big **ones**, please?

We use *and* to put things together.
We use *or* to talk about options.
We use *but* to say things are different.

I like apples **and** bananas.
I don't like apples **or** bananas.
I like apples, **but** I don't like bananas.

45

quiz

1. Choose the best sentence.

   (a) I baseball play.
   (b) Baseball I play.
   (c) I play baseball.

2. Choose the best sentence.

   (a) I TV don't watch.
   (b) I don't watch TV.
   (c) Don't I watch TV.
   (d) TV don't I watch.

3. Choose the best sentence.

   (a) Do you drink juice?
   (b) Do drink you juice?
   (c) Drink do you juice?
   (d) Drink you do juice?

4. Choose the best answer.

   Where are you?

   (a) I'm at the hotel.
   (b) I'm in the hotel.
   (c) I'm on the hotel.
   (d) (a) and (b)

5. Choose the best answer.

   Where are you?

   (a) I'm at the beach.
   (b) I'm in the beach.
   (c) I'm on the beach.
   (d) (a) or (c)

6. Choose the best answer.

   Where are you?

   (a) I'm at the living room.
   (b) I'm in the living room.
   (c) I'm on the living room.
   (d) (a) or (b)

7. Choose the best answer.

   When is the concert?
   (a) It's at Saturday.
   (b) It's in Saturday.
   (c) It's on Saturday.
   (d) (a) or (c)

8. Choose the best answer.

   When does the concert start?
   (a) It starts at 8PM.
   (b) It starts in 8PM.
   (c) It starts on 8PM.
   (d) (a) or (c)

9. Choose the best sentence.

   (a) I was born at January.
   (b) I was born in January.
   (c) I was born on January.
   (d) (a) or (c)

10. Choose the best sentence.

    (a) I was born at 1992.
    (b) I was born in 1992.
    (c) I was born on 1992.
    (d) (a) or (c)

11. Choose the best sentence.

(a) I'm black hair.
(b) I have black hair.
(c) I go black hair.
(d) I get black hair.
(e) (a), (c) or (d)

12. Choose the best sentence.

(a) I'm home at 6.
(b) I have home at 6.
(c) I go home at 6.
(d) I get home at 6.
(e) (a), (c) or (d)

13. Choose the best question.

(a) Am you live in Germany?
(b) Is you live in Germany?
(c) Are you live in Germany?
(d) Do you live in Germany?
(e) Does you live in Germany?

14. Choose the best question.

(a) Am you hungry?
(b) Is you hungry?
(c) Are you hungry?
(d) Do you hungry?
(e) Does you hungry?

15. Choose the best question.

(a) Am she from Korea?
(b) Is she from Korea?
(c) Are she from Korea
(d) Do she from Korea?
(e) Does she from Korea?

16. Choose the best question.

(a) Am he read books?
(b) Is he read books?
(c) Are he read books?
(d) Do he read books?
(e) Does he read books?

17. Choose the best question.

(a) Am they read books?
(b) Is they read books?
(c) Are they read books?
(d) Do they read books?
(e) Does they read books?

18. Choose the best question.

(a) Am you have a brother?
(b) Is you have a brother?
(c) Are you have a brother?
(d) Do you have a brother?
(e) Does you have a brother?

19. Choose the best sentence.

(a) I don't have sister.
(b) I don't have a sister.
(c) I don't have the sister.

20. Choose the best sentence.

(a) He helps I.
(b) He helps me.
(c) He helps my.

21. Choose the best sentence.

(a) We speak English.
(b) Us speak English.
(c) Our speak English.

22. Choose the best question.

(a) Which it do you want?
(b)Which them do you want?
(c) Which one do you want?
(d) Which ones do you want?
(e) (a) and (b)
(f) (c) and (d)

23. Choose the best question.

(a) Do you eat pumpkins?
(b) Do you eat pumpkin?

24. Choose the best question.

    (a) Do you eat grapes?
    (b) Do you eat grape?

25. Choose the best sentence.

    (a) I like your furnitures.
    (b) I like your furniture.
    (c) all of the above.

26. Choose the best sentence.

    (a) I eat an egg every morning.
    (b) I eat eggs every morning.
    (c) I eat egg every morning.
    (d) all of the above.

27. Choose the best question.

    (a) He plays trumpet.
    (b) He plays a trumpet.
    (c) He plays the trumpet.

28. Choose the best answer.

    What does Layla drink?
    (a) She drinks water.
    (b) She drinks a water.
    (c) She drinks the water.

29. Choose the best question.

    (at the dinner table)
    (a) Can you pass pepper please?
    (b) Can you pass a pepper please?
    (c) Can you pass the pepper please?

30. Choose the best sentence.

    Connor has a sister.
    (a) His sister's name is Lucy.
    (b) The sister's name is Lucy.
    (c) A sister's name is Lucy.
    (d) Her name is Lucy.

6

Tenses
present and past

introduction to verb forms

Different verb forms are used to give different information about time.
The following sections explore these verb forms and their uses.

The first verb of the sentence gives us **basic information** about the time we are referring to.
The first verb is either in the present form or past form.
We will look at these two forms in more detail in this section.

present form
(See page 52.)

be/am/are/is
have/has
go/goes
get/gets
say/says
do/does
make/makes
know/knows
think/thinks
take/takes
see/sees
want/wants
look/looks
use/uses
find/finds
give/gives

We add the *s* when the subject is a he, she or it.
The meaning of the verb is the same, but the
subject is different.

I **eat** breakfast. / He **eats** breakfast.
I **live** in England. / She **lives** in England.

past form
(See page 54.)

was/were
had
went
got
said
did
made
knew
thought
took
saw
wanted
looked
used
found
gave

Some common verbs have past forms that are
different to the present form.
With most verbs, we use the present form + *-ed*.

I **ate** breakfast this morning.
She **lived** in England last year.

We use the -ing form or -en form to add **extra information**.

-ing form
(See page 58.)

being
having
going
getting
saying
doing
making
knowing
thinking
taking
seeing
wanting
looking
using
finding
giving

All -ing form verbs end in *-ing*.

I'm eating breakfast (now).
She**'s living** in England (now).

-en form
(See page 70.)

been
had
gone
gotten
said
done
made
known
thought
taken
seen
wanted
looked
used
found
given

Some verbs have a separate form often ending in
-en, -ne or -n. However, **most verbs** use the same
form as the past form.

I've eaten breakfast.
She**'s lived** in England.

present form

The verbs in the sentences we have looked at so far have been in the present form.

What is it?

present form	past form	-ing form	-en form
eat	ate	eating	eaten
work	worked	working	worked
have	had	having	had
play	played	playing	played

What does it mean?

We talk about things that are generally true.

Things that are generally true are true in the **present-future**.
They may be true in the past too.

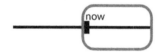

How do we use it?

We use the present form to talk about things that happen **many times**.

I **eat** breakfast.

We use the present form to talk about things that are generally **permanent**.

I **live** in England.

Subject	Verb	Object	Place/Time	
We	**eat**		at work.	We eat at work.
She	**works**		on Wednesdays.	She works on Wednesdays.
They	**live**		in Sweden	They live in Sweden.
You	**like**	swimming.		You like swimming.
He	**has**	breakfast	at 7:30.	He has breakfast at 7:30.
I	**play**	soccer	on Sundays.	I play soccer on Sundays.

We talk about things that are always true. These are **facts**.

Water **boils** at 100°C.
Cows **don't** eat rabbits.
Is Mt Everest the tallest mountain in the world?

We talk about things that are true now. These are **descriptions**. We describe things in the present.

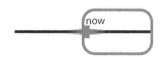

This **tastes** delicious!
He **doesn't** have a hat.
Are you hungry?

Things may be generally true because they are **fixed**, and can't be changed or controlled. These are **scheduled events**. We often add a **future time** to make this clear.

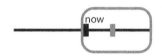

The meeting **starts** at 4PM.
I **don't** work this Sunday.
When **does** the bus leave?

We talk about quick actions or events that finish as the speaker is speaking. We say what happens **as it happens**. We talk about these actions and events when giving **commentary** and **telling stories**.

(James is watching soccer on TV) Commentator: He **shoots**... He **scores**!

Amy **wakes** up and **goes** downstairs. She **opens** the door...

Stories are in the past or in our imaginations, so we usually use the past form. However, storytellers sometimes use the present form to bring the story into the present for dramatic effect.

Practice

Choose the best timeline for the sentence.

1. We eat at work.
2. They live in Sweden.
3. She works on Wednesdays.
4. I'm hungry.
5. She arrives at 3PM tomorrow.
6. He eats breakfast at 7:30.
7. She wins the race.
8. You like swimming.
9. I play soccer on Sundays.

(a)  things that happen many times

(b) things that are always true or generally permanent

(c) things that are true now

(d) things in the future

(e)  saying what happens as it happens

past form

What is it?

present form	past form	-ing form	-en form
eat	ate	eating	eaten
work	worked	working	worked
have	had	having	had
play	played	playing	played

What does it mean?

Verbs in the past form show us we are NOT referring to the present-future.

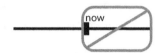

How do we use it?

We use verbs in the past form to refer to the past. Actions and events that happened in the past are **finished**.

We use the past form to talk about things that happened at a **point** of time in the past.

I **ate** breakfast at 6AM.

We use the past form to talk about things that happened over a **period** of time in the past.

I **lived** in England last year.

We are talking about a specific time in the past, so we often need to say when it was.

Subject	Verb	Object	Place	Time	
We	**ate**	eggs		this morning.	We ate eggs this morning.
She	**worked**			on Wednesday.	She worked on Wednesday.
They	**lived**		in Sweden	in 2007.	They lived in Sweden in 2007.
You	**liked**	swimming		last week.	You liked swimming last week.
He	**had**	breakfast		at 7:30.	He had breakfast at 7:30.
I	**played**	soccer		on Sunday.	I played soccer on Sunday.

Sometimes exactly when doesn't matter. We know it is in the recent past.

I **got** a new bike! The listener knows that this must have happened recently.

We also use the past form to describe things that were true in the past.

He **had** a hat.
In the past. He might not have a hat now.
The hat **was** new.
In the past. The hat might not be new now.
They **were** hungry.
In the past. They might not be hungry now.
That **tasted** delicious!
In the past. We have finished eating.

We add *did* (the past form of *do*) to make questions and negative sentences.

Questions

Did you **eat** eggs this morning?

Did she **work** on Wednesday?

Did they **live** in Sweden in 2007?

Did you **like** swimming last week?

Did he **have** breakfast at 7:30?

Did you **play** soccer on Sunday?

Negatives

We **didn't eat** eggs this morning.

She **didn't work** on Wednesday.

They **didn't live** in Sweden in 2007.

You **didn't like** swimming last week.

He **didn't have** breakfast at 7:30.

I **didn't play** soccer on Sunday.

> Notice that only the **first verb** gets changed to the **past form.** The first verb provides us with the essential information, so the other verbs stay in the basic **present form.**

Practice

Complete the sentences using the past form.

Example: I ___*did*___ (do) yoga last Friday.

1. I _____ (go) to school yesterday.
2. I _____ (not eat) breakfast this morning.
3. _____ (you play) golf last week?
4. _____ (he go) to work this morning?
5. They _____ (not go) on vacation in July.
6. She _____ (not live) in South Africa last year.
7. We _____ (have) a good day on Sunday.

Other basic verbs:	
present form	**past form**
do	→ did
does	→ did
am	→ was
is	→ was
are	→ were
have	→ had
has	→ had
go	→ went

Compare the past form and the present form.

We use the *past form* for descriptions in the past.
We use the *present form* for descriptions in the present-future.

Nara **was** the capital of Japan. (true in the past)
I **wasn't** hungry after work. So I didn't eat.
Were they delicious? There are none left.

Tokyo **is** the capital of Japan. (true in the present)
I**'m not** hungry.
Are they delicious?

We use the *past form* for events in the past (the past can't be changed) and the *present form* for fixed events in the future (these things can't be changed). We say or know when they happen.

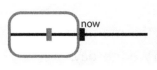

The meeting **started** at 10:30.
The game **wasn't** on Sunday.
When **did** the bus leave?

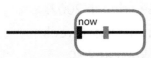

The meeting **starts** at 10:30.
The game **isn't** on Sunday.
When **does** the bus leave?

We use the *past form* for actions that happened in the past.
We use the *present form* for actions that happen in the present, as the speaker speaks. (These things finish in the present; they finish before we finish speaking.)

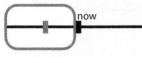

I **went** shopping.
He **didn't** lock the door.
Did you play golf?

She **doesn't** pass the ball.
She **shoots**.
Does it have the distance?

When we use the *present form* and don't know exactly when an action happens, we understand that the speaker is speaking **generally** and it happens **many times**. (This is the most common.)

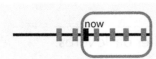

I **go** shopping.
He **doesn't** lock the door.
Do you play golf?

Practice

Complete the conversation.

1. A: Where do you work?
2. B: I _____ (work) in a restaurant, but I _____ (not work) yesterday.
3. A: What _____ (you do) yesterday?
4. B: I _____ (play) golf.
5. A: Where _____ (you play)?
6. B: At the golf club. How about you? What sport _____ (you like)?
7. A: I _____ (not like sport). I _____ (play tennis) last week, but I _____ (not like) it.

56

7

Unfinished actions
progressive aspect

-ing form

What is it?

present form	past form	-ing form	-en form
eat	ate	eating	eaten
work	worked	working	worked
have	had	having	had
play	played	playing	played

All verbs in the -ing form end in -*ing*.

What does it mean?

We are talking about things that are **not finished**.

How do we use it?

We use *be* with the -ing form.

We talk about things that have **started** and are **not finished**.

We talk about things that have **not started** and are **not finished.**
We know or say when.

We use the present form of *be* (*am/are/is*) and the -ing form to talk about unfinished actions.

I'm eating breakfast.

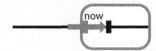

This **started** in the **past** and **finishes** in the **future**. It is happening **now**.

I'm eating breakfast at 6AM.

This **starts** and **finishes** in the **future**. It is happening in the **future**.

We also talk about things that started in the past and finish in the future that are not happening right now.

I'm learning Spanish.
We know that it isn't happening right now. I'm speaking English now.

Sometimes exactly when doesn't matter. We know it is in the near future.

I'm getting a new bike!
This is in the future. We know that it isn't happening in the present.

The present form of be (am/are/is) shows us this is in the **present-future**.
We use the verb be because we are referring to the whole person or thing.

Subject	be	Verb	Object	Place/Time	
We	**are**	**eating**	eggs.		We're eating eggs.
She	**is**	**working.**			She's working.
I	**am**	**living**		in Sweden.	I'm living in Sweden.
He	**is**	**having**	breakfast	at 7:30 tomorrow.	He's having breakfast at 7:30 tomorrow.
You	**are**	**playing**	soccer	on Sunday.	You're playing soccer on Sunday.

The -ing form shows us these actions are **not finished**.

finish

We put be (am/are/is) first to make it a question.

be	Subject	Verb	Object	Place/Time	
Are	you	**eating**	eggs?		Are you eating eggs?
Is	she	**working?**			Is she working?
Are	you	**living**		in Sweden?	Are you living in Sweden?
Is	he	**having**	breakfast	at 7:30 tomorrow?	Is he having breakfast at 7:30 tomorrow?
Are	you	**playing**	soccer	on Sunday?	Are you playing soccer on Sunday?

We add not to make it negative.

Subject	be not	Verb	Object	Place/Time	
We	**are not**	**eating**	eggs.		We aren't eating eggs.
She	**is not**	**working.**			She isn't working.
I	**am not**	**living**		in Sweden.	I'm not living in Sweden.
He	**is not**	**having**	breakfast	at 7:30 tomorrow.	He isn't having breakfast at 7:30 tomorrow.
You	**are not**	**playing**	soccer	on Sunday.	You aren't playing soccer on Sunday.

Practice

Complete the sentences using am/are/is and the -ing form.

Example: I'm doing (do) yoga next Friday.

1. I _____ (not eat) breakfast this morning.
2. _____ (you play) golf next week?
3. _____ (he work) this morning?
4. They _____ (not go) on vacation in July.
5. She _____ (not live) in South Africa.
6. We _____ (swim) in the lake on Sunday.
7. A: Where _____ (you go)?
   B: I _____ (go) to school.

59

Compare the past form and *am/are/is* + -ing form.

We use the past form for **finished** actions in the past.
We use *am/are/is* + -ing form for actions that are **not finished** in the present-future.

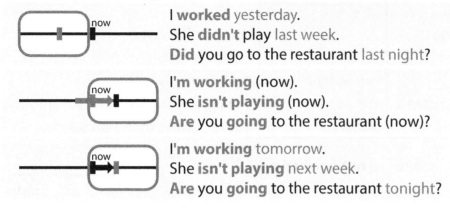

I **worked** yesterday.
She **didn't** play last week.
Did you go to the restaurant last night?

I'm **working** (now).
She **isn't playing** (now).
Are you **going** to the restaurant (now)?

I'm **working** tomorrow.
She **isn't playing** next week.
Are you **going** to the restaurant tonight?

Practice

Complete the conversation with the past form or *am/are/is* and the -ing form of the verb in brackets.

A: (1) What _____ (you do) next weekend?

B: Nothing. Why?

A: (2) I _____ (have) a barbecue. Do you want to come?

B: Yeah maybe. (3) What _____(you cook)?

A: (4) I _____ (cook) sausages and steak last time. (5) The steak _____ (be) very popular,
   (6) so I _____(do) that again.

B: (7) Yeah, it _____(be) very tasty. (8) I _____(like) the sausages last time too.

A: (9) I _____(try) something new this time. (10) I _____(make) hamburgers.

B: Sounds good.

A: (11) What _____(you do) now?

B: (12) I _____ (watch) TV.

A: Me too. (13) I_____(watch) the rugby.

B: (14) Who _____(win)?

A: The All Blacks… (15) They _____ (win) last week too.

Compare the present form and *am/are/is* + -ing form.

We use the present form when we are talking **generally**. Actions generally happen **many** times.
We use *am/are/is* + -ing form to talk about something that is **not finished**. We are talking about
something that is happening **at** or happening **during** a **specific** time.

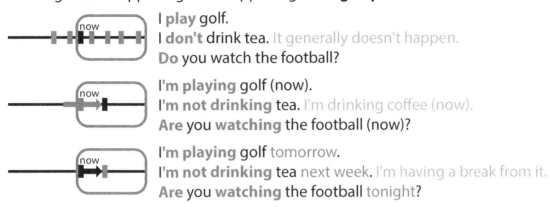

I **play** golf.
I **don't** drink tea. It generally doesn't happen.
Do you watch the football?

I'm **playing** golf (now).
I'm **not drinking** tea. I'm drinking coffee (now).
Are you **watching** the football (now)?

I'm **playing** golf tomorrow.
I'm **not drinking** tea next week. I'm having a break from it.
Are you **watching** the football tonight?

We use the present form for **general
descriptions**.

She **has** a baby.
general description: what she has.

I **live** in England.
This is generally **permanent**.
We are **not** thinking about it finishing.

We use *am/are/is* + -ing form for things that are
not finished. These things finish in the future.

She **is having** a baby.
action: what she is doing – giving birth.
This action **finishes** in the **future**.
(She may be giving birth now or pregnant now
and giving birth in the future.)

I'm **living** in England.
This is **temporary**. We are focusing on **now**.
We are thinking about it **finishing**.

Practice

Complete the telephone conversation with the present form or *am/are/is* and the -ing form.

A: Hello.
B: Hi. How are you doing?
A: Great. (1) I_____ (walk) in the mountains. (2) I_____ (not work) this week!
B: Sounds good. (3) You usually _____(work) really hard. Are you on vacation?
A: Yeah. (4) I_____ (really enjoy) myself. How are you?
B: Not great, (5) I _____ (have) a headache. How's the weather?
A: (6) It_____ (not usually snow) much at this time of year, (7) but it_____ (snow) a
lot today, (8) so I_____(go) skiing tomorrow.
B: (9) I'm envious. I _____ (love) the mountains.
A: Sorry, I have to go. The bus _____ (come).

unfinished in the past

We use the past form of *be* (*was/were*) with the -ing form to talk about things that were **not finished** at a time in the past.

We talk about things that had **started** and were **not finished** at a time in the past.

I **was eating** breakfast at 6AM.

We talk about things that had **not started** and were **not finished** at a time in the past.

I woke up at 4:30 yesterday because I **was meeting** a friend at 6AM.

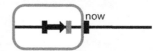

The past form of *be* (*was/were*) shows us this is **NOT** in the **present-future**. We use the verb *be* because we are referring to the whole person or thing.

Subject	*be*	Verb	Object	Place	Time	
She	**was**	**working**			on Saturday.	She was working on Saturday.
I	**was**	**living**		in Sweden	in 2010.	I was living in Sweden in 2010.
He	**was**	**having**	breakfast		at 6AM.	He was having breakfast at 6AM.
They	**were**	**playing**	soccer		on Sunday.	They were playing soccer on Sunday.

The -ing form shows us these actions are **not finished**.

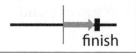
finish

The context often tells us if the action had started or not.

My mother called yesterday but I couldn't talk long because we **were having** dinner with friends.
Dinner was not finished. It was happening **at** the time of the phone call. It had **started**.

I went shopping yesterday. I bought a nice dessert because we **were having** dinner with friends.
Dinner was not finished. It was happening **after** shopping. It had **not started**.

There are lots of situations when we talk about things that were not finished.

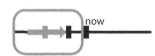

What **were** you **doing** at 6AM yesterday?
I **was having** breakfast.
Something was not finished at a specific time.

We **were waiting** for the bus when my phone rang.
She found $20 when she **was cleaning** the car.
Something was not finished when something else happened.

The sun **was shining** and the birds **were singing**. Kate **was walking** through the forest. She saw a squirrel...
We set the scene of a story. These things had started but were not finished when the story began.

We talk about things happening after something else in the past.

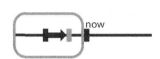

He took his golf clubs because he **was playing** golf that afternoon.
They **were going** hiking on Sunday so they rested on Saturday.
These things were not finished and hadn't started. We know or say when.

We emphasize the time things took.

He **was playing** golf all afternoon.
They **were hiking** for six hours.
We emphasize a period of time by saying something was not finished during that period.

Practice

Complete the sentences with *was/were* and the -ing form.

1. A: I tried to call you yesterday but you didn't answer your phone.
    B: Sorry, I didn't hear it. I _____(watch) the football.
2. We packed our bags because we _____ (leave) the next day.
3. I found my wallet when I _____ (clean) my room.
4. We _____ (wait) all day but the package didn't come.
5. Did you see Steve at the party? He _____ (wear) a cowboy hat.
6. Did I tell you about the time I rescued a koala? I _____ (live) in Byron Bay and....
7. We _____ (listen) to music so we didn't hear the doorbell.
8. We renewed our passports because we _____ (go) abroad.

Compare *am/are/is* + -ing form **and** *was/were* + -ing form.

We use *am/are/is* + -ing form for actions that are **not finished** at a time in the present-future.
We use *was/were* + -ing form for actions that were **not finished** at a time in the past.

We talk about things that have/had started.

She's **singing**.
She **isn't dancing**.
What **is** he **doing**?

The first time I saw her, she **was singing**.
She **wasn't dancing** when I saw her.
I heard something about 10 minutes ago. **Was** your phone **ringing**?

We talk about things that haven't/hadn't started.

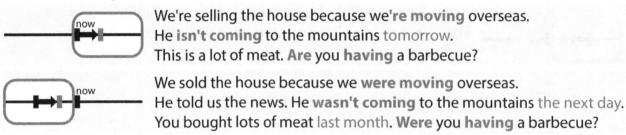

We're selling the house because we**'re moving** overseas.
He **isn't coming** to the mountains tomorrow.
This is a lot of meat. **Are** you **having** a barbecue?

We sold the house because we **were moving** overseas.
He told us the news. He **wasn't coming** to the mountains the next day.
You bought lots of meat last month. **Were** you **having** a barbecue?

Practice

Complete the conversations. There may be more than one answer.

A: (1) What _____ you _____ (do) tomorrow?
B: (2) I_____ (apply) for a driver's license. (3) I _____ (go) to do it yesterday but
   (4) I _____ (study) English and I lost track of the time.

A: (5) I_____ (live) in America now but (6) I _____ (live) in Canada last year.
B: (7) What _____ you _____(do) in Canada?
A: (8) I _____ (work) at a ski field. (9) I _____(save) money because
   (10) I _____ (start) college later in the year.
A: How is college?
B: Boring. (11) I_____ (quit) and (12) _____ (move) back to Canada next month.

Compare the **past form** and *was/were* + *-ing* form.

We use the past form for **finished** actions in the past.
We use *was/were* + *-ing* form for actions that were **not finished** at a time in the past.

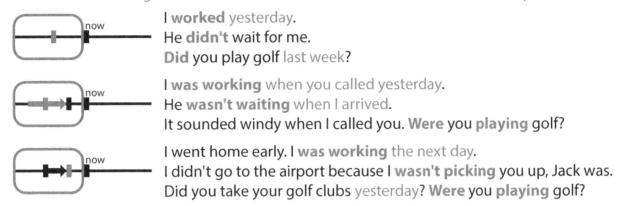

I **worked** yesterday.
He **didn't** wait for me.
Did you play golf last week?

I **was working** when you called yesterday.
He **wasn't waiting** when I arrived.
It sounded windy when I called you. **Were** you **playing** golf?

I went home early. I **was working** the next day.
I didn't go to the airport because I **wasn't picking** you up, Jack was.
Did you take your golf clubs yesterday? **Were** you **playing** golf?

When we talk about something that happened over a period of time we can say it **simply** with the past form, or we can **emphasize** how long it took with *was/were* + *-ing* form. It doesn't matter which way you choose to say it. We all think in different ways.

We **talked** for about three hours.
We **didn't** wait for long.
Did you play all night?

We **were talking** for about three hours.
We **weren't waiting** for long.
Were you **playing** all night?

Practice

Complete the narratives. There may be more than one answer.

I was on the train last Monday. (example) I __was reading__ (read) a book. (1) A man
_____ (sit) next to me and (2) he _____ (talk) on the phone.

(3) We _____ (go) to the pet shop last week to buy a dog. (4) There _____ (be) so many cute
dogs. (5) Some of them _____ (scratching). (6) Some of them _____ (sniff) each
other. (7) Then one dog _____ (catch) my eye. (8) She _____ (look) at me. (9) I _____
(know) from the minute I saw her that (10) she _____ (be) the dog for me.

(11) I _____ (drive) home from work yesterday and (12) it _____ (start) snowing. (13) It
_____ (snow) so heavily that (14) I _____ (have) to stop the car because (15) I _____
(can't) see.

-ing form: as a subject

When we use the -ing form we are talking about something happening. We can use it as a noun.

hiking

When we talk about an activity, we talk about the activity happening, not the activity being complete.

We can use the activity as as a subject.

Subject (activity)	Verb	Object	Description	
Hiking	is		fun.	Hiking is fun.
Drawing	requires	skill.		Drawing requires skill.

Hiking is fun: The fun part is doing the activity, not the fact that it finishes.

The -ing form is used in the same way as other subjects for questions and negatives too.

	Subject (activity)	Verb	Object	Description	
Is	**hiking**			fun?	Is hiking fun?
Does	**drawing**	require	skill?		Does drawing require skill?
	Hiking	isn't		fun.	Hiking isn't fun.
	Drawing	doesn't require	skill.		Drawing doesn't require skill.

The -ing form may have an object of its own.

Subject (activity)		Verb	Object	Description	
Verb	Object				
Driving	**cars**	is		fun.	Driving cars is fun.
Drawing	**pictures**	requires	skill.		Drawing pictures requires skill.

Practice

Complete the sentences.

1. _____ (cook pasta) **is easy.**
2. _____ (smoke) **causes health problems.**
3. _____(help people) **feels good.**
4. **Is** _____(snowboard) **your favorite winter sport?**
5. _____(learn English) **is fun.**

-ing form: as an object

We also use the -ing form to refer to an activity as an object.

dancing

We often talk about liking or not liking the activity, with *like*, *enjoy*, *love* or *hate*.

Subject	Verb	Object (activity)	Place/Time	
I	love	**dancing.**		I love dancing.
She	likes	**swimming**	in the sea.	She likes swimming in the sea.

We make questions and negative statements the same way as usual.

	Subject	Verb	Object (activity)	Place/Time
Do	you	love	**dancing?**	
	She	doesn't like	**swimming**	in the sea?

The activity may have an object of its own.

Subject	Main Verb	Object (activity)		Place/Time
		Verb	Object	
She	**likes**	playing	the guitar.	
He	**enjoys**	watching	TV	in the evening.

These statements are **generally true**. The main verb is in the present form. We **generally** like and enjoy these things.

The sentence pattern below is similar, but different. The main verb is different.

Subject	*be*	Main Verb	Object	Place/Time
She	is	**playing**	the guitar.	
He	is	**watching**	TV	in the evening.

In these sentences with *be (am/are/is)*, the main verb is in the -ing form. We are talking about an action happening in the **present-future**. It is **not finished**.

Practice

Complete the sentences.

1. I like _____ (swim).
2. They love _____ (eat oysters).
3. He likes _____ (play darts).
4. We love _____ (run).
5. She enjoys _____ (watch sport).

67

go + -ing form

We often use *go* with the -ing form when we go somewhere and do an activity.

I **go fishing** on Sundays.

Subject	Verb (*go*)	Activity (-ing)	time/place
I	**go**	**running**	every day.
They	**went**	**shopping**	at the mall.
He	**goes**	**fishing**	in the river.
She	**is going**	**scuba diving**	tomorrow.

	Subject	Verb (*go*)	Activity (-ing)	time/place
Do	you	**go**	**running**	every day?
Did	they	**go**	**shopping**	at the mall?
Does	he	**go**	**fishing**	in the river?
Is	she	**going**	**scuba diving**	tomorrow?

Subject	Verb (*go*)	Activity (-ing)	time/place
I	**don't go**	**running**	every day.
They	**didn't go**	**shopping**	at the mall.
He	**doesn't go**	**fishing**	in the river.
She	**isn't going**	**scuba diving**	tomorrow.

Note: We use *go* with *to* when we go to a destination (a place or an event).
Example: I go **to the park** on Sundays. (See page 202.)

Practice

Complete the conversation. Use *go/went/be going* and the -*ing form*.

A: Hi.
B: Hi. How are you doing?
A: Good. How was your day?
B: Good. (1) I _____(shop) this morning. (2)_____ you _____(shop) this morning too?
A: No. (3) I _____(swim) instead.
B: (4) _____ you _____(swim) every week?
A: Yes, most weeks. Are you doing anything tonight?
A: (5) I _____ (club). Do you want to come?

68

8

Results of actions
perfect aspect

-en form

What is it?

Many common verbs have an -en form. These words end in *-en*, *-ne* or *-n*.

present form	past form	-ing form	-en form
eat	ate	eating	eaten
do	did	doing	done
know	knew	knowing	known

Some verbs change vowels for their different forms and have a *u* (*n* upside-down) for the *-en form*.

present form	past form	-ing form	-en form (u)
drink	drank	drinking	drunk
swim	swam	swimming	swum

However, **most verbs don't have a separate -en form**. We use the same form as the past form.

present form	past form	-ing form	-en meaning
wash	washed	washing	washed
have	had	having	had
love	loved	loving	loved

We know it has the meaning of the -en form because of where it is used in the sentence, often after *have*. (The past form is used directly after the subject.)

I **washed** the car yesterday. (past form)
I've **washed** the car. (-en form meaning)

What does it mean?

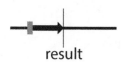
result

We use the -en form to shift focus away from an action.
Details of the action, such as when it happened, are not important.
We use *have* and the -en form to focus on the **result** of an action.

How do we use it?

We often use it with *have*. We have results in the present.

We talk about **recently completed actions**.

I **have eaten** breakfast.

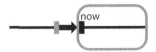

Breakfast is complete.
When it happened isn't important.
The result is important:
I don't need to eat now.

We talk about **experiences**.

I **have lived** in England.

I lived in England sometime in the past.
When it happened isn't important.
The result is important:
I have the experience now.

We are talking about the present. If we say when, we add a time that includes the present.

I **have eaten** breakfast today.

I **have lived** in England this year.

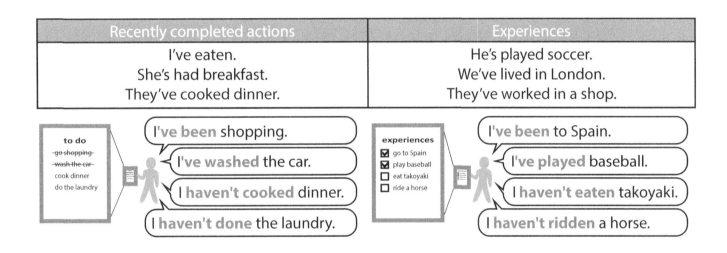

Recently completed actions	Experiences
I've eaten. She's had breakfast. They've cooked dinner.	He's played soccer. We've lived in London. They've worked in a shop.

to do
~~go shopping~~
~~wash the car~~
cook dinner
do the laundry

I've been shopping.
I've washed the car.
I haven't cooked dinner.
I haven't done the laundry.

experiences
☑ go to Spain
☑ play baseball
☐ eat takoyaki
☐ ride a horse

I've been to Spain.
I've played baseball.
I haven't eaten takoyaki.
I haven't ridden a horse.

We use *have* with the -en form.

The present form of *have* shows us this is in the **present-future**.
We are talking about what we have **now**, in the **present**.

Subject	*have*	Verb	Object	Place	
We	**have**	**eaten**	eggs.		We've eaten eggs.
She	**has**	**worked**		in a bank.	She's worked in a bank.
I	**have**	**lived**		in Sweden.	I've lived in Sweden.
He	**has**	**had**	breakfast.		He's had breakfast.
You	**have**	**played**	soccer.		You've played soccer.

The -en form focuses on the **results** of actions.
Exactly when it happened is not important.

71

We put *have* first to make it a question.

have	Subject	Verb	Object	Place	
Have	you	**eaten**	eggs?		Have you eaten eggs?
Has	she	**worked**		in a bank?	Has she worked in a bank?
Have	you	**lived**		in Sweden?	Have you lived in Sweden?
Has	he	**had**	breakfast?		Has he had breakfast?
Have	you	**played**	soccer?		Have you played soccer?

We add *not* to make it negative.

Subject	have not	Verb	Object	Place	
We	**haven't**	**eaten**	eggs.		We haven't eaten eggs.
She	**hasn't**	**worked**		in a bank.	She hasn't worked in a bank.
I	**haven't**	**lived**		in Sweden.	I haven't lived in Sweden.
He	**hasn't**	**had**	breakfast.		He hasn't had breakfast.
You	**haven't**	**played**	soccer.		You haven't played soccer.

Been and *gone* are used when we talk about people going places.

When we use *been* the person **was** somewhere or **was** doing something. They are not there or doing it now.

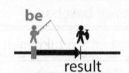
result

He's ***been*** fishing.
He **was fishing** sometime in the past.
He isn't fishing now.
She's ***been*** to Seoul.
She went **to Seoul** sometime in the past.
She **was** in Seoul. **She isn't in Seoul now.**

When we use *gone* the person **went** somewhere so we **don't know** exactly **where** they are now.

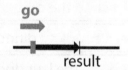
result

He's ***gone*** fishing.
He **went fishing** sometime in the past.
He isn't here now.
She's ***gone*** to Seoul.
She **went to Seoul** sometime in the past.
She isn't here now.

Practice

Complete the sentences using *have* and the -en form.

Example: I *haven't eaten* (not eat) breakfast yet.

1. _____ (you play) golf?
2. I _____ (send) you a letter.
3. _____ (you be) to Europe?
4. _____ (you hear) the news?
5. She _____ (not live) in South Africa.
6. I watched The Shawshank Redemption last night. _____ (you see) it?

adding a length of time

When we talk about experiences, we can add a time period to show how much experience we have. This is the amount of experience we currently have in the present. We often assume we are still gaining experience in these things.

Subject	*have*	Verb	Object	Place/Time	Time period
She	**has**	**worked**		in a bank	**for seven years.**
It	**has**	**rained**			**for the last few days.**
I	**have**	**lived**		in Sweden	**since 2010.**
He	**has**	**played**	soccer		**since he was five.**
It	**has**	**been**		a while	since I've seen you.

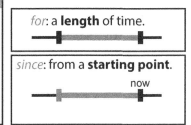

for: a **length** of time.

since: from a **starting point**.

now

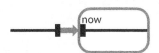

now

How long **has** she **worked** in a bank? She's worked in a bank for seven years.
She started working in the bank seven years ago. She still works there now.
It's **rained** for the last few days.
It started raining a few days ago. It is still raining now.
How long **have** you **lived** in Sweden? I've lived in Sweden since 2010.
I moved to Sweden in 2010. I still live there now.
He's a good soccer player. He's **played** soccer since he was five.
He started playing soccer when he was five. He still plays soccer now.
It's **been** a while since I've seen you.
I haven't seen you for some time.

This pattern is also used for recently completed actions. We often add a time period when we think the action has happened for long enough and we want it to end now.

Subject	*have*	Verb	Object	Place/Time	Time period
I	**have**	**waited**			**for two hours.**
I	**have**	**cooked**		every night	**for three months.**
He	**hasn't**	**eaten**	anything		**since Monday.**

I've **waited** for two hours. It's too long.
I've **cooked** every night for three months. Can you do the cooking for a change?
He **hasn't eaten** anything since Monday. He really should eat something.

Practice

Complete the conversation.

1. A: Nice house! How long _____ you _____ (live) here?
2. B: I_____ (live) here _____ about three years.
   A: You have a piano! Do you play it?
3. B: Yes, I_____ (play) it _____ I was a child. I love it.

ever and never

When we want to make it clear we are talking about experiences, we use *ever* with questions and *never* with negatives. (*never* means *not ever*)

When we are obviously talking about experiences we don't need *ever* and *never*, but we can use them to be clear. Either way is ok.

Experiences	Experiences
Has he played soccer?	Has he **ever** played soccer?
He hasn't played soccer.	He's **never** played soccer.
Have you lived in London?	Have you **ever** lived in London?
We haven't lived in London.	We've **never** lived in London.
Have they worked in a shop?	Have they **ever** worked in a shop?
They haven't worked in a shop.	They've **never** worked in a shop.

We can add *ever* and *never* to make it clear we are talking about an experience, and not a recently completed action.

Recently complete actions	Experiences
Have you cooked dinner?	Have you **ever** cooked dinner?
I haven't cooked dinner.	I've **never** cooked dinner.
	My wife always cooks.

Have you cooked dinner? (today) Or do I need to buy something for dinner?
I haven't cooked dinner. (not today) I often cook.

Have you **ever** cooked dinner? (at any time in your life)
I've **never** cooked dinner. (not even once)

Practice

Complete the conversation using *have* and the -en form. Use *ever* and *never* if you can.

Example:
A: I'm hungry. I _haven't eaten_ (not eat) since breakfast.
1. B: I _____ (not eat) either.
   A: Do you want to get something to eat?
2. B: Sure. _____ you _____ (have) Mexican food?
3. A: Yes. I_____ (have) tacos.
4. B: Have you _____ (have) a burrito?
5. A: No. I_____ (have) one.
   B: They're really good. There's a good burrito place near here.
   A: Ok, let's go there.

already and yet

We use *already* to emphasize that something happened at a point in time before now, before the time we are talking about, or before we expected.

I've **already** done the dishes. I did the dishes sometime before now.
When we got home it was **already** dark. It got dark before we got home.
Oh, you're here **already**! You are here earlier than I expected.
Are you at work **already**? I didn't expect you to be there now.

Yet is similar to *already*, but *yet* refers to the period of time up to now.
We often use *yet* in **questions** and **negative** statements.

Have you finished **yet**? (sometime up to now)
I haven't seen the movie **yet**. (not at any time up to now)
It's the best **yet**. (the best up to now) There may be a better one later.

Already shows something is done, it is not happening later.
Not yet shows something is not done, it is happening later.
Using *yet* in a question asks if something is done, or if it is happening later.

We sometimes use *already* or *yet*, and sometimes don't. It depends on the situation.

-en form only	-en form with *already* or *yet*
now result	now done or not
Teacher: Have you done your homework? Student: Yes, I've done it. The student completed their homework on time. It is due **now**. It could **not** have happened **later**.	Mother: Do your homework. Child: I've **already** done it. The child did the homework **before** now. Doing it **later** would have been ok.
Teacher: Have you done your homework? Student: No, I haven't done it. The student didn't complete their homework on time. It is due **now**. It can **not** happen **later**.	Mother: Have you done your homework **yet**? Child: No, **not yet**. The child hasn't done their homework. The child will do it **later**.

Practice

Complete the conversation using *already* or *yet*.

Example:
A: It's *already* the 26th! Not long to go.
1.   Have you renewed your passport _____?
2.   B: Yes, I have and I've _____ got a visa.
3.   A: You got the visa _____? That was quick.
4.   B: Yeah. Have you booked the flights and the hotel _____?
5.   A: Well, I've booked the flights but I haven't booked the hotel _____.
6.   B: The flights were easy because they _____ had our details from when we booked last time.

Compare *have/has* + -en form **and the** past form.

We use the *have/has* + -en form to talk about results we have in the present.
We use the past form to talk about a specific time in the past.

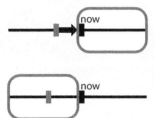

I've been to Africa.
He **hasn't eaten** lunch. (not yet: he may eat it in the future)
Have you **done** your homework?

I went to Africa last year.
He **didn't eat** lunch yesterday. Lunch time was in the past.
Did you **do** your homework? (in the recent past)

We often ask questions with the *have/has* + -en form. We don't know which time in the past to talk about so we talk about the present. We then use the past form to get the specific details.

A: **Have** you **been** to Africa? (interested in experience that you have in the present)
B: Yes, I **went** there last year. (giving details about when I got this experience: in the past)

We use the have/has + -en form with a period of time up to the present.
We use the past form to talk about a period of time that finished in the past.

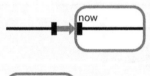

She **has worked** here for a year. She works here now.
He **hasn't eaten** since yesterday.
Have you **lived** here for more than a year?

She **worked** here for a year. (finished: she doesn't work here now)
He **didn't** eat for three days. (in the past: he eats again now)
Did you **stay there** for more than a week?

Practice

Complete the conversations.

1. A: _____ (you ever be) to South America?
   B: Yes, I have. Once.
2. A: When _____ (you go) there?
3. B: I _____ (go) there last year with my family.

4. A: _____ (you ever save) someone's life?
5. B: No, I haven't, but I _____ (save) a dog's life.
6. A: What _____ (you do)?
7. B: I _____ (pull) it out of the path of a moving car.

76

Compare *have/has* + *-en* form **and the** present form.

We use the *have/has* + *-en* form to talk about **specific experiences** (results we have in the present).
We use the present form to talk about things **generally**.

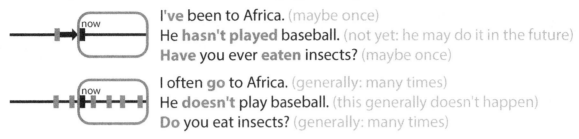

I've been to Africa. (maybe once)
He **hasn't played** baseball. (not yet: he may do it in the future)
Have you ever **eaten** insects? (maybe once)

I often **go** to Africa. (generally: many times)
He **doesn't** play baseball. (this generally doesn't happen)
Do you eat insects? (generally: many times)

We often talk about what generally happens then more specifically about experiences in the same conversation.

A: **Do** you ski? (present form)
B: Yes.
A: **Have** you ever **skied** in Europe? (have/has + -en form)

Practice
Complete the conversations.

A: (1) What music _____ (you like)?
B: (2) I _____ (like) Muse.
A: (3) _____ (you hear) their new album?
B: No, I haven't.

A: (4) _____ (you ever play) futsal?
B: Yes, I have.
A: (5) I_____ (play) on Sundays. Come along.

A: Guess what? (6) I _____ (get) a new car! (7) I _____ (love) it. (8) I _____ (drive) it every day, so (9) my husband _____ (not drive) it yet. (10) _____ (you want) my old car?
B: No thanks, (11) I _____ (just buy) a new car too.

Compare *have/has* + -en form **and** *am/are/is* + -ing form.

We use *have/has* + -en form for **recently completed actions**.
We use *am/are/is* + -ing form for unfinished, but **soon to be completed actions**.

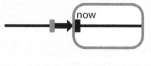

I**'ve** fixed the door.
I **haven't mopped** the floor.
Have you **washed** the windows?

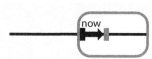

I**'m mopping** the floor. (started or not started)
I**'m not fixing** the door. It isn't broken.
Are you **washing** the windows? I hope you plan to do it soon.

We use *have/has* + -en form for **experiences** we have in the present.
We use *am/are/is* + -ing form for things that are unfinished: **definite future experiences**.

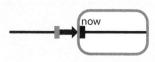

I**'ve ridden** a motorcycle.
I **haven't been** to Salt Lake City.
Have you **seen** Star Wars?

I**'m riding** a motorcycle next week. I am experiencing it soon.
I**'m not going** to Salt Lake City. I am never having the experience.
Are you **watching** Star Wars soon? Are you experiencing it soon?

We use *have/has* + -en form with *for* or *since* to talk about a period of time up to **now**.
We use *am/are/is* + -ing form with *for* to talk about periods of time from start to **end**.

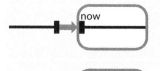

I**'ve lived** here for a month. (to now: from when I moved to now)
I **haven't worked** here for long. I'm new here.
How long **have** you **been** in Costa Rica? (from arriving to now)

I**'m living** here for a month (total: from when I moved to when I leave)
I**'m not working** here for long. I have a short contract.
I'm in Costa Rica now. How long **are** you **staying** in Costa Rica?*

*We answer by saying the total time, 'For a month total', or additional time, 'For two more weeks'.

Practice

Complete the conversations.

1. A: _____(you ever be) to Alaska?
2. B: No, but I _____(go) there next month.

3. The oven _____(heat up) so don't put the potatoes in yet.
4. Wait until it _____(heat up).

5. A: How long _____ (you be) here?
6. B: I _____ (be) here since Monday.
7. A: How long _____ (you stay)?
8. B: I _____ (stay) for three weeks.

9. A: _____(you ever study) English?
10. B: Yes! I _____ (study) English now.

78

9

Results of actions 2
perfect aspect

have got / have

Got is the past form of *get*. We use *have got* (*have* + -en form meaning) in many of the same situations we use *have*. Both of these sentences are referring to the present.

She**'s got** a hat.   =   She **has** a hat.

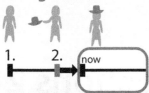

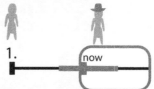

1. She didn't have a hat.
2. She **got** a hat.
now: She**'s got** a hat. ('s got = has got)

1. She **didn't have** a hat.
now: She **has** a hat.

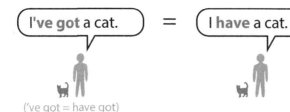

('ve got = have got)

	Subject	*have*	Verb(*got*)	Object	Place	
	We	**have**	**got**	eggs.		We've got eggs.
Have	you		**got**	a soccer ball?		Have you got a soccer ball?
	He	**has**	**got**	blue eyes.		He's got blue eyes.

Everything has a beginning. We get something, then we have it. We use either *have got* or *have*.

We**'ve got** eggs. = We **have** eggs.
Have you **got** a soccer ball? = **Do** you **have** a soccer ball?
He**'s got** blue eyes. = He **has** blue eyes. He got his blue eyes from his mother.

However, there is a difference in how we use *have got* and *have*.

Have got refers to things we got in the past and have in the present.

What **have** you **got** for lunch?
(your lunch today)

Have may refer to things we have in the present or things that generally happen (many times).

What do you **have** for lunch?
(**generally**: every day) (your lunch today)

Practice

Complete the sentences using *have*. Then complete each sentence again using *have got*.

1. I *have* a car.
2. My brother _____ a boat.
3. We _____(not) a jet ski.
4. We _____ a daughter.
5. _____ you _____ a sister?

1. I *'ve got* a car.
2. My brother _____ a boat.
3. We _____(not) a jet ski.
4. We _____ a daughter.
5. _____ you _____ a sister?

80

have done / have to do

Here we have a 'to do' list. The items that are crossed out are complete. The items that are not crossed out are important, but not complete, so we - *have* - *to do* - them in the present-future.

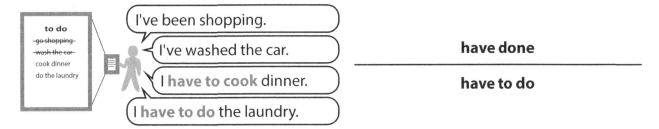

	Subject	Verb		Verb	Object	Place/Time	
		have	*to*	(goal)			
	I	**have**	**to**	**wash**	my hair.		I have to wash my hair.
	She	**has**	**to**	**leave**	the party	early.	She has to leave the party early.
	They	**have**	**to**	**work**		tomorrow.	They have to work tomorrow.
Do	you	**have**	**to**	**go?**			Do you have to go?

Either *have to* or *have got to* can be used.

	Subject	Verb		Verb	Object	Place/Time	
		have got	*to*	(goal)			
	I	**have got**	**to**	**wash**	my hair.		I've got to wash my hair.
	She	**has got**	**to**	**leave**	the party	early.	She's got to leave the party early.
	They	**have got**	**to**	**work**		tomorrow.	They've got to work tomorrow.
Have	you	**got**	**to**	**go?**			Have you got to go?

People often say *gotta* instead of *got to*. We use *have to* in formal English.

We can use these patterns to describe anything that is necessary or must be done.

Practice

Complete the sentences using *have* with the *-en form* and *have to (verb)*.
Using *have got to (verb)* is fine too.

    A: How are the preparations for our Asia trip coming along?
1. B: Good. How about you? _____ you _____(get) your passport?
2. A: Not yet. ____ I _____ (get) a visa too?
3. B: Yes. You _____(get) a visa for China.
4. A: Ok. _____ you _____ (book) the flights and the hotel?
5. B: I _____(book) the flights but I _____(still) (book) the hotel.
    A: Ok then.

adding *to*

We use *to* to connect two places in sequence.

We went from Barcelona to Madrid.

from A   to B

We use *to* to connect two verbs in sequence.

I want to learn.

now to goal

We can connect as many as we like.

I want to learn to dance to impress girls.

now   to next   to next   to goal

Some verbs (such as *have, got, want* and *need*) are often used with *to* before another verb.

Subject	Verb 1		Verb 2	Object	Place/Time
	Verb (now)	*to*	(goal)		
We	**have**	**to**	**buy**	food.	
She	**has got**	**to**	**go.**		
I	**want**	**to**	**help**	you.	
They	**need**	**to**	**work**		tomorrow.
She	**offered**	**to**	**do**	the gardening.	
I	**promise**	**to**	**take**	you	swimming.

now   to goal

We are talking about things happening in sequence.

We **have** to **buy** food. 1. We **have** the task. 2. We **buy** food.
She**'s got** to **go**. 1. She **has got** the task. 2. She **goes**.
I **want** to **help** you. 1. I **want** it. 2. I do it; I **help** you.
They **need** to **work** tomorrow. 1. They **need** it. 2. They do it; they **work** tomorrow.
She **offered** to **do** the gardening. 1. She **offered**. 2. She (possibly) **does** it.
I **promise** to **take** you swimming. 1. I **promise**. 2. I do it; I **take** you swimming.

Practice

Add *to* only where needed. Leave other spaces blank.

Example: I ___ want _to_ buy a hamster.

1. He ___ has ___ go home.
2. She ___ wants ___ a rabbit.
3. They ___ jog ___ keep fit.
4. We ___ want ___ learn ___ speak English.

82

When we use verbs in this way, each verb may have an object.

Subject	Verb 1				Verb 2	Object/Description
	(*not*)	Verb	Object	*to*	(goal)	
I	**don't**	**have**	money	**to**	**buy**	clothes.
We		**have**	conversations	**to**	**practice**	English.

Some common expressions are formed with *be*, a description, and *to*, and used before a verb. These expressions give us information relating to the goal.

Subject	Expression			Verb	Object/Description	Place/Time
	be	Description	*to*	(goal)		
I	**am**	**supposed**	**to**	**work**		on Friday.
He	**was**	**able**	**to**	**find**	a job.	
It	**is**	**bound**	**to**	**be**	good.	
It	**is**	**about**	**to**	**rain.**		
The President	**is**		**to**	**visit**	Africa	next month.

We add verbs with *to* to sentences with verbs in the -ing form and -en form too.

Subject	Verb 1			Verb 2	Object	Place/Time
		Verb	*to*	(goal)		
I	**have**	**decided**	**to**	**go**		to Africa.
I	**am**	**planning**	**to**	**go**		next year.
They	**haven't**	**come**	**to**	**get**	the car	yet.
They	**are**	**coming**	**to**	**get**	the car	on Tuesday.
We	**are**	**going**	**to**	**have**	a barbecue.	

The actions and events after *to* happen in the future. We often use this pattern with *be going to* to talk about the future. (See page 153.)

Practice

Combine the sentences using *to*.

1. Now: He eats vegetables. Goal: He loses weight. *He eats vegetables to lose weight*   .
2. Now: I am trying. Goal: I find a solution. _____.
3. Now: They have gone. Goal: They get some milk. _____.
4. Now: We're about... Goal: We go home. _____.
5. Now: I have... Goal: work tomorrow. _____.

to or -ing?

Some verbs are often used when we talk about **two** things happening in sequence. We use *to*.

Subject	Verb 1	*to*	Verb 2	Object etc.
I	**want**	**to**	**go**	snorkeling.
She	**is learning**	**to**	**drive.**	
We	**'ve decided**	**to**	**take**	a holiday.

now   to goal

I **want** to **go** snorkeling.
1. I **want** it. 2. I (possibly) **go** snorkeling.
She **is learning** to **drive**.
1. She **learns**. 2. She **drives**.
We**'ve decided** to **take** a holiday.
1. We **decide**. 2. We **take** a holiday.

Some verbs talk about one thing happening. We use the -ing form as the object. (Page 67)

Subject	Verb	Object (activity)
I	**enjoy**	**walking.**
She	**is practicing**	**parking.**
We	**considered**	**going to Egypt.**

The object is the thing that we *enjoy, are practicing, considered* etc.

The object often doesn't end in *-ing*.
I enjoy **walks** in the park.
She is practicing **the piano**.
We considered **the option**.

The meaning of the first verb is important. Some verbs go with *to*, some with *-ing*, some with either.

In some situations, some verbs can be followed by a verb with *to* or an activity (-ing form). The overall meaning is the same.

Subject	Verb 1	*to*	Verb 2	Object etc.
I	**love**	**to**	**sing.**	
She	**likes**	**to**	**go**	to Europe.

now   to goal

I **love** to **sing**.
1. Reason: I **love** it. 2. What I do: I **sing**.

Subject	Verb	Object (activity)
I	**love**	**singing.**
She	**likes**	**going to Europe.**

I **love singing**.
Singing is the thing I love.

Sometimes only one option fits.

Subject	Verb 1	*to*	Verb 2	Object etc.
I	**like**	**to**	**close**	the windows.

now   to goal

Before I go out, I **like** to **close** the windows.
1. Reason: I **like** having the windows closed.
2. What I do: I **close** the windows.
I like having the windows closed so I close them. Closing windows is **not** my hobby.

Subject	Verb	Object (activity)
I	**like**	**living in Melbourne.**

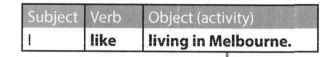

I **like living** in Melbourne.
I like this one thing: living where I live.
It is **not** an **activity** that I do from time to time. It is something permanent.

Sometimes the meaning is different in different situations.

A: What do you do for fun?
B: I love to figure skate. I love it. I do it.
or:
B: I love figure skating: I love the sport.
We assume I do it because of the context.
= I love to figure skate. (in this situation)

A: Do you like the Winter Olympics?
B: Yes, I love figure skating. I love the sport.

Many people who love the sport don't actually do it. They love watching it.

Sometimes the meaning is completely different.

Subject	Verb 1	to	Verb 2	Object etc.
I	**stopped**	**to**	**talk**	to Michelle.

Two things happening in sequence.
1. I **stopped** doing what I was doing.
2. I **talked** to Michelle.

Subject	Verb	Object (activity)
I	**stopped**	**talking to Michelle.**

One thing I stopped: talking to Michelle. We often talked in the past but I do not talk to her anymore.

Remember to lock the door before you leave.
I will lock the door in the future.
1. Remember. 2. Lock the door.

Where's my key? I **remember locking** the door, so I had it when I left.
One thing I remember: I locked the door.

I **tried to open** the window, but it was stuck.
I couldn't get the window open.
1. I try. 2. Goal: open the window - It was stuck so I didn't reach my goal.

It's so hot. I **tried opening** the window but it didn't help.
One thing I tried: I opened the window, but the house was still hot.

We **regret to inform** you that your services are no longer required.
1. We feel regret because your services are no longer required. 2. We inform you.

I **regret** not **studying** harder.
One thing I regret in the past: I feel regret because I didn't study hard enough.

Practice

Complete the sentences with a *verb* (with *to*) or a *noun* (a verb in the -ing form). There may be more than one answer.

1. I promise _____ (help) you.
2. I recommend _____ (go) to the museum.
3. Sorry, I forgot _____ (get) a cake.
4. I don't like _____ (run).
5. Keep _____ (go).
6. What will they choose _____ (do)?
7. We're planning _____ (go) to the theater.
8. Stop _____ (write) and hand in your exam!

results in the past

We talk about results in the past the same way we talk about results in the present (*have* and the -en form - See page 70). We use *had* (past of *have*) to show we are talking about a time in the past.

I **had eaten** breakfast.

I **had lived** in England.

We add **more information** so the listener knows when we are referring to.

I'd eaten a big breakfast **so I wasn't hungry at lunch time**. (referring to lunch time: in the past)
I wasn't hungry at lunch time. I'**d eaten** a big breakfast.
I'**d lived** in England **so I was comfortable speaking English in America**.
I lived in America last year. I'**d lived** in England before that.

We use *had* with t*he* -en form.

| *Had* is used because we are talking about what we had at a time in the **past**. | 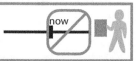 |

Subject	*have*	Verb (-en)	Object	Place	
She	**had**	**worked**		in a bank	before she got her current banking job.
I	**had**	**lived**		in Sweden	so I knew a little Swedish.
He	**had**	**had**	breakfast		so he didn't eat anything.
You	**had**	**played**	soccer		before Ashley became your coach.

| The -en form focuses on the **results** of actions. Exactly when it happened is not important. | 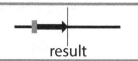 |

We use this pattern to talk about results at a time in the past. These things happened before the time we are referring to. We can talk about experiences or actions.

Experiences
He was much better than the other players because they were beginners but he**'d played** soccer before.
The new employee was very slow because he **hadn't worked** in a shop before.
A: We went to the USA last year. B: Great, **had** you **been** there before?

Actions
Dave offered me a sandwich yesterday but I wasn't hungry because I**'d** already **eaten**.
I made her lunch. She was very hungry because she **hadn't had** breakfast.
So you got home at 6PM, **had** they **cooked** dinner?

Adding a time

When we talk about experiences, we can add time information to show how much experience we had. This is the amount of experience we had at that time in the past. People often continued gaining experience in these things.

Subject	*have*	Verb (-en)	Object	Place	Time period
She	**had**	**worked**		in a bank	**for seven years.**
I	**had**	**lived**		in Sweden	**for ten years.**
He	**had**	**played**	soccer		**since he was five.**

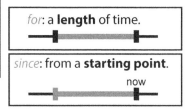

for: a **length** of time.	
since: from a **starting point.**	

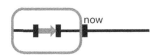

She'**d worked** in the bank for seven years so the boss offered her a promotion.

I'**d lived** in Sweden for ten years and decided it was time for a change. I sold my house and moved to Germany.

Gary was the captain of the team because he'**d played** soccer since he was five.

This pattern is also used for **actions** and **events**. We use *had* and the -en form to show that something happened before something else in the past. We add time information to show the time between the two actions or events.

Subject	*have*	Verb (-en)	Object	Time/Time period
I	**had**	**eaten**		**ten minutes before.**
Sally	**had**	**arrived**		**at 8:00.**
They	**hadn't**	**taken**	a vacation	**since they were 25.**

Dave offered me a sandwich yesterday but I wasn't hungry because I'**d eaten** ten minutes before. I ate something. Ten minutes after that, Dave offered me a sandwich.

I arrived at 8:30. I thought I was the first one there but Sally **had arrived** at 8:00. Sally arrived first.

Sue and Glen took a vacation last week. It had been a long time. They **hadn't taken** a vacation since they were 25. Their last vacation was when they were 25.

Practice

Complete the sentences using *had* and the -en form.

1. Everyone got lost except Andrea because she_____ (be) there when she was a child.
2. I was late to work because I _____ (be) stuck in traffic for two hours.
3. When I got home, I realized I _____ (forgot) my bag.
4. After the rain _____ (stop), the children went out to play.
5. She got good grades because she _____ (work) so hard on all her assignments.
6. I tried papaya the other day. I _____ (not have) it before.

Compare *had* + -en form **and the** past form.

We use *had* + -en form for things that happened **before** something else.
We use the past form for things that happened in the **past**. Sometimes either can be used.

A: **Had** you ever **eaten** pizza for lunch before you met me?
B: Yes I **had**.
We are talking about what happened before an event in the past.

A: **Did** you ever **eat** pizza for lunch before you met me?
B: Yes I **did**.
We are talking about a time in the past: your life before you met me.

We use *had* + -en form to make it **clear** that something happened before something else.
We often just use the past form and use **common sense** to put things in order.

I got to work on time but I **had forgotten** to go to the bank.
The order is clear. The plan was: go to the bank before work.
I got to work on time but I **forgot** to go to the bank.
Two things that happened in the past. Common sense tells us the order they happened.

Had + -en form is sometimes needed because the past form suggests that things happened in a different order.

When I arrived, the show **had started**.
The show started **before** I arrived. We often say 'the show had already started' to be clearer.
When I arrived, the show **started**.
We use *when* to say the order things happened. The part with *when* happened first. The other part happened immediately after. **1.** I arrived. **2.** The show started.
He **hadn't lived** in America when I met him. (**before** I met him)
He **didn't** live in America when I met him. (**at** the time I met him) He may have lived there before.

Practice

Complete the narrative with *had* + -en form or the past form. There may be more than one answer.
(1) I _____(finish) work late and (2) _____ (rush) to the train station, hoping to catch the last train. Luckily, (3) the train _____ (leave). (4) I _____ (put) my hand in my pocket but (5) _____ (can't) find my wallet. (6) I _____ (leave) it in the office. (7) Then I _____(realize) (8) I _____ (leave) my phone in the office too. (9) This is a real problem, (9) I _____ (do) the same thing the week before too.

88

10

Shifting focus
passive sentences

be + -en form

We use the -en form to shift focus.

We use *be (am/are/is/was/were)* and the -en form to focus on what the verb relates to, rather that who or what does it.

Subject	Verb	Object	Place/Time
I	**ate**	**breakfast**	at 6:00.

I ate **breakfast** at 6:00.
We say **who** ate and **what** they ate.

Subject	*be*	Verb (-en)	Place/Time
Breakfast	**was**	**eaten**	at 6:00.

Breakfast was eaten at 6:00.
We focus on **breakfast**.
Who ate it is not important.

In the first sentence, *breakfast* is the **object**. In the second sentence, *breakfast* is the **subject**. Making *breakfast* the subject gives it more focus.

We use *be (was)* because we are referring to breakfast as a whole. We are talking about breakfast and describing what happens to it.

Compare the -ing form and the -en form.

The chicken is **eating**.
We are saying what the chicken is doing.
(now)

The chicken is **eaten**.
We are saying what happens to the chicken.
(generally)
Who or what does it is not important.

Compare *be (is)* and *have*.

Fish **is eaten** at this restaurant.

People eat fish at the restaurant.

Fish **have eaten** at this restaurant?!

Fish have eaten food at the restaurant.

We use the present form of be to talk about things that are generally true. We also add by to say who or what does it.

Subject	be	Verb (-en)	Person/Method	Place/Time
These bags	**are**	**made**		in Denmark.
Elephants	**aren't**	**found**		in this region.
The website	**is**	**updated**	**by our staff**	every day.

We use the past form of be to talk about things that happened in the past.

Subject	be (past)	Verb (-en)	Person/Method	Place/Time
These bags	**were**	**made**		in Denmark.
He	**was**	**born**		in 1951.
My camera	**was**	**stolen**		last week.
Electricity	**was**	**discovered**	**by Benjamin Franklin**	in 1752.
The bags	**were**	**sewn**	**by hand.**	

We also say:

Benjamin Franklin discovered electricity in 1752. This puts focus on Benjamin Franklin. He did it.

When we use be and the -en form we don't need to say who did it:
Electricity was discovered in 1752. We are just focusing on electricity.

Practice

Complete the sentences with be and the -en form. These things are generally true or things that happened in the past.

1. My guitar _____ (make) in Indonesia.
2. Christmas _____ (celebrate) in December.
3. The Starry Night _____ (paint) by Vincent Van Gogh.
4. The lost dog _____ (return) to his owner.
5. Her music _____ (enjoy) by people all over the world.
6. The telephone _____ (invent) by Alexander Graham Bell.
7. The winner _____ (announce) last night.

with other sentence patterns

We use *be* and the -en form with other sentence patterns.

We change the form of *be*.

Subject		Verb	Object
Lachlan		eats	chicken.
Lachlan		ate	chicken.
Lachlan	is	eating	chicken.
Lachlan	has	eaten	chicken.
Lachlan	is going to	eat	chicken.

Subject		*be*	Verb (-en)	
Chicken		is	eaten.	generally
Chicken		was	eaten.	past
Chicken	is	being	eaten.	not finished
Chicken	has	been	eaten.	result
Chicken	is going to	be	eaten.	future plan

Subject		Verb	Object
Lachlan	doesn't	eat	chicken.
Lachlan	didn't	eat	chicken.
Lachlan	isn't	eating	chicken.
Lachlan	hasn't	eaten	chicken.
Lachlan	isn't going to	eat	chicken.

Subject		*be*	Verb (-en)	
Chicken		isn't	eaten.	generally
Chicken		wasn't	eaten.	past
Chicken	isn't	being	eaten.	not finished
Chicken	hasn't	been	eaten.	result
Chicken	isn't going to	be	eaten.	future plan

Practice

Change the sentences to change the focus. You don't need to say who did/does it.

Example: We have finalized the sale.
The sale _has been finalized_____.

1. The boss has arranged a meeting for Thursday.
   A meeting_____.
2. The police are going to investigate the incident.
   The incident _____.
3. The department hasn't received your application.
   Your application _____.
4. They are building a new shopping center.
   A new shopping center _____.
5. The bank has declined your credit card.
   Your credit card _____.
6. We're notifying successful applicants by email.
   Successful applicants _____.
7. We are not considering other options.
   Other options _____.

92

get + -en form

We also use *get* with the -en form. We use *get* to talk about changes. (See page 20.)

Be can also be used in these sentences. There is a small difference in meaning (*be* describes how it is, *get* describes a change), but both can be used to describe the same things.
Be is used in formal situations. We often use *get* when speaking casually and there is a change.

Subject	*be*	Verb (-en)
Chicken	**is**	**eaten.**

≈

Subject	*get*	Verb (-en)
Chicken	**gets**	**eaten.**

Subject		*get*	Verb (-en)	Person/Method	Place/Time
She		**gets**	**rewarded**		for her hard work.
We		**got**	**invited**		to lunch.
The package	is	**getting**	**delivered**		on Friday.
Amelia	has	**gotten**	**bitten**	by a mosquito.	
The USA	are going to	**get**	**beaten**	by Canada	tonight.

Subject		*get*	Verb (-en)	Person/Method	Place/Time
She	doesn't	**get**	**rewarded**		for her hard work.
We	didn't	**get**	**invited**		to lunch.
The package	isn't	**getting**	**delivered**		on Friday.
Amelia	hasn't	**gotten**	**bitten**	by a mosquito.	
The USA	aren't going to	**get**	**beaten**	by Canada	tonight.

Practice

Change the sentences to change the focus using *get*. You don't need to say who did/does it.

Example: He drove me to the station.
I *got driven to the station* .

1. The mechanic is fixing my car next week.
   My car _____.
2. When are you going to pay us?
   When are we _____?
3. A car didn't hit the dog.
   The dog _____ by a car.
4. There was an accident, but it hurt nobody.
   There was an accident, but _____.
5. We didn't wash the sheets.
   The sheets _____.
6. The driver delivered the pizza to the wrong address.
   The pizza _____.
7. They accepted me for an interview.
   I _____.

feelings

We often use *be* and the -ing form to say how we feel. We use *be* and the -en form to say how someone or something makes us feel.

We talk about what is happening.

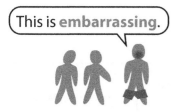

This is **embarrassing**.

The situation is embarrassing.
We describe the situation in its unfinished state.

We talk about the result of what happened.

I'm **embarrassed**.

I feel embarrassed.
This feeling is the result of something that happened.

Subject	*be*	Description (-ing form)
They	**are**	**interesting.**
He	**was**	**annoying.**
She	**is**	**amazing.**

They are interesting.
They make other people interested.

He was annoying.
He makes other people feel annoyed.

She is amazing.
She amazes people. She is a great singer.

Subject	*be*	Description (-en meaning)
I	**am**	**interested.**
She	**was**	**annoyed.**
We	**are**	**amazed.**

I'm interested.
They made me interested.

She was annoyed.
He made her feel annoyed.

We are amazed.
How we feel. We just listened to a great singer.

Practice

Complete the sentences with the -ing form or the -en form.

Example: Don't eat at that restaurant. We ate there last week. The food was __*disgusting*__ (disgust).

1. They had so many chances but they couldn't score. It was really _____ (disappoint).
2. The news was very _____ (shock).
3. This drink is really _____ (refresh).
4. The new album comes out tomorrow. I'm really _____ (excite).
5. I was _____ (shock) when I read what happened.
6. I just had a massage. I feel _____ (relax).
7. I watched a movie on Saturday. It was _____ (inspire).

11

Putting it together
perfect aspect and progressive aspect

have + been + -ing

We use *have* + -en form **and** *be* + -ing form together.

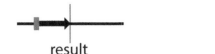

result

finish

We use *have* (present form) + the -en form to talk about results in the present.
We use *be* + -ing form to talk about an activity in its unfinished state.

It may **not** be **finished**.
This is useful when talking about **recent activities**. We are focusing on doing the activity, not finishing it.

A: What have you been doing recently?
B: **I've been reading** a book.

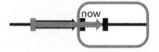

It is not finished, but I have a result in the present (I have read some).

It may be **finished**.
Doing this activity causes a result. The activity causes the result, not its completion.

A: Why are you wet?
B: **I've been swimming**.

The activity (swimming) caused the result (wet). It is finished. It is obvious that I'm not swimming now.

Subject	*have*	*be* (en)	Verb (-ing)	Object	
She	**has**	**been**	**waiting.**		She's been waiting. (result: She is next)
I	**have**	**been**	**watching**	TV.	I've been watching TV. (result: news)
He	**has**	**been**	**drinking.**		He's been drinking. (result: He is drunk)

have	Subject	*be* (en)	Verb (-ing)	Object	
Has	she	**been**	**waiting?**		Has she been waiting?
Have	you	**been**	**watching**	TV?	Have you been watching TV?
Has	he	**been**	**drinking?**		Has he been drinking?

Subject	*have not*	*be* (en)	Verb (-ing)	Object	
She	**hasn't**	**been**	**waiting.**		She hasn't been waiting.
I	**haven't**	**been**	**watching**	TV.	I haven't been watching TV.
He	**hasn't**	**been**	**drinking.**		He hasn't been drinking.

When we ask someone how they are we often say:

How are you? (describing now)

We often use other sentence patterns too. These are used a lot in friendly conversations. The meanings are slightly different, but because they are simply used to start a conversation it doesn't usually matter which one you use.

How are you doing? (now and into the future)
How have you been? (past: up to now)
How have you been doing? (past: up to now, now and into the future)

We often use ask questions with *have + been doing* in friendly conversations.

A: Hi. How have you been doing?
B: Good thanks.
A: What have you been doing recently?
B: I've been playing a lot of sport.

We often use *up to* instead of *doing*. *Doing* and *up to* are both common in casual speech.

What are you **up to**? ≈ What are you **doing**?
What have you been **up to**? ≈ What have you been **doing**?

There is a subtle difference: *doing* is about action, *up to* suggests we have completed part of something. We use *up to* to describe the next point. When talking about life in general we have completed part of our life up to a point.

Adding a time

We can add a **time period** to show how long these things have been happening. These things are not finished.

Subject	*have*	*be* (en)	Verb (ing)	Object	Time period
She	**has**	**been**	waiting		**for ten minutes.**
I	**have**	**been**	watching	TV	**all day.**
He	**has**	**been**	drinking		**since noon.**
It	**has**	**been**	raining		**since yesterday.**

We are talking about what we have in the present. We can say how recent these things are by adding a time that includes the present.

Subject	*have*	*be* (en)	Verb (ing)	Object	Time
She	**has**	**been**	swimming		**this morning.**
He	**hasn't**	**been**	drinking		**this week.**
It	**has**	**been**	raining		**today.**

Compare *have + been + -ing* form **and** *have + -en* form.

We use *have + been + -ing* form **to talk about recent activities** (completed or not).
We use *have + -en* form **to talk about results of recently completed actions.** These are finished.

My eyes are tired. **I've been looking** at the computer all day.
If I say this at the end of the day we assume it is finished.

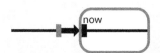

I **have been writing** a book.
We assume this is not finished.
What **have** you **been doing** (this week)?
We are asking about the time up to now, it doesn't matter if it's finished. This is friendly.

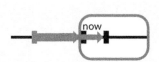

I **have looked** at the computer. You need to do an update. I've finished.
I **have written** a book. This is finished.
What **have** you **done** (this week)?
We are asking about something that finished recently with a result in the present. A boss might ask this when wanting to know what is complete.
Oh no! What **have** you **done?**
We question something that someone did in the past that has a negative impact on the present.

We use both sentence patterns with *for* and *since*. *Have + -en* form **simply refers to a period of time up to the present.** *Have + been + -ing* form **refers to something that is not finished, that has lasted a period of time up to the present.** In most situations either can be used.

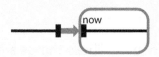

I **have been playing** basketball since I was a child.
Up to now, this finishes in the future.
I **have been living** in Japan for a year. This will finish, I'll move somewhere else someday.

I **have played** basketball since I was a child. Up to now, We aren't thinking about it finishing.
I **have lived** in Japan for a year. We are not thinking about it finishing.
I **have lived** for 30 years. We are not thinking about it finishing.

Practice

Complete the conversation. There may be more than one answer.

1. A: Hi. What _____ you been doing this week?
2. B: I _____ (play) a lot of guitar.
3. A: _____ you _____ (write) any new songs?
4. B: I_____ (work) on a new one but it isn't finished yet.
5. _____ you _____(hear) the song I wrote last week?
6. A: Yeah, I listened to it this morning. It's so catchy. I _____ (hum) the melody all day.
7. B: How about you? What _____ you _____(do)?
8. A: Not much, I'm sick. I_____ (be) sick for the last few days.
9. So, I _____ (lie) around the house, _____(sleep) and _____(watch) TV.
10. B: How long _____ you _____ (feel) sick?
    A: Since Tuesday.

Compare *have + been + -ing form* **and** *am/are/is + -ing form.*

We use *have + been + -ing form* to talk about recent activities. They may or may not have finished.
We use *am/are/is + -ing form* to talk unfinished actions. They may or may not have started.
We know if it has started or finished because of the **context**.

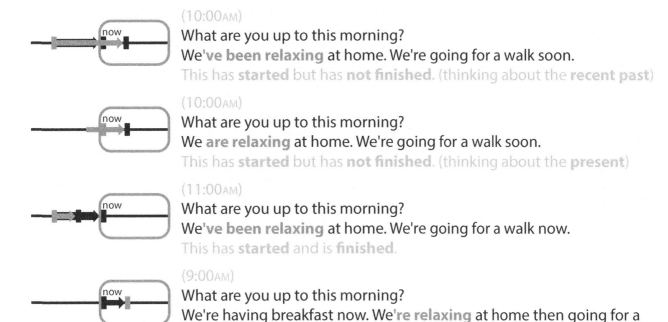

(10:00AM)
What are you up to this morning?
We**'ve been relaxing** at home. We're going for a walk soon.
This has **started** but has **not finished**. (thinking about the **recent past**)

(10:00AM)
What are you up to this morning?
We **are relaxing** at home. We're going for a walk soon.
This has **started** but has **not finished**. (thinking about the **present**)

(11:00AM)
What are you up to this morning?
We**'ve been relaxing** at home. We're going for a walk now.
This has **started** and is **finished**.

(9:00AM)
What are you up to this morning?
We're having breakfast now. We**'re relaxing** at home then going for a walk. This has **not started** and is **not finished**.

Recent activities have started. We can think about them in two ways. Both fit the same situation. Some people may tend to use one more than the other.

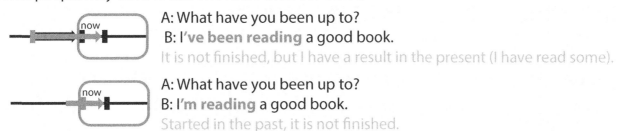

A: What have you been up to?
 B: I**'ve been reading** a good book.
It is not finished, but I have a result in the present (I have read some).

A: What have you been up to?
B: I**'m reading** a good book.
Started in the past, it is not finished.

Practice

Complete the chat conversation. There may be more than one answer.

1. A: Hi. It's been a while. What _____ you _____ (do) recently?
2. B: Lots. We _____ (move) to Ireland next week.
3.   So we_____(pack) and _____(get) ready to move.
4. A: Great! I_____ (live) in Ireland now!
5.   Which part of Ireland _____ you _____ (move) to?
    B: Dublin.
6. A: I_____(live) in Dublin!
7. B: How long _____ you _____ (live) there?
8. A: Since April. I _____ (work) at a hotel but I don't really like it.
9.   So, I_____(look) for a new job for the last few weeks.
10. B: How long _____ (work) at the hotel?
    A: Only about one month.

had + been + ing

We use *had* (past form) + the -en form. We are talking about results in the past.
We use *be* + -ing form to talk about an activity in its unfinished state.

It may not have been finished at a time in the past. We talk about what we were doing leading up to a time in the past.

Last time I saw you **you'd been reading** a good book.

It was not finished, but I had a result in the past (I had read some).

It may have been finished at a time in the past. Doing this activity caused a result. The activity causes the result, not its completion.

A: **Why were you wet** when I saw you?
B: **I'd been swimming**.

The activity (swimming) caused the result (wet). It was finished. It was obvious that I wasn't swimming when you saw me.

Context	Subject	*have*	be (-en)	Verb (-ing)	Object/Time/Place etc.
When I saw her	she	**had**	**been**	**waiting**	for an hour.
My eyes were tired.	I	**had**	**been**	**looking**	at a screen all day.
He came home at 4:00.	He	**had**	**been**	**drinking.**	

Compare *had* + *been* + -ing form and *was/were* + -ing form.

Sometimes *had* + *been* + -ing form and *was/were* + -ing form may fit the same situation.

Last time I saw you **you'd been reading** a book.
We talk about the result of something that was **not finished**.

Last time I saw you **you were reading** a book.
We talk about something that was **not finished**.

Had + *been* + -ing form and *was/were* + -ing form **may have very different meanings.**

A: **Why were you wet** when I saw you?
B: **I'd been swimming**.
I was swimming **before** you saw me. I had **finished**.

A: **Why were you wet** when I saw you?
B: **I was swimming**.
I was in the water. I had **not finished**.

Compare *had + been + -ing form* **and** *had + -en form*.

These things **didn't finish** at the time in the past; they continued to happen. We can often think about the same situation in either way.

When you met your wife, how long **had** you **been living** here?
Talking about period of time in the past. The activity was not finished (you are still living here now).

When you met your wife, how long **had** you **lived** here?
Talking about period of time in the past: from moving to the time you met your wife. We assume you continued living here after that.

Compare *had + been + -ing form* **and the** past form.

These things **finished** at or before the time in the past. We can often think about the same situation in either way.

I **had been waiting** for twenty minutes when the bus finally arrived.
We emphasize the activity happening over a period of time before the time in the past (when the bus arrived).

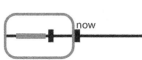

I **waited** for twenty minutes then the bus finally arrived.
We talk about two things in the past in sequence. The period of time finished, then the next thing happened.

Practice

Complete the conversation. There may be more than one answer.

    A: Hi Greg. How are you doing?
    B: Good thanks.
1. A: Last time I saw you you said you_____ (study) Spanish, how is that coming along?
2. B: It's going really well. I had a test last month so I_____ (read) books in Spanish and _____ (practice) with my tutor every day leading up to that.
    A: So how did the test go?
3. B: I think I'll pass. How's it all going with you? Last time you said you_____ (look) for a new job.
4. A: Yeah, I_____(look) for about five months.
5. I_____ (take) interview after interview and was getting nowhere, but then I got a call back for a job in a warehouse. So, I'm starting that next week.
    B: Congratulations. I hope it goes well.

12

Review of verb forms
tense and aspect

review of verb forms

present form
general use

We use the present form to refer to things that are generally true in the **PRESENT-FUTURE**.

happens many times

is permanent

descriptions true now

happens at a fixed time

happens as speaker is speaking

We use the present form when another verb tells us when it happens.

past form
not present-future

We use the past form to refer to something **NOT** in the **PRESENT-FUTURE**.

We describe how something was at a time in the past.

We talk about actions and events that are **FINISHED**.

-ing form
not finished

We use be and the -ing form to refer to an action or event that is **NOT FINISHED.**

It may have started.

It may happen later.

It has **started** but is **not finished** now.

It had **started** but was **not finished** (past).

It has **not started** and is **not finished** now.

It **hadn't started** and was **not finished** (past).

-en form
shifting focus

We use have and the -en form to shift focus from the action to the **RESULT**.

It may have finished.

It may continue to happen.

We talk about **results** in the present.

We talk about **results** in the past.

We talk about a period up to the present.

We talk about a period up to a time in the past.

We use be or get and the -en form to shift focus away from the person or thing that does the action.

examples

I **play** football in the park.
We **go** shopping on Mondays.

Do you **eat** fish?
Does he **drink** coffee?

She **doesn't read** books.
We **don't cook** dinner at home.

London **is** the capital of the UK.
We **have** a dog.

Where **does** she **live**?
Is he short?

We **don't like** tennis.
I **don't have** to write emails.

I'm hungry.
This **looks** good.

Are you ready?
Does it sound good?

It **isn't** hot.
It **doesn't** taste bad.

Our flight **departs** at 6:30.
The meeting **is** at 10.

What time **does** it **finish**?
When **is** the party?

The concert **doesn't start** at 6.
They **don't arrive** at 5:20.

He **wakes** up...
He **goes** downstairs...

Does he go to the fridge?...
Does he drink something?...

He **doesn't drink** anything...
He **doesn't eat** breakfast.

I have to **go**.
I wanted to **play** tennis.

Do you **want** a drink?
Did you **have** a good day?

I don't **play** the piano.
I didn't **drink** tea yesterday.

I **had** to go.
I **wanted** to play tennis.
We **were** on vacation last week.
It **looked** good.

Were you ready?
Did it sound good?
Did you have a good day?
Was it cold yesterday?

It **wasn't** hot.
It **didn't** taste bad.
I **didn't** know her.
I **didn't** like heavy metal.

She **ate** six eggs yesterday.
We **went** to an island.
He **played** golf on Sunday.
They **ate** sushi last night.

Did they play sport last week?
Did they go swimming?
Did she clean her room?
Did he call my name?

He **didn't** go to work today.
I **didn't** eat this morning.
She **didn't** open the window.
We **didn't** drink coffee.

She**'s drinking** tea.
We**'re watching** the baseball.

Is he **running**?
Are they **cooking** pasta?

She **isn't watching** TV.
I**'m not listening**.

When I saw her,
she **was drinking** tea.

Were they **cooking** pasta last
night?

When I talked to him,
he **wasn't watching** TV.

I**'m going** to Norway tomorrow.
We**'re having** a BBQ on Sunday.

Are we **going** home soon?
When **are** you **starting** work?

I**'m not playing** tennis next week.
She **isn't having** a party.

I didn't drink much beer because
I **was driving**.

Why did you pack your towels?
Were you **going** swimming?

She **wasn't having** a party so we
didn't get her a present.

I**'ve been** to Hong Kong.
They**'ve done** the laundry.
She**'s got** a boat.

Have you ever **been** to Sweden?
Has she **washed** the car?
Have they **eaten**?

We **haven't been** to Vietnam.
She **hasn't received** the letter.
He's never **driven** a truck.

She went out to play because she
had already **done** her homework.

You played so well! **Had** you
played before?

I went to Vietnam last month. I
hadn't been there before.

I**'ve been** in Hong Kong for a day.
I**'ve played** soccer **since** I was six.

How long you **been** in Sweden?
How long have you **waited**?

She **hasn't received** any letters
for a week.

I met an old friend in Hong Kong. I
had only **been** there **for** a day.

So you left Sweden, **how long**
had you **been** there?

I called them because I **hadn't**
received any letters for a week.

It **was made** in Indonesia.
My shirt **got caught** on the fence.

Did it **get stolen**?
Were they **rescued**?

They **didn't get paid**.
 It **wasn't painted** by me.

quiz

1. Choose the best picture for the word *have*.
   (a)   (b)

2. Choose the best picture for the word *be*.
   (a)   (b)

3. I play tennis on Mondays.

   When are we referring to?
   (a) last Monday
   (b) next Monday
   (c) probably both (a) and (b) and others
   (d) we don't know which Monday

4. We went shopping on Wednesday.

   When are we referring to?
   (a) last Wednesday
   (b) next Wednesday
   (c) probably both (a) and (b) and others
   (d) we don't know which Wednesday

5. She's going cycling on Saturday.

   When are we referring to?
   (a) last Saturday
   (b) next Saturday
   (c) probably both (a) and (b) and others
   (d) we don't know which Saturday

6. He's worked on Sunday.

   When are we referring to?
   (a) last Sunday
   (b) next Sunday
   (c) probably both (a) and (b) and others
   (d) we don't know which Sunday

7. _____ you live in Malaysia now?

   (a) Are
   (b) Do
   (c) Have
   (d) Did

8. _____ you watch TV yesterday?

   (a) Are
   (b) Do
   (c) Have
   (d) Did

9. _____ you lived in Brazil?

   (a) Are
   (b) Do
   (c) Have
   (d) Did

10. _____ you watching TV?

    (a) Are
    (b) Do
    (c) Have
    (d) Did

11. _____ you eaten lunch?

    (a) Are
    (b) Do
    (c) Have
    (d) Did

12. _____ you sleep well last night?

    (a) Are
    (b) Do
    (c) Have
    (d) Did

13. Which of these sentences can be used to talk about tomorrow?

    (a) He walked home.
    (b) He's walking home.
    (c) He's walked home.
    (d) all of the above

14. Which of these sentences can be used to talk about yesterday?

    (a) He walks home.
    (b) He walked home.
    (c) He's walking home.
    (d) all of the above

15. Which of these sentences can be used to talk about today?

    (a) He walked home.
    (b) He's walking home.
    (c) He's walked home.
    (d) all of the above

16. Which of these sentences can be used to talk about every day?

    (a) He walks home.
    (b) He's walking home.
    (c) He's walked home.
    (d) all of the above

17. She's cooking dinner.

    What does 's mean?
    (a) has
    (b) is

18. She's cooked dinner.

    What does 's mean?
    (a) has
    (b) is

19. Which of these refers to the future?

    (a) The show starts at 10:00.
    (b) The show started at 10:00.
    (c) The show is starting at 10:00.
    (d) both (a) and (c)

20. Choose the best answer.

    What are you doing tomorrow?
    (a) I go fishing.
    (b) I went fishing.
    (c) I'm going fishing.
    (d) I've been fishing.

21. Choose the best answer.

    What did you do yesterday?
    (a) I go fishing.
    (b) I went fishing.
    (c) I'm going fishing.
    (d) I've been fishing.

22. Choose the best answer.

    Do you have any brothers or sisters?
    (a) Yes, I have one sister.
    (b) Yes, I've got one sister.
    (c) Yes, I'm a sister.
    (d) (a) and (b)

23. Choose the best answer.

    What do you drink with breakfast?
    (a) I have a cup of coffee.
    (b) I've got a cup of coffee.
    (c) I'm a cup of coffee.
    (d) (a) and (b)

24. Choose the best answer.

    Do you have a bicycle?
    (a) Yes, I have.
    (b) Yes, I've got.
    (c) Yes, I do.
    (d) (a) and (b)

25. Choose the best answer.

Do you like Taiwan?
(a) I don't know, I haven't been there.
(b) I don't know, I've never been there.
(c) Yes, I do. I went there last year.
(d) all of the above

26. am

(a) I _____ a child.
(b) I _____ hungry.
(c) I _____ talking.
(d) all of the above

27. have

(a) I _____ a child.
(b) I _____ hungry.
(c) I _____ talking.
(d) all of the above

28. jogging

(a) I'm _____.
(b) _____ is fun.
(c) I like _____.
(d) all of the above

29. jogged

(a) I've _____.
(b) _____ is fun.
(c) I like _____.
(d) none of the above

30. Do you _____ pizza?

(a) likes
(b) like
(c) liked
(d) liking

31. Have you _____ my keys?

(a) see
(b) saw
(c) seeing
(d) seen

32. Did you _____ my pasta?

(a) eat
(b) ate
(c) eating
(d) eaten

13

Options and possibilities 1
modal verbs

the verbs

When there are options or possibilities we often use the following verbs:

can/could
to say something is an option or a possibility. (See page 112.)

will/would
to say what we decide or predict. (See page 118.)

shall/should
to say something is the right thing to do. (See page 124.)

may/might
to say there is more than one option or possibility. (See page 128.).

must
to say there is only one reasonable option or possibility. (See page 132.)

We put these verbs before the other verbs in the sentence.
These verbs have different meanings and change the meaning of the sentence.

Subject	Verb	Verb (present)	Place
I	can	wait	at the airport.
I	could	wait	at the airport.
I	will	wait	at the airport.
I	would	wait	at the airport.
I	shall	wait	at the airport.
I	should	wait	at the airport.
I	may	wait	at the airport.
I	might	wait	at the airport.
I	must	wait	at the airport.

the past form isn't just for the past

When we think about options and possibilities we think about them being either **real** or **hypothetical**.

When we talk about **real** options and possibilities we use the present form.
(*can*, *will*, *shall*, *may* and *must*)

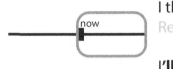

I think I **am** lucky.
Reality: I am lucky.

I**'ll** have a beer. (I'll = I will)
Reality: beer.

The past form refers to things that are NOT in the PRESENT or FUTURE. It is mainly used for the past, but is also used for **hypothetical** situations. These are things we are **imagining**.

I wish I **was** lucky.
Imagining: I am lucky.
Reality: I am not lucky.

When we talk about **hypothetical** options and possibilities we use the past form.
(*could*, *would*, *should* and *might*)

I **would** have a beer, but I'm driving today.
Imagining: having a beer.
Reality: no beer, I'm driving.

 # can/could

We use *can* (present form) to talk about things that are generally possible.

It **can** get really hot here in summer. It is possible. It doesn't always get hot, but it does happen.
Can wombats be found in this region? Is it possible to find wombats in this region?

I **can** drive a truck.

It is possible. I have the **ability**.

I **can't** drive a truck.

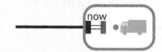

It is NOT possible. I don't have the **ability** (or a license).

	Subject	*can*	Verb	Object/Description
Can	I	**can**	play	the trombone.
	she		run	fast?
	He	**can't**	fly	a plane.

We use *could* (the past form of *can*) to talk about things that were possible in the **past**.

Before we installed the air conditioner, this room *could* get really hot in summer. It was possible.
Could wombats be found in this region in the 1960s? Was it possible?

I **could** drive a truck when I was 22.

It was possible. I had the **ability**.

I **couldn't** drive a truck when I was 22.

It wasn't possible. I didn't have the **ability**.

	Subject	*could*	Verb	Object/Description	Time
Could	I	**could**	play	the trombone	when I was twelve.
	she		run	fast	before the accident?
	He	**couldn't**	fly	a plane	when he got the job.

112

 # could

We also use *could* to talk about **hypothetical** possibilities.

I'm so hungry I **could** eat a horse.

I'm not really going to eat a horse.
It is **possible** in my **imagination**.

I think I **could** drive a truck. I have never done it but I **imagine** it is possible.
If we didn't have the air conditioner, this room **could** get really hot in summer. I am imagining.
Could wombats be found in this region again if we make it a conservation area? Imagining the future.

	Subject	*could*	Verb	Description	Time
Could	The package	**could**	arrive		any day now.
	it		rain		tomorrow?
	It	**couldn't**	be	easier.	

The package could arrive any day now. I imagine this is possible.
Could it rain tomorrow? Is it possible? Is there a chance?
It couldn't be easier. It is as easy as possible. We can't imagine an easier way.

Practice

Complete the sentences with *can* or *could*. There may be more than one answer.

1. _____ you drive a car?
2. A: Where are they?
   B: I don't know. They _____ be stuck in traffic or something.
3. He _____ play the piano when he was six.
4. I_____ come to see you tomorrow.

113

real or hypothetical?

There are situations when we use either *can* or *could*. We can think in a real or hypothetical way. Saying something in a hypothetical way is less direct and more polite.

We use *can* to ask if something is an option in the present-future

Can I open the window?

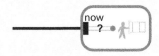

We use *could* to ask if something is hypothetically an option.

Could I open the window?

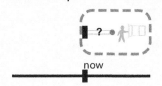

can	Subject	Verb	Object
Can	I	borrow	your phone?
Can	you	turn off	the TV?
Can	I	have	some salad?

≈
≈
≈

could	Subject	Verb	Object
Could	I	borrow	your phone?
Could	you	turn off	the TV?
Could	I	have	some salad?

more direct → *more polite*

The meaning is basically the same. *Can* is more direct, it is talking about something real. It is more polite to express what we want less directly—as something we are imagining. *Could* is used in more formal situations.

Can is more common in some situations.

'*Can* I help you?'
What I am offering **is an option** in the present-future.

We often use the past form to be less direct.

Do you want a drink? ≈ **Did** you want a drink?
Do you need some help? ≈ **Did** you need some help?
What **is** your name? ≈ What **was** your name?

Practice

Complete the sentences with *can* or *could*. There may be more than one answer.

1. A: Hi, _____ I help you?
2. B: Yes, _____ I have a coffee please.
3. _____ you please make it extra strong?
4. A: Ok. _____ I get you anything else?
5. B: Yes, _____ I have some cake, please.
   A: Ok.

114

could have done

We use *could* to imagine different options or possibilities. We can imagine how things could be different as a result of something being different in the past.

A: My legs are so sore.
B: I don't know why you walked. You **could have taken** the bus.

A different past (taking the bus instead of walking) means a different present (no sore legs). Taking the bus was an option.

	Subject	*could*	*have* -en	Description	Time
Could	The package	**could**	have arrived		by now.
	it		have rained?		
	It	**couldn't**	have been	easier.	

The package could have arrived by now. It could be waiting in my office. It is possible.
Could it have rained? It looks a little wet, but there are no clouds in the sky? Is it possible?
It couldn't have been easier. It was very easy. Being easier was not possible.

We also say *could've* instead of *could have*.

Practice

Complete the sentences with *could*, *have* and *the* -en form.

    A: How was your job interview?
Ex. B: Ok, but it <u>*could have been*</u> (be) better.
1. A: Why? What _____ you _____ (do) differently?
2. B: I _____ (answer) the questions faster and I _____ (be) more direct.
    A: Do you think you'll get the job?
3. B: I _____ (get) it, but I'm not very confident.
4. A: Yeah, you don't look very well presented. You _____ (wear) a tie.

Options and possibilities 2
modal verbs

 will

We use *will* when we think about options and possibilities. We say the chosen option (a decision) or the possibility that we believe is really happening (a prediction).

We use *will* when there are options or possibilities in the future. (I'll = I will)

I'**ll** open the window.

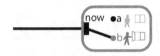

It'**ll** be sunny today.

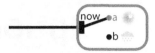

Options: (a) leave it shut (b) open it   **Possibilities:** (a) sunny (b) rain etc.

It'**ll** be warm next week. Possibilities: (a) cold (b) cool (c) warm (d) hot
There are so many people coming tonight. It'**ll** be a great party! Possibilities: (a) great (b) ok etc.
I'**ll** buy a new shirt. I've just decided: (a) new shirt (b) no new shirt. I've chosen an option.

Subject	*will*	Verb	Object	Time
She	'**ll**	wait.		
I	'**ll**	watch	TV	all day.
He	**won't**	drink	coffee	today.

We use *will* when we think about options and make a **decision** and when we think about possibilities and make a **prediction**. *Won't = will not.*

Decisions	Predictions
I'**ll** have a coffee.	It'**ll** rain tomorrow.
We'**ll** buy a new bed.	We'**ll** have flying cars in 2050.
Will we go out for lunch today?	**Will** it be sunny tomorrow?
We **won't** eat chicken again.	We **won't** be home by 7PM.

We also use *will* when there are options or possibilities in the present.

Madison said she's coming to visit us. She wants to...
(knock knock)
Ah, that'**ll** be her now.
I don't know who is at the door, it may be Madison or someone else. I think it is Madison.

IMPORTANT: *Will* is only used when we are thinking about options and possibilities.
There are often options and possibilities in the future, so we often use *will* when we talk about the future. However, there are many ways of talking about the future. (See page 152.)

 # would

We use *would* (the past form of *will*) to talk about options and possibilities we are **imagining**.

I **would** open the window, but my legs are too sore from all that walking.

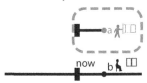

I won't actually open the window.

Subject	would	Verb	Object	but...
I	**would**	buy	a hat	but I don't have enough money. So I won't.
She	**would**	turn off	her phone	but the button is broken. So she won't.
He	**would**	go	skiing	but he has hurt his back. So he won't.

We use *wouldn't* when we talk about an option or possibility in the past that didn't happen. We often wanted it to happen. (wouldn't = would not)

I tried many times but the car **wouldn't** start. I conclude that it wasn't possible.
I asked him nicely but he **wouldn't** give me any pizza. He had options. He decided not to.

When we think about the past, we consider options we had at the time. We use *would* to say what often happened. (See page 161.)

Time	Subject	would	Verb	Object/Place	Time
When we lived in China	we	**would**	use	chopsticks	every day.
When he didn't read at school	he	**would**	often read	at home.	
When she was a student	she	**would**	work		in the evening.

We don't need to use would. Saying 'When we lived in China we used chopsticks every day.' is fine. There are different ways of thinking about it.

Practice

Complete the sentences with *will* or *would*. Use the short forms (*'ll* and *'d*) where possible.

1. I_____ cook dinner tomorrow.
2. I_____ cook dinner tomorrow but I can't because I have to work.
3. When I was young we _____ often go swimming in summer.
4. A: Imagine winning the lottery. What _____ you do?
   B: I _____ buy a new car for my mother. I _____ also give money to charity.
5. A: What time _____ Alex get here?
   B: He_____ be here in about an hour.
6. I_____ have the pasta, please.

will be doing

Will is a very useful word when we are thinking and talking about the unknown.
We use *be* + -ing form to make **predictions** about things that are **not finished**.

We talk about things we can't see that we think are happening **now**.

Don't call her now, she**'ll be eating** breakfast.

I don't know for certain, but I predict she is eating breakfast now.

We talk about things that we think are happening at a time in the **future**.

A: I'll come to your house at 7:00 tomorrow.
B: Ok, but I**'ll be eating** breakfast then.

When you come to my house, my breakfast will not be finished.

Subject	*will*	*be* + -ing	Object	Place	Time
She	'll	**be working**			on Saturday.
I	'll	**be living**		in Sweden	by the time I am 30.
He	'll	**be leaving**	the office		now.
They	'll	**be playing**	soccer		next week.

I don't think she'll come. She'll be working on Saturday.
I'll be living in Sweden by the time I am 30.
He should be here soon. He'll be leaving the office now.
They'll be playing soccer next week. We are focusing on the activity.

Practice

Complete the sentences with *will* and the verbs in the -ing form.

1. Don't come next month, we_____ (travel) Asia then.
2. We have to go now. Fred _____ (wait).
3. You_____ (work) hard in the office tomorrow, I_____ (sit) on the beach.
4. The next time you see me, I _____ (wear) a new uniform.

will have done

We use *will* and *have* + -en form to talk about the **result** of something at the time we are thinking about. We make **predictions** about what happens before.

We talk about things we think have happened that have a result in the **present**.

You can call her now, she'**ll have eaten** breakfast.

I don't know for certain, but I think her breakfast will be finished now.

We talk about results at a **future** time we are thinking about.

A: I'll come to your house at 7:00 tomorrow.
B: Ok, I'**ll have eaten** breakfast by then.

When you come to my house, my breakfast will be finished.

Subject	will	have + -en	Object	Place	Time
She	will	**have worked**			on Saturday.
I	will	**have lived**		in Sweden	by the time I am 30.
He	will	**have left**	the office		by now.
They	will	**have played**	soccer		by next week.

She'll be tired on Saturday because she will have worked.
I'll have lived in Sweden by the time I am 30.
He should be here soon. He'll have left the office by now.
They'll have played soccer by next week. We don't know exactly when.

Practice
Complete the sentences with *will* and the verbs in the -en form.

1. Come in September, we_____ (be) back for a while then.
2. We have to go now. Fred's flight_____ (land).
3. I'm reading a book now, but I_____ (finish) it by the time you get here.
4. They _____ (fix) the problem by now.

would like

We use *would* (with *like*) to offer and ask for things in a polite way. We are not directly telling someone to do something, we are expressing what we are imagining.

> **Would** you like anything to drink?

> I'**d** like a coffee.

> I'**d** like some juice.

I'd = I would

When we politely ask people if they want things, we ask with *would*.

Do you want a drink? (very direct)
Would you like a drink? (much more polite) Imagine having a drink, do you like that thought?

When we say we want something there are different ways we can ask. All of the sentences below are very common and fit this situation. Speaking hypothetically is more polite.

	present form (real)	past form (hypothetical)
can/could (is it an option?)	**Can** I have a coffee?	**Could** I have a coffee?
will/would (what we decide)	I'**ll** have a coffee.	I'**d** like a coffee.

To politely say we don't want something, we say 'No, thank you' or 'I'm fine, thank you'.

Practice

Complete the conversation with *will* or *would*. Use the short forms ('*ll* and '*d*) when possible.

   Waiter: Hi, are you ready to order?
Ex. Customer A: Yes, We'<u>d</u> like something to drink. What <u>would</u> you recommend?
   Waiter: The house red is very good.
1. Customer A: We_____ have a bottle of that, please.
2. Waiter: What _____ you like to eat?
3. Customer A: I_____ like the steak.
4. Customer B: I_____ have the chicken curry.
5. Waiter: _____ you like any salads?
   Customer B: No, thank you.
6. Waiter: Ok, so a bottle of house red, the steak and the chicken curry. Your meals _____ be ready soon.
   Customer A: Thank you.

would have done

We use *would* to talk about things that were not options or possibilities in the past. We can imagine how things would be different as a result of something being different in the past.

A: My legs are so sore.
B: I don't know why you walked. I **would have taken** the bus.

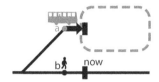

My decision would have been to take the bus. It wasn't an option because I'm not you.

Subject	*would*	*have* -en	Object/ Description	*but...*
The package	**would**	have arrived,		but the address was wrong.
I	**wouldn't**	have eaten	that last pie,	but no one else was going to eat it.
It	**would**	have been	easy,	but I didn't have my tools.

The package would have arrived, but the address was wrong. So, it didn't arrive.
I wouldn't have eaten that last pie, but no one else was going to eat it. So, I ate it.
It would have been easy but I didn't have my tools. So, it wasn't easy.

We also say *would've* instead of *would have*.

Practice

Complete the sentences with *would* or *would have* and the -en form.

A: I didn't see you at the barbecue yesterday.
1. B: I didn't go. I _____ (go) but I didn't have enough money.
   A: I could have lent you some.
2. B: I _____ (not enjoy) myself anyway. I had a bad headache.
3. A: _____ you like to go out for a drink tonight?
4. B: I _____, but I already have plans. How about tomorrow night?

 shall 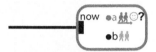 should

We use *shall* to say something is the RIGHT thing to do. We often use it in questions when we make suggestions.

Shall we go soon?

We are asking if going soon is the right thing to do. We want someone else's opinion.

We use *should* (the past form of *shall*) in hypothetical situations.
We say what is the right option, hypothetically speaking.

We use *should* to ask for advice.

Should we get him a present?

We are asking if it is the right thing to do, hypothetically speaking.

We use *should* to give advice or to tell people to do the right thing.

You **should** get a haircut.

I think it is the right option. You can choose to get a haircut, but that is up to you.

Subject	*should*	Verb	Object/Description
I	**should**	buy	a hat.
You	**should**	turn off	your phone.
He	**should**	be	quiet.
It	**should**	be	good.

We sometimes use *should* when we know the right thing to do, but do something else.

I **should** go to the gym tonight... but I want to watch the football on TV so I won't.
Going to the gym is the right thing to do. I won't do it though.
A: Would you like another slice of cake?
B: I **shouldn't**, I'm on a diet. But, it is a special occasion... ok.
Not eating cake is the right thing to do according to this person's diet.

We also use *should* when we consider possibilities.

The bus ***should*** arrive soon. This is the possibility I expect - assuming everything goes right.

124

should have done

We use *should* to talk about mistakes in the past and what we think was the right thing to do. We can imagine how things could be different as a result of doing the right thing in the past.

A: My legs are so sore.
B: I don't know why you walked. You **should have taken** the bus.

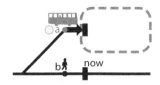

I think walking that far was a bad idea. Taking the bus was the **right** option.

Subject	*should*	*have* -en	Object/Description	Time
The package	should	have arrived		by now.
I	shouldn't	have eaten	that last pie.	
It	should	have been	easier.	

The package should have arrived by now (but the courier didn't follow their schedule correctly).
I shouldn't have eaten that last pie. It was the wrong thing to do. I ate too much and feel sick.
It should have been easier. It was too hard.

We also say *should've* instead of *should have*.

Practice

Complete the sentences with *shall*, *should* or *should have* and the -en form.

A: I'm going to Japan next week.
B: It's a very different culture. You _should be_ (be) careful.

1. I went into someone's house with my shoes on. I _____(take) them off at the door.
2. A: Haha, really? You wore your shoes inside? Everyone knows you _____ (not do) that!
3. B: I know. I just forgot. You _____(bow) to people too.
4. You _____ (not try) to shake hands.
5. A: Yeah ok. Anyway, _____ we get a coffee?
6. B: You _____(ask) me earlier. I've just had one.

ought

Ought is a very unusual verb; it has **no** present form. We use *ought* (past form) when we think **hypothetically** and say what is **expected**. Verbs ending in *-ought/-aught* are common past forms (*thought, bought, brought, taught* etc.).

Subject	Verb 1		Verb 2	Object	
	Verb	*to*			
I	**ought**	**to**	buy	a hat.	I need a hat so I will do it, as expected.
You	**ought**	**to**	turn off	your phone.	Appropriate behavior: what is expected.
He	**ought**	**to**	be	quiet.	Appropriate behavior: what is expected.
It	**ought**	**to**	be	good.	Saying how I expect it to be.

There are many situations where *ought* or *should* can be used. *Ought* is less direct (talking about a **general expectation**), so it is used in more formal situations. We use *should* when we think about options or possibilities and give an **opinion** about **what is right**. There are different ways of thinking and both are acceptable, but *should* is far more common.

You **ought** to get a haircut. You are **expected** to do this.
You **should** get a haircut. You have options. I think this is **the right thing** for you to do.
We **ought** to be home soon. This is what is **expected** given the situation.
We **should** be home soon. This is a possibility. What I expect if everything goes **right**.

Should is much more common than *ought*   **Frequency (2008)**

...should...   764428652
...ought...   45275332

Ought (to) is actually more common than *should* when followed by *punch you*! We often use *ought* in this way when we talk about something that we don't think is right that is said in frustration. *Ought (to)* is also more common than usual when followed by *slap you*, *kick you* and *beat you*. These things are clearly not right, but we may hypothetically expect them to happen to someone if they behave inappropriately.

I ought to punch you. This is hypothetical. I'm not really going to punch you, but I'm saying people generally expect someone to do this in this situation. I don't do it because I don't think it is right.

When *ought* is more common than *should*   **Frequency (2008)**

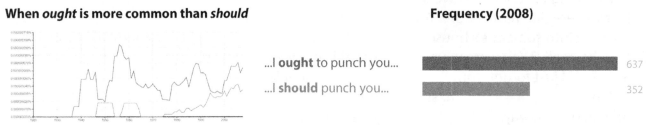

...I **ought** to punch you...   637
...I **should** punch you...   352

Data from Google Ngrams: https://books.google.com/ngrams/

15

Options and possibilities 3
modal verbs

may  might

We use *may* when there are other options or possibilities. We haven't decided or are uncertain. There are other things that may happen.

I **may** see you this afternoon.

I **may not** see you this afternoon.

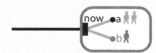

Might (the past form of *may*) is used in hypothetical situations. We use *might* when something is hypothetically an option or possibility; it is an option or possibility we are imagining.

I **might** see you this afternoon.

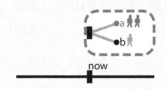

I **might not** see you this afternoon.

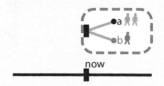

When we say something is undecided or uncertain we can use either *may* or *might*.

I *may* see you this afternoon. ≈ I *might* see you this afternoon.

Subject	*may*	Verb	Object etc.		Subject	*might*	Verb	Object etc.
I	**may**	see	you this afternoon.	≈	I	**might**	see	you this afternoon.
We	**may**	arrive	early.	≈	We	**might**	arrive	early.
You	**may**	find	this interesting.	≈	You	**might**	find	this interesting.
I	**may not**	have	pasta for dinner.	≈	I	**might not**	have	pasta for dinner.

Which should I use?

May is considered slightly more likely; it refers to a real possibility.
Might is considered slightly less likely; it refers to a possibility we are imagining.
However, it is personal preference, and you will find people using both in similar situations.
I use *might* more when speaking; I go straight from what I imagine in my mind to my mouth.
I use *may* more when writing; I take my time, and think more about what may really happen.

may have done / might have done

We use *might have* when we know what happened.
We imagine a different possibility and a different hypothetical result.

We **might have won** if Mason wasn't injured.

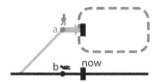

In reality, Mason was injured and we lost. We are talking about a hypothetical possibility.
We can also say, 'We might have won if Mason hadn't been injured'. (See page 142.)

We use *may have* or *might have* when we don't know exactly what happened.
We offer a possible solution, real or hypothetical. We can talk about it either way.

A: How did she get here so quickly?
B: She **may have taken** a taxi.

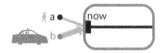

This is a real possibility.

A: How did she get here so quickly?
B: She **might have taken** a taxi.

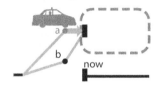

This is a hypothetical possibility.
We don't know what really happened.

Subject	*may/might*	*have* -en	Object etc.	Time
The package	**might**	have arrived		by now.
He	**may**	have eaten	that last pie.	
She	**might not**	have seen	you.	

The package might have arrived by now. It is a possibility. I'm not sure.
He may have eaten that last pie. It is a possibility. It may have been someone else. I'm not sure.
She might not have seen you. It is a possibility. I'm not sure.

Practice

Complete the sentences with *might have* or *may have* and the -en form, or *may* or *might*.
There may be more than one answer.

1. I knocked but there is no answer. They _____ (be) asleep or they _____ (go) out.
2. I found $50. I _____ (go) out for lunch today.
3. I'm not feeling well so I _____ (not be) able to make it to dinner.
4. I can't find my phone. I _____ (leave) it at the restaurant.
5. They didn't put the dishes away. They _____ (not know) where they go.
6. Olivia isn't at work. She _____ (quit).
7. I _____ (take) a break.

129

permission- can, could and may

We use *can* or *may* to give someone permission to do something.

You can go out tonight.

≈   **You may go out tonight.**

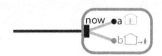

You have my permission.
There is nothing stopping you.

You have my permission.
I am making this option available to you.

Subject	*can*	Verb	Object etc.
You	**can**	borrow	my phone.
You	**can**	have	some salad.
You	**can't**	have	chocolate.

≈
≈
≈

Subject	*may*	Verb	Object etc.
You	**may**	borrow	my phone.
You	**may**	have	some salad.
You	**may not**	have	chocolate.

We often use *can* because *can* is a very common word, it is simple and more direct.
May is less direct, so we use *may* when we want to be more polite.

When we ask for permission, we use *can*, *could* or *may*.

Can I borrow your phone?   ≈   **Could I borrow your phone?**   ≈   **May I borrow your phone?**

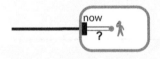      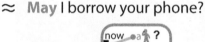

One option:
I borrow your phone.
Is it an option?

One option:
I borrow your phone.
Is it hypothetically an option?

More than one option:
(a) I borrow your phone.
(b) I don't borrow your phone.
Is option (a) one of my options?

can	S.	Verb	Object etc.
Can	I	borrow	your phone?
Can	I	have	some salad?
Can	I	help	you?

≈
≈
≈

could	S.	Verb	Object etc.
Could	I	borrow	your phone?
Could	I	have	some salad?
Could	I	help	you?

≈
≈
≈

may	S.	Verb	Object etc.
May	I	borrow	your phone?
May	I	have	some salad?
May	I	help	you?

more direct ——————————————————————————————→ *more formal/polite*

In some very formal situations *might* is used. 'Might I borrow your phone?'
Might is far less direct, asking if something is hypothetically one of my options.

But remember, *may* and *can* are two different words with two different meanings.

Can means something is an option or is possible. There is nothing stopping it from being an option or possibility.

A: It's been too long. We should see each other soon.
B: I'm busy today, but I **can** see you tomorrow.

One option:
Seeing each other tomorrow.
It is ok with me.

I'm sorry, I'm very busy. I **can't** see you tonight.

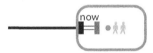

It is not possible / not an option.

May means there is more than one option or possibility. We use *may* to say something is undecided or uncertain.

A: When will we see each other again?
B: I **may** see you tomorrow.
(or: I might see you tomorrow.)

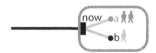

More than one possibility:
(a) seeing each other tomorrow.
(b) not seeing each other tomorrow.
We're not sure what will happen.

I **may not** see you tonight.

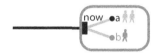

We plan to see each other, but not seeing each other is also a possibility.

Practice

Complete the sentences with *may*, *might*, *can* and *could*. There may be more than one answer.

1. A: Do you have any plans this evening?
   B: Maybe. Levi and I _____ go to a restaurant.
2. Hey Amy, _____ I borrow your car?
3. _____ I take your order?
4. _____ you do me a favor?
5. It looks like it _____ rain.
6. _____ I help you with your bags?
7. _____ I please have some dessert?

 must

We use *must* when there is only one option.

You **must** wear a seatbelt.

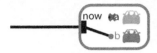

Not wearing a seatbelt is unacceptable.

We add *must* when we make rules. We are very clear and direct. There is no other reasonable option. Not doing it would result in negative consequences.

Subject	*must*	Verb	Object/Place/Description	Time
You	must	be	home	before 10PM.
Staff	must	wear	uniforms.	
Applicants	must	be	over 18 years of age.	
Passengers	must not	use	cellphones.	

We use *must* when we have a strong opinion. There is only one option in our mind.

Subject	*must*	Verb	Object/Place/Description	Time
I	must	phone	my father.	
I	mustn't	forget	the PIN number.	
You	must	go	home	now.

We use *must* when the subject doesn't have any other options.

Subject	*must*	Verb	Object/Place/Description	Time
We	must	breathe	to stay alive.	
They	must	cross	the desert.	

We use *must* when there is only one reasonable possibility.

Subject	*must*	Verb	Object/Place/Description	Time
He	must	be	her husband.	
It	mustn't	be	ready	yet.

Must only has one form: the present form, no past form. Must: only one option.

must have done

We use *must* when there is only one possibility. We conclude what happened in the past based on what we see or hear in the present.

A: How did she get here so quickly?
B: She **must have taken** a taxi.

This is the only reasonable explanation.
We make our conclusion based on what we heard or saw: she got here quickly.

Subject	*must*	*have* -en	Object/Description	Time
The package	**must**	have arrived		by now.
He	**must**	have eaten	that last pie.	
She	**mustn't**	have seen	you.	

The package **must have** arrived by now.
We sent it a long time ago. This is the only reasonable explanation.
He **must have** eaten that last pie.
There is no one else here that could have eaten it. This is the only reasonable explanation.
She **mustn't have** seen you.
If she saw you she would have said "Hello". She isn't rude. This is the only reasonable explanation.

Practice

Complete the sentences with *must*, *have* and the -en form or just *must*.

1. A: I lived in downtown New York in 2010.
   B: Sounds good. It _____ (be) convenient.
2. We've been traveling all day. We _____ (be) almost home.
3. We _____ (not leave) the door open.
4. Your hands are dirty. You _____ (wash) your hands.
5. His hands are clean. He _____ (wash) his hands.
6. I knocked but there's no answer. They _____ (be) out.
7. I knocked but there's no answer. They _____ (go) out.

must / have to

In many situations, *have to* or *must* can both be used.

Have to refers to a task given to a person to do. They may have given themself the task or someone else may have given them the task.

Subject	*have to*	Verb	Object/Place/Description	Time
You	**have to**	be	home	before 10PM.
Staff	**have to**	wear	uniforms.	
Applicants	**have to**	be	over 18 years of age.	
I	**have to**	phone	my father.	
I	**have to**	remember	the PIN number.	
She	**has to**	go	home.	

Must shows that there are no other options. It is very clear and direct so it sounds stronger. If it does not happen, there will be negative consequences.

Subject	*must*	Verb	Object/Place/Description	Time
You	**must**	be	home	before 10PM.
Staff	**must**	wear	uniforms.	
Applicants	**must**	be	over 18 years of age.	
I	**must**	phone	my father.	
I	**must**	remember	the PIN number.	
You	**must**	go	home.	

Must is more serious than *have (to do something)*.

I **must** work tomorrow. If I don't work tomorrow there will be negative consequences.
I **have to** work tomorrow. This is the shift I've been given. In most situations this is better.

We also use *have got to* when speaking casually. (See page 81.)

I**'ve got to** work tomorrow.

Which should I use?

Must is used more in formal situations and writing. We think about it more and decide there are no other options.
Have to is used more in speaking. We also use *have to* when someone tells us what to do. "I have to wear a tie at work" - someone has decided that I do this but in my mind this is not the only option.
Have got to is also used in speaking and is very common in casual speech. We use *gotta* for short.

mustn't / don't have to

In negative sentences, *have to* and *must* have very different meanings.

Don't have to shows a person hasn't been given the task to do. So, it is ok if they do it or if they don't do it.

I **don't have to do** anything.

Doing anything is ok.

Subject	*don't have to*	Verb	Object/Place/Description	Time
You	**don't have to**	be	home	before 10PM.
Staff	**don't have to**	wear	uniforms.	
Applicants	**don't have to**	be	over 18 years of age.	
I	**don't have to**	phone	my father.	
I	**don't have to**	remember	the PIN number.	
She	**doesn't have to**	go	home.	

Must not shows that there are no other options. If it does happen, there will be negative consequences. It is **not** ok if the person does it.

Subject	*mustn't*	Verb	Object/Place/Description	Time
You	mustn't	be	home	before 10PM.
Staff	mustn't	wear	uniforms.	
Applicants	mustn't	be	under 18 years of age.	
I	mustn't	phone	my father.	
I	mustn't	forget	the PIN number.	
You	mustn't	go	home.	

Mustn't and *don't have to* have different meanings.

I **mustn't** work tomorrow. If I work tomorrow there will be negative consequences.
I **don't have to** work tomorrow. It's ok if I stay home.

Practice

Complete the sentences with *must, have to, have got to, mustn't* or *don't have to* using the verb in brackets. There may be more than one answer.

1. You _____ (be) here on time tomorrow.
2. A: I'll see you tomorrow. What should I bring?
   B: You _____ (not bring) anything. We've got it covered.
3. I _____ (get) a present for my nephew.
4. We _____ (not forget) to call Jane.
5. You _____ (wash) everything by hand. We have a dishwasher.
6. I _____ (go) shopping this afternoon.

135

making deductions

We use *must* when we make deductions. Our conclusion is the only reasonable possibility.

The only reasonable possibility: It must be (d).

A: I haven't eaten since this morning. B: You **must** be hungry.
Phillip isn't here. The train **must** have been delayed.

We use *can't (can not)* when we deduce that something is not possible. Based on what I know, I don't believe it is possible.

This is not possible.

You've just eaten a whole pizza! You **can't** be hungry.
Emma takes the same train as Phillip. She's here so the train **can't** have been delayed.

We are sometimes unsure. We use *may* or *might* to say something is one of many possibilities.

 or *or* *or* *or...*

This is a possibility. We are unsure.

We should prepare some food. The guests **might** be hungry.
Phillip isn't here. The train **might** have been delayed.
We should prepare some food. The guests **may** be hungry.
Phillip isn't here. The train **may** have been delayed.

We often combine *may* and *be* into one word and put it first.

Maybe the guests are hungry. = The guests **may be** hungry.
Maybe the train has been delayed. = The train **may** have **been** delayed.
Maybe they're rich. = They **may be** rich.

When we are unsure we can also use *could* to say something is hypothetically possible.

We should prepare some food. The guests **could** be hungry.
Phillip isn't here. The train **could** have been delayed.

had better

Must has no past form, so when we want to speak about what is hypothetically the only option or possibility we use *had better*.

You**'d better** wear a seat belt.

This is hypothetically the only reasonable option. We imagine that there would negative consequences if you didn't wear your seatbelt, so not wearing a seatbelt would be unacceptable.

Must, *had better* and *should* are often used in similar situations.

You **must** wear a seatbelt.
Not wearing a seatbelt is unacceptable.

You**'d better** wear a seatbelt.
Hypothetically speaking: not wearing a seatbelt would be unacceptable.

You **should** wear a seatbelt.
Wearing a seatbelt is hypothetically the right thing to do.

strong ————————————————→ *soft*

We use *had better* to talk about options or possibilities. This is the only reasonable option or possibility that fits with what we are imagining.

I**'d better** go soon.
This is hypothetically my only option.
≈ I need to go soon.
If I don't go soon, the plan I am imagining is not going to happen.

Oliver is running late.
(knock knock)
That**'d better** be him.
This is hypothetically the only possibility.
If the person at the door is not Oliver, the plan I am imagining is not going to happen.

Why do we use two words?

There is no single word that has this meaning so the meanings of *had* and *better* are combined.

We use *have* because the subject **has to do** something or something **has to be true** to fit in with what we are imagining.

We use the past form (*had*) because we are thinking **hypothetically**.

We use better because we consider and **compare** options and possibilities.

We also use *had better not*.

He**'d better not** say anything.
Not saying anything is the better option.

He**'d better not** be late.
Not being late the better possibility.

Practice

Complete the sentences with *must, can't, may, might, maybe* or *could*. There may be more than one answer.

1. A: I can't find my shoes.
   B: You always leave them by the front door. They _____ be there somewhere.
2. A: I can't find my laptop.
   B: It _____ be in the bedroom, you sometimes use it there.
3. A: I can't find my pen.
   B: You just had it so it _____ be far away.
4. Wow! What an amazing house. They _____ be rich.
5. A: Can we meet up tomorrow?
   It _____ be ok. Let me check with my husband.
6. A: Can we meet up tomorrow?
   _____. Let me check with my husband.
7. A: The air conditioner is making strange noises.
   B: That _____ be good. We should get it repaired.

Practice

Complete the sentences with *must, had better* or *should*. There may be more than one answer.

1. Come and look at this bird. It'll probably go soon, you_____ come quick!
2. He got me a present for my birthday so I_____ get him something.
3. All staff_____ wear suits. Anyone who doesn't wear a suit will be fired.
4. He was so sick, he _____ have died but he recovered and now he's healthy again.
5. We're getting busier all the time. We_____ hire some more staff.
6. We'll leave at 5:00 sharp. You_____ (not) be late.

16

if
conditional sentences

if

We use *if* to talk about consequences of options and possibilities we have at a time in the present-future.

If we leave now, we'll be home in time for the game.

Option: leave
Consequence: we'll be home in time for the game

If the traffic is bad, we won't be home in time.

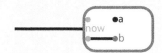

Possibility: bad traffic
Consequence: we won't be home in time

We can speak **hypothetically** about something that is less likely or impossible.
We use the past form for hypothetical situations. (*leave - left, will - would*)

If we left now, we would be home in time for the game.

Hypothetical option: leave
Hypothetical consequence: we would be home in time for the game

If I were you, I would watch the game here.

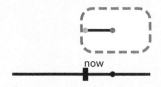

Not possible, but hypothetically: I am you
Hypothetical consequence: I would watch the game here. ('If I was you' is also fine - See page 143)

We can put either part first.

if	Subject	Verb	Ob./Desc.	Time	S.	*will*	Verb	Ob./Place	Place/Time
If	we	**leave**		now,	we	**will**	be	home	in time for the game.
If	the traffic	**is**	bad,		we	**won't**	be	home	in time.
If	I	**were**	you,			I	**would**	watch	the game	here.

S.	*will*	Verb	Ob./Place	Place/Time	if	Subject	Verb	Ob./Desc.	Time
We	**will**	be	home	in time for the game	**if**	we	**leave**		now.
We	**won't**	be	home	in time	**if**	the traffic	**is**	bad.	
I	**would**	watch	the game	here	**if**	I	**were**	you.	

We'll be home in time for the game if we leave now.
We won't be home in time if the traffic is bad.
I'd watch the game here if I were you.

We also use *can/could*, *may/might*, *shall/should* and *must/had better* in *if* sentences. We use these the same way we use *will/would*.

If we leave now, we **can** watch the game at home.
If we leave now, we **could** watch the game at home.
If we leave now, we **may** be home in time for the game.
If we leave now, we **might** be home in time for the game.
Shall we leave now **if** we want to watch the game at home?
If we want to watch the game at home, we **should** leave now.
If we want to watch the game at home, we **must** leave now.
If we want to watch the game at home, we **had better** leave now.

We use *if* to talk about something that happens because something else happens, a **consequence**. These things generally happen, many times, so the verbs are in the present form.

If it rains, I *get* wet.

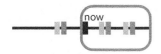

Possibility: rain
Consequence: I get wet.

Practice

Circle the correct words in brackets to complete the sentences.

1. I'm not rich, but if (I'm) (I was) rich, (I buy) (I'll buy) (I'd buy) a big house.
2. If (I am) (I were) you, (I'll get) (I'd get) a new job.
3. (We'll go) (We'd go) shopping if it (rains) (rained) tomorrow.
   If it (doesn't rain) (didn't rain), (we'll go) (we'd go) fishing.
4. A: Shall we do something tonight?
   B: Maybe, but I might have to work late. If I (finish) (finished) on time, (I'll call) (I'd call) you.
5. If you (can have) (could have) any super power, what power (will) (would) you have?
   What (will) (would) you do if you (have) (had) super powers?
6. A: Are you going out tonight?
   B: I'd like to, but I'm feeling a bit sick. I (won't) (wouldn't) go out if (I'm) (I was) still feeling sick.
7. A: It's great to see you out. Are you still feeling sick?
   B: I'm feeling great! I (won't) (wouldn't) be out if (I'm) (I was) feeling sick.

would have... if...

We can talk about how things could have been different if we made a different decision in the past.

My legs wouldn't have been **sore if** I had taken **the bus.**

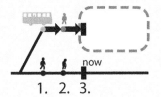

What **really** happened:
1. I walked.
2. My legs were sore because I had walked.
3. My legs **have been** sore.

Subject	*would*	*have* -en	Object etc.	if	Subject	*had* -en	Object etc.
The package	would	have arrived		if	the address	had been	correct.
I	wouldn't	have eaten	that last pie	if	someone	had wanted	it.
It	would	have been	easy	if	I	had had	my tools.

...**if the address had been correct.** The address wasn't correct so it didn't arrive.
...**if someone had wanted it.** No one wanted the last pie so I ate it.
...**if I'd had my tools.** I didn't have my tools, so it wasn't easy.

We often simplify and use the *past form* in the *if* part.
We use the *past form* when something happened at a time in the past. The listener knows we are talking about another option or possibility before something happened.

This structure is common, especially in spoken English, but people may find it ungrammatical.
In formal writing or exams the more traditional structure above with *had* is recommended.

My legs wouldn't have been **sore if** I took **the bus.**

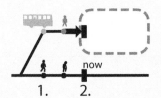

What **really** happened:
1. I walked.

2. My legs **have been** sore.

Subject	*would*	*have* -en	Object etc.	if	Subject	Verb (past)	Object etc.
The package	would	have arrived		if	the address	was	correct.
I	wouldn't	have eaten	that last pie	if	someone	wanted	it.
It	would	have been	easy	if	I	had	my tools.

...**if the address was correct.** The address wasn't correct when it was written, so it didn't arrive.
...**if someone wanted it.** No one wanted the last pie at the time, so I ate it.
...**if I had my tools.** I didn't have my tools at the time, so it wasn't easy.

We can use *could,* instead of *would* to say something may have been possible. We use *may* or *might* if we are less certain.

We use had + -en form after *if...*

> We would have been home in time for the game if we'd left at 4.
> We could have been home in time for the game we'd left at 4.
> We may have been home in time for the game if we'd left at 4.
> We might have been home in time for the game if we'd left at 4.

or the past form after *if...*

> We would have been home in time for the game if we left at 4.
> We could have been home in time for the game if we left at 4.
> We may have been home in time for the game if we left at 4.
> We might have been home in time for the game if we left at 4.

If I were... **and** if I was...

Some people tend to use *were* when they are talking about something they are imagining. This helps separate the past and hypothetical. It is traditionally considered grammatically correct.

> If **I were** you, I would have traveled abroad. We know this is hypothetical because *were* is used.
> She'd ask for food if **she were** hungry. We know this is hypothetical because *were* is used.

There is no reason not to say *I was* or *she was* the same as when we talk about the past. We know it is hypothetical because of the context. These sentences are also very common.

> If **I was** you, I would have traveled abroad. We know this is hypothetical because of the context.
> She'd ask for food if **she was** hungry. We know this is hypothetical because of the context.

Practice

Complete the sentences to talk about how the past may have been different.

1. We_____ (go) shopping if it _____ (rain) yesterday.
2. If it _____ (not rain) we_____ (go) fishing.
3. Sorry I didn't call you. I had to work overtime. If I _____ (finish) on time, I _____ (call) you.
4. A: Did you go out last night?
   B: No, but I _____ (go) out if I _____ (not be) feeling sick.
5. A: You went out last night? Were you still feeling sick?
   B: I felt great! I _____ (not go) out if I _____ (be) feeling sick.

if: polite expressions

We use expressions with *if* to be less direct and more polite.

Asking for permission	Asking people to do things
If you don't mind, could I borrow some money?	**If you don't mind**, could you meet me tomorrow morning?
If it is ok (with you), could I borrow some money?	**If it is ok** (with you), could you meet me tomorrow morning?
Do you mind if I borrow some money?	**If you have time**, could you meet me tomorrow morning?
Is it ok (with you) *if* I borrow some money?	Could you meet me tomorrow morning **if you're free**?
Would it be ok if I borrowed some money?	**If it's not too much trouble**, could you meet me tomorrow morning?

There are many ways we can answer.

giving permission agreeing to do it	refusing permission refusing to do it
That's fine.	Polite: No, sorry.
That's ok.	Polite: Sorry, I don't have any.
Yes.	(giving a reason)
Sure.	Strong: No.

Do you mind questions are answered differently.

giving permission agreeing to do it	refusing permission refusing to do it
That's fine.	
That's ok.	Polite: Sorry, I don't have any.
	(giving a reason)
No, not at all.	Very strong: Yes. I do mind.

We follow these expressions with a verb in the *present form*. We are referring to this happening in the present-future.

> If you don't mind, could I **borrow** your car?

When we use *would* the *past form* is also possible. It depends on how you are thinking. There is a very small difference in meaning. Using the *past form* is less direct and a little more polite.

> Would it be ok if I **borrow** your car? I'm thinking about borrowing your car in the future.
> Would it be ok if I **borrowed** your car? I'm thinking hypothetically about borrowing your car.
> Both questions ask if it is hypothetically ok (using would).

Practice

Make polite questions. Use any of the expressions above. Ask questions rather than telling people what to do or telling people what you are doing.

Example: I'm opening the door! ___*Do you mind if I open the door?*___

1. Help me with something. _____
2. I'm using your phone. _____
3. Buy some milk. _____
4. Do me a favor. _____
5. I'm taking the day off tomorrow. _____
6. We're meeting at 10 tomorrow, instead of 9. _____
7. Cook dinner tonight. _____

17

Review of options and possibilities
modal verbs

review of options and possibilities

Modal verbs

The words *can*/*could*, *may*/*might*, *must*, *shall*/*should* and *will*/*would* are used to talk about options and possibilities.

	REAL	**HYPOTHETICAL**

can/could
to say something is an option or possibility.
(See page 112.)

I **can** drive a truck.

I'm so hungry
I **could** eat a horse.

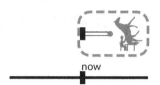

---

will/would
to say the chosen option or possibility.
(See page 118.)

I'll buy a dog.

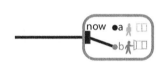

I **would** open the window, but my legs are sore.

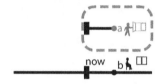

---

shall/should
to say something is the right option or possibility.
(See page 124.)

Shall we go?

You **should** get a haircut.

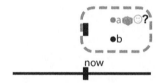

---

may/might
there is more than one option or possibility we are considering.
(See page 128.)

I **may** go out tonight.

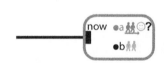

I **might** see you tonight.

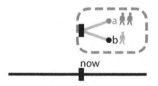

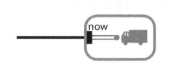

must
to say there is only one reasonable option or possibility.
(See page 132.)

You **must** wear a seatbelt.

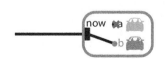
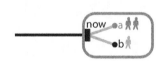

146

examples

I **can** speak English.
If you're free I **can** come now.
You **could** have left earlier.
I **could** help you if you like.

Can I have a milkshake, please?
Can we leave early if it's raining?
Could I have an apple, please?
If you don't mind, **could** I go now?

He **can't** be hungry, he's just eaten.
If you don't help you **can't** go out.
I looked but I **couldn't** find it.
I'm full, I **couldn't** eat another bite.

I'**ll** see you soon.
If I'm free I'**ll** visit you tomorrow.
I **would** have left earlier.
I **would** help but I'm busy.

Will you be married in 10 years?
Will you still come if it's raining?
Would you like a drink?
If you were rich, **would** you buy a car?

I **won't** have a coffee.
Sorry, I **won't** be able to make it.
I **wouldn't** do that if I was you.
I asked but he **wouldn't** help.

We **should** think about other options.
If it rains, we **should** reschedule.
You **should** have asked me earlier.
They **should** be here soon.

Shall we go soon?
Where **shall** we go?
What **should** we do if we're late?
Should I get them a gift?

You **shouldn't** do that.
I **shouldn't** have told you.
That box **shouldn't** be here.
You **shouldn't** go out if you're sick.

I **may** be able to help.
You **may** like this.
I **might** get a new car.
We **might** have won if we tried hard.

May I have a banana, please?
If you don't mind, **may** I go now?
What **might** happen next?
Who **might** that be?

I **may not** have told you, but...
You **may not** go out tonight.
You **might not** like it.
We **might not** be able to make it.

She **must** be the new boss.
It **must** have been amazing.

Must they be so loud?
What **must** we do?

You **mustn't** be late.
That **mustn't** have been him.

quiz

1. I am unsure.

    (a) I can see you tomorrow.
    (b) I will see you tomorrow.
    (c) I may see you tomorrow.
    (d) I must see you tomorrow.

2. I have decided.

    (a) I can see you tomorrow.
    (b) I will see you tomorrow.
    (c) I may see you tomorrow.
    (d) I must see you tomorrow.

3. It is possible.

    (a) I can see you tomorrow.
    (b) I will see you tomorrow.
    (c) I would see you tomorrow.
    (d) I must see you tomorrow.

4. It is the only option.

    (a) I can see you tomorrow.
    (b) I will see you tomorrow.
    (c) I may see you tomorrow.
    (d) I must see you tomorrow.

5. What is the right thing to do?
    (I want your opinion)

    (a) Can we leave soon?
    (b) Will we leave soon?
    (c) Shall we leave soon?
    (d) May we leave soon?

6. Are you hot? _____ I open the window?

    (a) Shall
    (b) Should
    (c) Can
    (d) Could
    (e) Any of the above.

7. If you _____ have any car in the world, what car would you have?

    (a) shall
    (b) should
    (c) can
    (d) could
    (e) Any of the above.

8. If you can't move your car...

    (a) I'll call the police.
    (b) I'll call a tow truck.

9. If you won't move your car...

    (a) I'll call the police.
    (b) I'll call a tow truck.

10. Can I get you anything to drink?

    (a) I'll like a cup of coffee.
    (b) I'd like a cup of coffee.
    (c) I'm like a cup of coffee.
    (d) I could like a cup of coffee.

11. Are you ready to order?

    (a) I'll have a chicken sandwich.
    (b) I'd have a chicken sandwich.
    (c) I could have a chicken sandwich.
    (d) Any of the above.

12. Would you like anything else?

    (a) Will I have some fries, please?
    (b) Would I have some fries, please?
    (c) Could I have some fries, please?
    (d) Any of the above.

13. Would you like a dessert?

    (a) Can I have some ice cream, please?
    (b) May I have some ice cream, please?

(c) Could I have some ice cream, please?
(d) Any of the above.

14. What will you be doing in 10 years?

(a) I'll be living in the mountains.
(b) I'd be living in the mountains.
(c) I may be living in the mountains.
(d) I might be living in the mountains.
(e) (a), (c) or (d)

15. What would you be doing if you didn't have to work?

(a) I'll be living in the mountains.
(b) I'd be living in the mountains.
(c) I may be living in the mountains.
(d) I can be living in the mountains.
(e) (a), (c) or (d)

16. I lost my job last week. I don't have much money,...

(a) I have to find another job soon.
(b) I must find another job soon.
(c) I'll find another job soon.
(d) Any of the above.

17. Can I see you tomorrow?

(a) Sorry, I have to be on vacation.
(b) Sorry, I must be on vacation.
(c) Sorry, I'll be on vacation.
(d) Any of the above.

18. A: Where are my glasses?
    B: You just had them, they _____ be far away.

(a) can't
(b) will
(c) may
(d) must

19. The bus will be late...

(a) if there is a lot of traffic.

(b) if there will be a lot of traffic.
(c) if there was a lot of traffic.
(d) if there would be a lot of traffic.

20. I'd tell them the truth...

(a) if I am you.
(b) if I will be you.
(c) if I was you.
(d) if I would be you.

21. I would have got you lunch...

(a) if you'd asked me earlier
(b) if you asked me earlier.
(c) if you would ask me earlier.
(d) (a) or (b)
(e) (b) or (c)

Practice

Complete the conversation with *can*, *could*, *shall*, *should*, *will* or *would*. Use the short forms of *will* and *would* ('*ll* and '*d*). There are many options.

A: I've got free tickets to travel anywhere in Europe! (1) Where _____ we go?
B: (2) We _____ go to Italy.
A: (3) That _____ be good. (4) I_____ like to go to Rome. (5) My aunt lives there and I really _____ visit her. (6) We _____ probably stay with her for a few days.
B: (7) We _____ go to Rome first, then other parts of Italy? (8) How long _____ we travel for?
A: One week. (9) So, we _____ stay in Rome for a few days, then go to Milan or Venice?
B: (10) I_____ like to go to another country for a few days, maybe Sweden?
A: (11) I think we _____ go somewhere closer to Italy. How about Spain?
B: (12) Yes, I_____ like to go to Spain. (13) I _____ speak some Spanish.
A: (14) Great, you _____ speak with the locals. (15) It_____ be good practice for you.
B: (16) I_____ translate for you.
A: (17) When _____ we go? How about summer?
B: (18) That_____ be good. (19) We _____ go to the beach.
A: (20) Ok great, so we_____ go to Rome for a few days, then we _____ have a few days in Spain.
B: Sounds great. (21) I _____ (not) wait.

Practice

Complete the telephone conversations with *must*, *shall*, *should*, *will*, *would*, *can*, *could*, *may* or *might*. There may be more than one answer.

A: Do you have any plans this evening?
B: (1) We _____ go to the cinema. I'm not sure. (2) I_____ like to see a good action movie. (3) _____ you like to come?
A: Sure, why not.

later...
A: (4) I'm just finishing work and I _____ leave the office in five minutes. (5) _____ you meet me outside?
B: (6) Ok, where _____ I wait?
A: (7) _____ you meet me in front of the office? It's number 37, Main St.

later...
B: (to self) Main St... (8) It _____ be around here... (9) Number 37, this _____ be the place.

later...
A: (10) Sorry, I _____ be a bit late. (11) _____ you go to the cinema and get the tickets? (12) I _____ be there in the next ten minutes. (13) _____ you be able to buy some drinks and snacks?
B: Ok. (14) _____ I get some chips?
A: Yes, that sounds good.

Ways of talking about the future

present simple, present progressive, *will* and *be going to*
tense, aspect, modality and quasi-modality for future

Ways of talking about the future

Aspect for future

am/are/is + -ing form (See page 58.)

We often talk about the future using *be (am, are, is)* and the -ing form to talk about something that is **not finished** (and has **not started** yet). This is a very simple way to talk about the future and can be used in many situations. We are talking about what is happening **after** the present time.

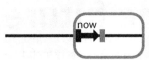

She**'s leaving** at 6:30.
We**'re having** a BBQ on Sunday.
Is he **working** on Saturday?
When **are** we **going** home?
I**'m not doing** yoga on Monday.
We **aren't going out** tonight.

Tense for future

present form (See page 52.)

We also talk about the future using a verb in the present form. We speak generally about things that just happen. These things are **fixed**, such as things that happen according to **schedule**.

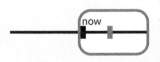

The bus **leaves** at 6:30.
The meeting **is** at 10.
Does he work on Saturday?
When **is** the party?
The concert **doesn't** start at 6.
They **don't** arrive at 5:20.

Practice

Complete the sentences. Use *am/are/is* + ing form or the present form.

1. A: What time does the show start?
   B: It _____ (start) at 7:30.
2. We _____ (have) a surprise party for Julia.
3. A: _____ you _____ (come) running tomorrow?
   B: Sorry, I can't. I _____ (have) an appointment.
4. The flight _____ (depart) at 11:54.
5. A: I _____ (go) on vacation next week.
   B: Great. Where _____ you _____ (go)?
6. Billy and Sandra have changed their plans. They _____ (not come) tomorrow.

will and be going to

We use *will* when we think about possibilities and make a prediction, and when we think about options and make a decision. (See page 118.)

We often make a decision to go somewhere. Then we go there, moving through space.

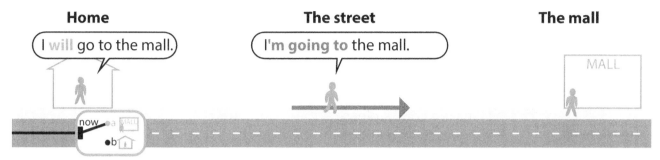

We talk about time the same way we talk about space. We make a decision to do something. Then we move through time until it happens in the future.

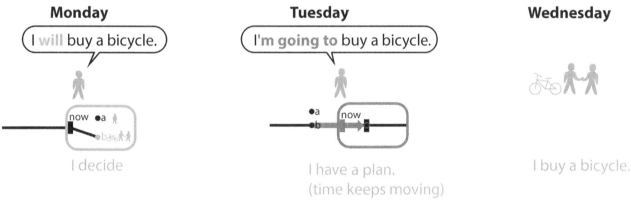

I'm *going to* (= not finished now) *do* something (= next step).
The next step is sometime in the future. We don't need to say when it is going to happen.

Subject	be going to	Verb	Object	Time	
She	**is going to**	wait.			She's going to wait.
I	**am going to**	watch	TV	all day.	I'm going to watch TV all day.
He	**isn't going to**	drink	coffee	today.	He isn't going to drink coffee today.

We can also use *be (am, are, is) + going to* for predictions based on clear evidence.
These things are controlled by laws of the universe. There are no other possibilities.

He**'s going to** fall off!
She doesn't have an umbrella. She**'s going to** get wet.

When people use *be going to* the words *going to* sometimes get blended together into *gonna*.

153

which one should I use?

There isn't one correct answer for every situation. The sentences we use depend on how we are thinking about the future. Here are some different ways we think and talk about the future.

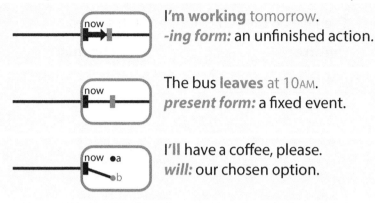

I'm **working** tomorrow.
-ing form: an unfinished action.

The bus **leaves** at 10AM.
present form: a fixed event.

I'**ll** have a coffee, please.
will: our chosen option.

I'm **going** to buy a bicycle.
am going: a future action or event we are on the path to.

Does the weather look good for our picnic?

No, it'**s going** to rain.

No, it'**ll** rain.

There are dark clouds in the sky.
Based on this evidence it is going to rain.
(This may also be based on other evidence such as a weather report.)

There are two possibilities:
a: It doesn't rain.
b: It rains.
This is what I think.
We say 'it might rain.' or 'it may rain' if we are less certain.

Dad, I'm hungry.

I know. We'**re going** to stop for lunch soon.

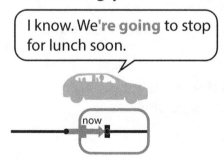

I know. We'**ll** stop for lunch soon.

Dad says what has already been decided.

There are several possibilities:
a: Don't stop for lunch.
b: Stop for lunch right now.
c: Stop for lunch soon.
Dad thinks about the possibilities and says what he thinks.

I saw the new James Bond movie last night.

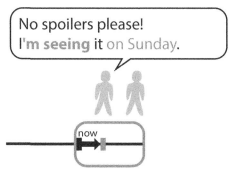

No spoilers please!
I'm **seeing** it on Sunday.

It is an unfinished action.

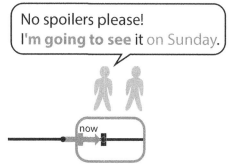

No spoilers please!
I'm **going to see** it on Sunday.

This has been decided: It is a plan.

Can I meet with you next week?

Sorry, I'm **going** to be in Morocco next week.

This has been decided: It is a plan.

Sorry, I'**ll** be in Morocco next week.

Thinking about possibilities: here or not.
We say 'I might be in Morocco.' or 'I may be in Morocco' if we are less certain.

Sorry, I'm in Morocco next week.

This is a fixed event - scheduled.

There are lots of ways we can think about the future, and lots of ways we talk about it. All of these sentences are very natural.

What's on tomorrow's agenda?

We'**re having** breakfast at 7:00, then golf.

These things are not finished.

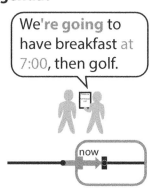

We'**re going** to have breakfast at 7:00, then golf.

These things have been decided.
We are on the path to these events.

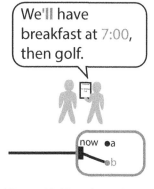

We'**ll** have breakfast at 7:00, then golf.

We are thinking about the possibilities and saying what has been decided.

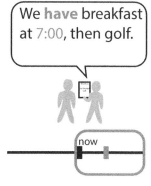

We **have** breakfast at 7:00, then golf.

These things are fixed.

Practice

Complete the sentences with *am/is/are + going to* or *will*.

1. A: Can you please wash the car?
   B: Yes, I_____ do it this afternoon.
2. A: Where do you want to go for our summer vacation?
   B: I want to go to the Netherlands.
   A: Me too. We_____ go to the Netherlands then.
3. A: What are your plans for the summer?
   B: We_____ go to the Netherlands.
4. A: Excuse me, do you know how to use the photocopier?
   B: Yes, I_____ show you.
5. A: Can you help me with the computer?
   B: I_____ show Lily how to use the photocopier now, so I_____ help you after that.
6. A: Why is she so happy?
   B: She just found out she's pregnant. She_____ have a baby.
7. It's my birthday so my wife_____ take me to a concert tonight.
8. A: Are you free on Sunday afternoon?
   B: No, sorry. I_____ go hiking.
9. A: Robert has an allergy so we can't have seafood tonight.
   B: Ok, I_____ cook chicken instead.
10. A: Why is he looking for his gloves?
    B: He_____ go skiing.

Practice

Which do you think is the best answer? Are the other answers acceptable?

1. There's nothing for dinner... I know!

   (a) I order a pizza.
   (b) I'll order a pizza.
   (c) I'm ordering a pizza.
   (d) I'm going to order a pizza.

2. Do you have any plans for tomorrow?

   (a) Yes, I go running.
   (b) Yes, I'll go running.
   (c) Yes, I'm going running.
   (d) Yes, I'm going to go running.

3. What time does the game start?

   (a) It starts at 6.
   (b) It'll start at 6.
   (c) It's starting at 6.
   (d) It's going to start at 6.

4. What do you think about the future?

   (a) We have more robots.
   (b) We'll have more robots.
   (c) We're having more robots.
   (d) We're going to have more robots.

5. Are you coming to pick me up?

   (a) Yes, I'm there in 5 minutes.
   (b) Yes, I'll be there in 5 minutes.
   (c) Yes, I'm being there in 5 minutes.
   (d) Yes, I'm going to be there in 5 minutes.

6. What are you doing next week?

   (a) I go to New Orleans.
   (b) I'll go to New Orleans.
   (c) I'm going to New Orleans.
   (d) I'm going to go to New Orleans.

7. When do you arrive?

   (a) I arrive at 11.
   (b) I'll arrive at 11.
   (c) I'm arriving at 11.
   (d) I'm going to arrive at 11.

8. We have some news...

   (a) We get married!
   (b) We'll get married!
   (c) We're getting married!
   (d) We're going to get married!

9. Oh no, you broke my watch!

   (a) Sorry, I buy you a new one.
   (b) Sorry, I'll buy you a new one.
   (c) Sorry, I'm buying you a new one.
   (d) Sorry, I'm going to buy you a new one.

10. Choose the best question.

   (a) Do you come to the party?
   (b) Will you come to the party?
   (c) Are you coming to the party?
   (d) Are you going to come to the party?

Understand the differences, understand the meaning each part adds.
There are lots of options. We all think differently.

before and after a time in the future

We talk about something happening **before** something else in the future.

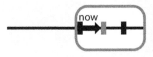

I'm going to a restaurant for lunch Sunday. I'll be hungry because I'**m playing** golf in the morning.
The listener uses common sense to make a connection between these two events.

I'm going to a restaurant for lunch on Sunday, I'll be hungry because I **will have** just played golf.
The hunger at the restaurant will be a result of playing golf.

We talk about something happening **after** something else in the future.

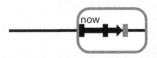

I have to leave the party early because I'**m working**.
Work is my reason for leaving. It is **not finished** at the time I leave (and not started either).

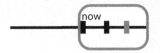

I arrive at 10:00 tomorrow. The interview **is** at 10:30, so I'll sit in the park and try to relax. I will try to relax to prepare for the interview: a **scheduled** event.

What they do **will** be remembered for generations.
There are **possibilities** at the time: (a) remember (b) forget.
After they do it, people will remember what they do.

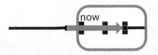

Bring lunch tomorrow because we'**re going** to go to the zoo.
The reason you bring lunch tomorrow is because we have the **plan** to go to the zoo.

Bring lunch tomorrow because we'**ll be going** to the zoo.
We are thinking about our options at a future time. The zoo trip is not finished.

We talk about something happening **at the same time as** something else in the future.

When you arrive I'**ll be reading** a book in front of the station.
We are thinking about options or possibilities at a future time. It **won't be finished** at the time. (It will have started)

19

Ways of talking about the past

past simple, present perfect, *would* and *used to*

tense, aspect, modality and quasi-modality for past

Ways of talking about the past

past form

The simplest way to talk about the **past** is to use a verb in the past form.

We talk about **periods** of time in the past.

I **lived** in England last year.

This **period** was some time last year. It may be the whole year or part of the year.

We talk about **actions** and **events** that happened once in the past and are **finished**.

She **went** to the park yesterday.

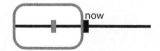

We are talking about **one time**.

We talk about things that happened many times over a period of time in the past.

She **went** to the park three times last month.

We **say** it happened **more than once** and **say when** it happened. If we don't say how many times, we assume it happened once.

have +-en form

We use *have* + -en form when we talk about things that happened **before** the present time, and the **result** in the **present** is **important**.

We talk about something that happened before now.

I **have been** to England.

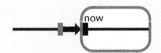

We are talking about the **present**: I have the experience **in the present**.

We say we have experienced something **more than once**.

I **have been** to England three times.

It happened **more than once**. We have experience **in the present**.

We talk about periods of time that **started in the past** and **include the present**.

She **has been** to the park three times this year.

It happened **more than once** over a period of time that includes the **present**.

used to and would

We use *used to* or *would* to talk about things that happened many times during **periods** of time in the **past**. We don't say how many times. Either can often be used in the same situation.

She **used to** go to the park.

We don't need to say when.

When she was a child, she **would** go to the park after school.

Would refers to options or possibilities at points in time. We add a period of time to show these things happened many times during the period.

The difference between *used to* and *would* can be seen in negative sentences.

I ***didn't used to*** talk in front of people.
We aren't talking about choice, just what happened.

When I was a child, I ***wouldn't*** talk in front of people.
This was an option, I chose not to do this.

Used to refers to **periods** of time. *Would* refers to options or possibilities at **points** in time.

We talk about things that were true for a **period** of time in the past.

I **used to** live in England.

This was true for a period of time in the past.

We use *wouldn't* to talk about **one point** in time in the past. These things were options or possibilities but they didn't happen.

I asked him nicely but he **wouldn't** listen.

He had the **option** of listening to us but he made the decision **not** to.

We also use *couldn't* in this way.

I looked everywhere but I **couldn't** find it.
Finding it was possible but it didn't happen.

The meaning of *used* has changed over time. *Used to* + verb and *used* + object are now different words. They are spelled the same but the pronunciation is different.

I **used to** live in England. The 's' makes a 's' sound. The 'd' is lost when it blends with the 't' in *to*.
I **used** a saw to cut the branches. The 's' is voiced and makes a 'z' sound. The 'd' is pronounced.

which one should I use?

There isn't one correct answer for every situation. The sentences we use depend on how we are thinking about the past. Here are some different ways we think and talk about the past.

We often don't say when something happened in the past. We use either the past form or *have + -en form*.

I'm sorry I'm late...

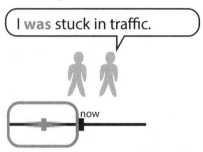

We know when it happened because of the context.

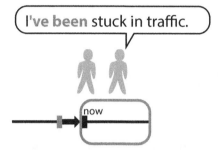

It is clear that we are talking about something that happened in the past with a result in the present.

In some situations we can use *didn't* (past form) or add *wouldn't* or *couldn't*.

The car **didn't** start so I took the bus.

It simply didn't happen.

The car **wouldn't** start so I took the bus.

I tried, but it wasn't possible for the car to start.
We also use couldn't:
'I couldn't get the car started so I took the bus.'

When we talk about things that were true for a period in the past we can use *the past form* or *used (to)*. When we use *the past form* the listener wants to know **when**. It is often not true in the present.

I'm going to Canada next week.

This was true for a period of time in the past. I don't live in Canada now.

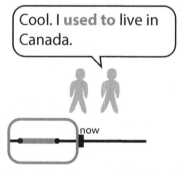

This was true for a period of time in the past. I don't live in Canada now.

However, it may be true in the present too.

I haven't been to this part of town for ages.
Last time I was here, **there was** a good cafe on this street. I hope it's still there.
Later...
Yes! It's still here!

I haven't been to this part of town for ages.
There **used to** be a good cafe on this street.
I hope it's still there.
Later...
Yes! It's still here!

When we talk about things that happened many times over a period of time in the past, we can use the past form, *would* or *used to*. When we use the past form or *would* the listener wants to know **when**. It often doesn't happen in the present.

Do you play sport? No, but...

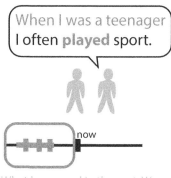

What happened in the past. We say when: many times during a period of time.

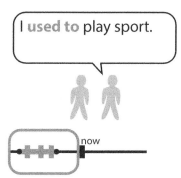

We can add the time to add more information:
when I was a teenager,
I **used to** play sport.

There were options and this is what I chose to do. We say when so we know we are talking about past, not a hypothetical situation.

However, it may happen in the present too.

When she was a child **she talked** like an adult.

When she was a child **she used to** talk like an adult.

When she was a child **she would** talk like an adult.

She **is** an adult now, it is very likely that she **still** talks like one.

We often start with *used to* (we don't need to say when) and then use the past form or *would* to add further information. We can use *used to* again but we usually use one of the other expressions because they are shorter and simpler.

In the summer **we used** to go to the coast...
(a) There was a river and we**'d** spend our days fishing. (*would*: remembering)
(b) There was a river and we **spent** our days fishing. (past form: at these times in the past)
(c) There was a river and we **used to** spend our days fishing. (*used to*: during a period in the past)

Practice

Complete the sentences with the *past form, have + -en form, used to* or *would*. There may be more than one answer.

1. A: Hi... Sorry I didn't reply to your email. I _____ (be) traveling around America.
   B: Awesome. Did you have a good time?
2. A: Yeah. I _____ (live) there so I _____ (go) out for drinks with some old friends.
   B: How are they all doing?
3. A: They're good. They've all got families so they don't go out as much as they _____. In the
4. old days we _____ (go) out for dinner, then we _____ (go) to a concert and party all night.

Practice

Complete the conversation with *used to*, *would* and/or the correct form of the verb in brackets. There may be more than one answer.

1. A: I _____ (live) in Australia now but I _____ (live) in Japan. It was great.
2.   We _____ (go) skiing a lot.
3. B: I _____ (live) there too.
4.   I _____ (go) snowboarding in the winter.
5.   We _____ (go) on weekdays and there _____ (be) no one there.
6. A: What _____ you _____ (do) in the summer?
7. B: We _____ (have) barbecues.

Practice

Which do you think is the best answer? Are the other answers acceptable? Do the sentences mean the same thing?

1. What did you have for dinner yesterday?

    (a) We had tacos.
    (b) We'd have tacos.
    (c) We used to have tacos.

2. When I was a child,...

    (a) we had tacos for dinner on Fridays.
    (b) we'd have tacos for dinner on Fridays.
    (c) we used to have tacos for dinner on Fridays.

3. I live in Scotland now.

    (a) Really? I lived in Scotland!
    (b) Really? I'd live in Scotland!
    (c) Really? I used to live in Scotland!

4. When I lived in Bangladesh,...

    (a) we often played cricket.
    (b) we'd often play cricket.
    (c) we used to often play cricket.

5. When I was young,...

    (a) I didn't eat mushrooms.
    (b) I wouldn't eat mushrooms.
    (c) I didn't used to eat mushrooms.

6. (a) I played the piano.
    (b) I'd play the piano.
    (c) I used to play the piano.

7. (a) I was good at playing the piano.
    (b) I'd be good at playing the piano.
    (c) I used to be good at playing the piano.

8. (a) Did you like coffee?
    (b) Would you like coffee?
    (c) Did you use to like coffee?

9. Where did you use to go for holidays?

    (a) We always went to the lake.
    (b) We'd always go to the lake.
    (c) We used to always go to the lake.

used to / be used to

We talk about things we *used to* do and things we *are used to* doing. Words change meanings over time. These two expressions include the same word (*used*) but they have very different meanings.

used to: a during a period of time in the past.
used to + verb

Greg used to work late.

This happened during a period of time in the past (many times).

be used to: comfortable with something (generally speaking).
be used to + noun

Greg is used to working late.

We are describing Greg. He is generally comfortable working late. This is something he often finds himself doing.

Helen used to live in Denmark.

This happened during a period of time in the past.

Helen is used to life in Denmark.

We are describing Helen. She is generally comfortable living in Denmark. She lived somewhere else before but lives in Denmark now.

We use *be used to* when we talk about a situation someone is often in and is comfortable with.

Subject	*be*	Description	
She	is	used to life in Denmark.	She is comfortable in Denmark.
We	are	used to using chopsticks.	We are comfortable with chopsticks.
He	isn't	used to this heat.	He isn't comfortable. It's too hot for him.
I	am	used to talking in front of people.	I've done it many times. I am comfortable.

Practice

Complete the sentences with *be(am, is, are) used to* or *used to*.

1. The new job is tough, but I _____ it now.
2. My old job was good, I _____ take long breaks.
3. He _____ drink too much soda.
4. She_____ working in a noisy place.
5. I _____ (not) like olives.
6. They _____(not) shoveling snow.

before and after a time in the past

We talk about something happening **before** something else in the past.

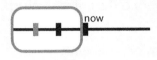

I went to a restaurant for lunch Sunday. I was hungry because I **played** golf in the morning.

The listener uses common sense to make a connection between these two events.

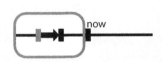

I went to a restaurant for lunch on Sunday. I was hungry because I **had** just **played** golf.

These two things are connected. The hunger at the restaurant was a result of playing golf.

There are many ways of thinking and talking about what happened **after** something in the past. These are the same words used when talking about the future (see page 158), but in the past form instead of the present form.

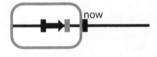

I had to leave the party early because I **was working**.

Work was my reason for leaving. It was not finished at the time I left (and not started either).

It was 10:00. The interview **was** at 10:30, so I sat in the park and tried to relax. I was trying to relax to prepare for the interview: a scheduled event.

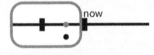

What they did **would** be remembered for generations.

There were options or possibilities at the time: (a) remember (b) forget. People remembered what they did.

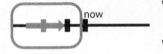

We were so excited, we **were going** to go to the zoo.

We were excited because we had the zoo plan.

We **were going** to go to the beach, **but** we got lost.

We had the plan, but It didn't happen because we got lost.

They didn't know it, but they**'d be going** to the zoo later that day.

We are thinking about something **not finished** and **unknown**. (there were other possibilities)

We talk about something happening **at the same time as** something else in the past.

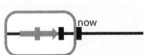

I **was reading** a book when she arrived.

It **wasn't finished** at the time. (It had started)

20

Review of future and past
using tense, aspect and modality

review of future and past

We refer to fixed times in the **present-future** or the **past**.
(tense)

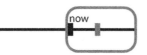

We use the present form for fixed future events that can not be changed.

We use the past form for the past. The past can not be changed.

We talk about things that have happened **before** now and things that are happening **after** now.
(aspect)

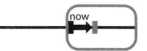

We use *be* + *-ing* form to talk about unfinished actions happening **after** now.

We use *have* + *-en* form to talk about results of thing that happened **before** now.

We talk about **options** and **possibilities**.
(modality)

• a: ?

• b: ?

or...

We use *will* when we make decisions and predictions.

We use *would* when we think about what often happened during a period of time in the past.

We talk about things **between** two **points** in time.
(quasi-modality)

We use *be going to* to talk about things that we planned in the past that happen in the future.

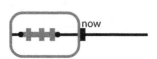

We use *used to* to talk about what generally happened during a period of time in the past.

168

examples

The show **starts** at 6:00.
The party **is** on Friday.
We **arrive** next month.

When **is** the festival?
Does it finish by 10:00?
When **does** it start?

I **don't** leave at 9:00.
The concert **isn't** this week.
I **don't** have any plans tomorrow.

They **ate** fish for dinner.
She **caught** the ball.
I **was** hungry yesterday morning.

Did you go to the park yesterday?
When you were a child, **were** you tall?
When **was** the ceremony?

I **didn't** go to get the car.
It **wasn't** ready.
The supermarket **wasn't** open.

I'**m working** tomorrow.
We'**re taking** a holiday next Friday.
He'**s playing** soccer tomorrow.

Are you **going** to the festival?
What **are** you **doing** on the weekend?
Where **are** you **going**?

She **isn't coming** next week.
I'**m not taking** a break.
We **aren't going** overseas next year.

We **have finished** the project.
I'**ve hiked** twice this month.
He'**s had** a haircut.

Have you **been** to Mali?
Have you **seen** her this morning?
Have you **done** the vacuuming?

I **haven't washed** the windows.
Her flight **hasn't landed** yet.
They **haven't been** to America.

It'**ll** rain tomorrow.
I'**ll** cook dinner tonight.
I'**ll** retire in ten years.

Will we have enough time?
When **will** we eat?
What **will** you give her?

She **won't** like it.
We **won't** go to the park.
They **won't** be home.

When I was a student I **would** stay up all night studying.

When you lived at the snow, **would** you ski more or snowboard more?

When I worked in the factory, we sometimes **wouldn't** get breaks.

Or, when something was an option or possibility in the past, but it didn't happen:
We **couldn't** see the mountain because it was cloudy.   We tried several times but the car **wouldn't** start.

We'**re going to** travel Europe.
I'**m going to** fix the car.
She'**s going to** study medicine.

Are you **going to** help?
Where **are** you **going to** go?
What **are** you **going to** do?

I'**m not going to** have time.
He **isn't going to** play tomorrow.
We **aren't going to** see it.

They **used to** play golf.
He **used to** be slim.
I **used to** live in Canada.

Did you **use to** like tomatoes?
Did you **use to** do your homework?
Did they **use to** go for walks?

I **didn't used to** have long hair.
I **didn't use to** study.
I **didn't use to** sleep much.

quiz

1. Which of the following sentences is about the future?

   (a) I feel good.
   (b) I felt good.
   (c) I'm thinking about music.
   (d) I'm going soon.

2. Which of the following sentences is about the past?

   (a) I feel good.
   (b) I felt good.
   (c) I'm thinking about music.
   (d) I'm going soon.

3. Choose the best answer.

   What are you doing tomorrow?
   (a) I go to school.
   (b) I'll go to school.
   (c) I'm going to school.

4. Choose the best answer.

   What did you do yesterday?
   (a) I went to school.
   (b) I used to go to school.
   (c) I would go to school.

5. Choose the best answer.

   I want to watch the game...
   (a) It starts at 6.
   (b) It's starting at 6.
   (c) It'll start at 6.
   (d) It'll be starting at 6.
   (e) any of the above.

6. Choose the best sentence.

   (a) I'll have time to help you next week.
   (b) I'm having time to help you next week.
   (c) (a) or (b)

7. Choose the best sentence.

   (a) Next time I see you we live in Asia.
   (b) Next time I see you we'll live in Asia.
   (c) Next time I see you we're living in Asia.
   (d) Next time I see you we'll be living in Asia.

8. Choose the best sentence.

   A: Have you sent the invitations?
   B: Sorry, I forgot!...
   (a) I do it this afternoon.
   (b) I'll do it this afternoon.
   (c) I'm doing it this afternoon.
   (d) I'll be doing it this afternoon.

9. Choose the best sentence.

   When I was a teenager...
   (a) I worked in a shop.
   (b) I'd work in a shop.
   (c) I used to work in a shop.
   (d) (a) or (c)
   (e) (a), (b) or (c)

10. Choose the best sentence.

    When I was a student I used to study every day...
    (a) I did my homework every evening.
    (b) I'd do my homework every evening.
    (c) I used to do my homework every evening.
    (d) (a) or (c)
    (e) (a), (b) or (c)

170

21

Think and say 1
content clauses: reported thoughts and reported speech

say

When we say what someone said we can use *say* and their **exact words**.

Todd says, "I live in San Francisco."

We use *said* for the past.

Todd said, "I live in San Francisco."

This style is often used in novels. We read exactly what each character said.

There is often no reason to use the exact words (we often don't remember them anyway!). The **meaning** is more important. We make a sentence with the same meaning.

Todd talks **about the present**.

1. "I **live** in San Francisco."
2. Todd says (that) he **lives** in San Francisco.

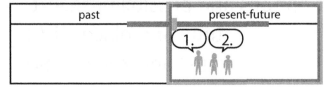

Todd talks **about the past**.

1. "I **lived** in San Francisco."
2. Todd says (that) he **lived** in San Francisco.

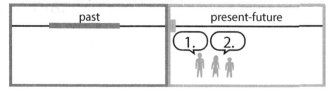

Todd would have used the word *I*, but we use *he* to make it clear we are referring to Todd.

● ●*that*   *That* is optional in these sentences. *That* is used to refer to a separate point.
That is not needed, but using *that* prepares the listener for the point that follows.

We say what Todd **said in the past**. This was true at the time he spoke (in the past) so we use the past form of *live (lived)*.

1. "I **live** in San Francisco."
2. Todd said (that) he **lived** in San Francisco.

We can use the present form if we think it is still true in the present.

1. "I **live** in San Francisco."
2. Todd said (that) he **lives** in San Francisco.

We often talk about what people **said in the past** and refer to the time in the past it was said. When there is more than one verb the first verb is in the past form.

Subject	Verb	(that)	Subject	Verb	Object etc.
She	said	(that)	"I **she**	**'ve finished** **'d finished**	work." work.
He	said	(that)	"I **he**	**'m watching** **was watching**	a movie." a movie.

172

It often doesn't matter which way we say it as long as we communicate the meaning.
In the following situation we can use *says* or *said*. There are different ways of thinking about it.

Says - The speaker's words are being passed on to the listener in the **present**.

Said - The person speaks, then you say what they said. They spoke in the **past**.

The above examples use *is* in the present from. When we are translating, the information is true in the present.

Practice

Tell your American friend what your Japanese friend says. Use *she*.

Example: (I play the piano.) **She says (that) she plays the piano** *or* **she said (that) she plays the piano.**

1. (My name is Yuki.) _____.
2. (I live in Tokyo.) _____.
3. (I'm studying science.) _____.
4. (I have been to America before.) _____.
5. (I went to North Carolina last year.) _____.
6. (My brother lives in Greensboro.) _____.

Practice

Tell your coworker what people said at the meeting last month. Things have changed since then.

Example: Brenda: The light in room six needs to be changed.
*Brenda said the light in room six needed to be changed*___.

1. Stephanie: Sales are down _____.
2. Raymond: We need to get more customers. _____.
3. Justin: Some customers are having trouble ordering. _____.
4. Stephanie: Delivery has been taking too long. _____.
5. Raymond: Customers have asked for cheaper products. _____.
6. Brenda: We have to hire new staff. _____.
7. Justin: I have a headache. _____.

We can also look at it from another perspective and say what we hear or heard.
We don't need to say who said it.

   I **heard** (that) Todd lives in San Francisco.

said about the past

We talk about people speaking in the past about something that happened **before they spoke**.

We can use the past form for both main verbs. We assume it happened **before** the person spoke.
This sentence pattern is common, but some people don't consider it grammatically correct.

1. "I **went** shopping on Sunday."
2. He said (that) he **went** shopping on Sunday.

Sunday	Monday	Tuesday	Wednesday	Thursday	Friday	Saturday	Sunday	Monday
SHOPPING MALL		1.				2.		

Or, we can use *had* + -en form to clearly say it happened before the person spoke.

1. "I **went** shopping on Sunday."
2. He said (that) he **had been** shopping on Sunday.

Sunday	Monday	Tuesday	Wednesday	Thursday	Friday	Saturday	Sunday	Monday
SHOPPING MALL		1.				2.		

Subject	Verb	(that)	Subject	Verb	Object etc.	Time
			"I	**played**	baseball	on Saturday morning."
He	said	(that)	he	**played**	baseball	on Saturday morning.
He	said	(that)	he	**'d played**	baseball	on Saturday morning.
			"We	**went**	to a restaurant	on Friday night."
She	said	(that)	they	**went**	to a restaurant	on Friday night.
She	said	(that)	they	**'d been**	to a restaurant	on Friday night.

Practice

Tell your friend what Kate and Daniel told you yesterday. There are two ways you can answer, use whatever makes more sense for you.

I saw Kate and Daniel yesterday...

1. Kate: We went away on vacation in December. _____.
2. Daniel: We went away for two weeks. _____.
3. Daniel: We had a great time. _____.
4. Kate: I got a new job last week. _____.
5. Kate: I got a haircut on Tuesday. _____.
6. Daniel: I ate a big sandwich for lunch on Sunday. _____.
7. Kate: We saw a good movie on Wednesday night. _____.

said about the future

We talk about people speaking in the past about something that happened **after they spoke**.

People speak about what is happening in the future using *am/are/is* + -ing form (1). When we say what they said we use *was/were* to make it clear we are referring to **after they spoke**, not after now (2).

1. "I**'m going** shopping on Thursday."
2. He said (that) he was going shopping on Thursday.

Sunday	Monday	Tuesday	Wednesday	Thursday	Friday	Saturday	Sunday	Monday
		1.		SHOPPING MALL		2.		

People speak about **scheduled events** in the future using the present form (1). However, when we say what someone said, we use *was/were* + -ing form to clearly say it happened **after they spoke** (2).

1. "We **arrive** on Thursday."
2. She said (that) they were arriving on Thursday.

Sunday	Monday	Tuesday	Wednesday	Thursday	Friday	Saturday	Sunday	Monday
		1.		arrive		2.		

When we say 'I spoke with her on Tuesday and she said they **were arriving** on Thursday' (as in the example above), we know she arrived the Thursday after I spoke with her. However, if we say 'I spoke with her on Tuesday and she said they **arrived** on Thursday,' it sounds like they had already arrived the Thursday **before** I spoke with her.

If it hasn't happened yet, we often use the present form (it happens in the future, **after now**).

1. "We **arrive** on Monday."
2. She said (that) they **arrive** on Monday.

Sunday	Monday	Tuesday	Wednesday	Thursday	Friday	Saturday	Sunday	Monday
		1.				2.		arrive

For the top example, we can also say 'He said he**'s going** shopping on Thursday' if he is going shopping in the future.

Practice

Tell your friend what Kate and Daniel told you yesterday. There may be more than one answer.

1. Kate: We're going away on vacation in July. _____.
2. Daniel: We leave on the 6th. _____.
3. Kate: I'm starting my new job today. _____.
4. Daniel: I'm going to eat a big sandwich for lunch. _____.

said about options and possibilities

When we say what someone said in the past, we use *could*, *might* or *would* to talk about what was an option or possibility at the time.

1. "I**'ll** go shopping on Thursday."
2. He **said** he **would** go shopping on Thursday.

Sunday	Monday	Tuesday	Wednesday	Thursday	Friday	Saturday	Sunday	Monday
		a or (1.) b		SHOPPING MALL		(2.)		

a: shopping
b: something else

If it is still an option or possibility we can use the present form.

1. "I**'ll** go shopping on Monday."
2. He **said** he'll go shopping on Monday.

Sunday	Monday	Tuesday	Wednesday	Thursday	Friday	Saturday	Sunday	Monday
		(1.)				a or (2.) b		SHOPPING MALL

a: shopping
b: something else

Or, we can use the past form. It was also an option or possibility in the past when it was said.

1. "I**'ll** go shopping on Monday."
2. He **said** he **would** go shopping on Monday.

Sunday	Monday	Tuesday	Wednesday	Thursday	Friday	Saturday	Sunday	Monday
		a or (1.) b				(2.)		SHOPPING MALL

a: shopping
b: something else

We use the past forms of *can (could)*, *may (might)* and *will (would)*.

	Subject	Verb	(that)	Subject	Verb	Object etc.
Monday: Tuesday:	He	said	(that)	"We they	**can** play **could** play	baseball." baseball.
Monday: Tuesday:	John	said	(that)	"Alice Alice	**may** win **might** win	an award." an award.
Monday: Tuesday:	She	said	(that)	"I she	**'ll** have **'d** have	a coffee." a coffee.

176

The past form is used for things that are not in the present-future. When we use *could*, *would*, *should* or *might*, we know if it is in the **past** or **hypothetical** because of the context.

2. George said he would pick me and he did.

2. Michael said he would pick me up if he had more time.

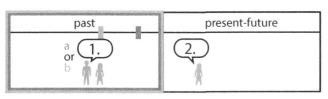

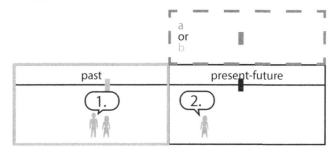

1. "I'll pick you up." (a promise in the past)

1. "I'd pick you up if I had more time." (hypothetical)

We add *have + -en form* to say something happened before a time in the past, or before the hypothetical present (hypothetical in the past).

2. She said George would have picked Sarah up.

2. Michael said he would have picked me up if he had more time.

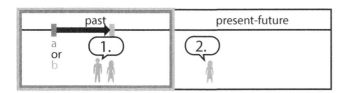

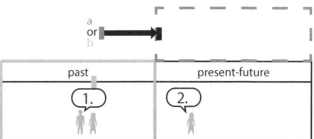

1. "George will have picked Sarah up."
A prediction about before a time in the past.

1. "I'd pick you up if I had more time".
This was hypothetical in the past, said before pick up. Pick up was in the past so it's not a hypothetical option anymore.
or "I would have picked you up if I had more time". This was said after pick up, hypothetical before a time in the past.

Practice

Complete the sentences. Say what the people said. There may be more than one answer.

Example:

We'll go out for dinner.   → She said we'd go out for dinner.

1. "I can play the drums."   → He said _____.
2. "I might watch the football."   → She said _____.
3. "I'll buy him a present."   → I said _____.
4. "We could have rice for dinner." → She said _____.
5. "I'll be late."   → He said _____.
6. "I might go if I have the money." → He didn't go. He said _____ if he had the money.
7. "I'd like a sandwich."   → She said _____.

time and place

We often talk about what someone said (in the past) about another time in the past. We clearly state the time so the listener knows when these things happened.

We use other words to say something happens in relation to another time.

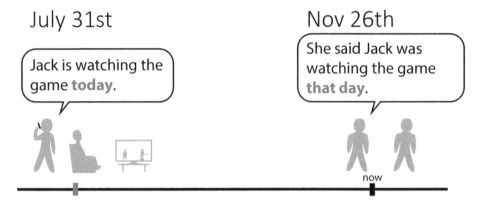

July 31st

> Jack is watching the game **today**.

Nov 26th

> She said Jack was watching the game **that day**.

now

We use words like *yesterday*, *today* and *tomorrow* in relation to **now**.

Sunday	Monday	Tuesday	Wednesday	Thursday	Friday	Saturday	Sunday	Monday
					yesterday	**now** today	tomorrow	

We use other words in relation to other times. These times may be in the **past** or **future**.

Sunday	Monday	Tuesday	Wednesday	Thursday	Friday	Saturday	Sunday	Monday
	the day before	that day	the next day			**now**		

from now	from another time
last week	the week before
this week	that week
next week	the next week

from now	from another time
last month	the month before
this month	that month
next month	the next month

from now	from another time
last year	the year before
this year	that year
next year	the next year

Next week and *the next week* sound similar, but refer to different times.
We can say *the following week* to be clear.
We can also say *the following day*, *the following month* and *the following year*.

	Subject	Verb	(that)	Subject	Verb	Object etc.	Time
May:				"I	played	baseball	yesterday."
August:	He	said	(that)	he	played	baseball	the day before.
May:				"We	're going	to a restaurant	next week."
August:	She	said	(that)	they	were going	to a restaurant	the next week.
	She	said	(that)	they	were going	to a restaurant	the following week.
May:				"Alice	won	an award	last month."
August:	John	said	(that)	Alice	won	an award	the month before.
2012:				"I	'm going	to Europe	this year."
This year:	You	said	(that)	you	were going	to Europe	that year.

I saw Sam last week. He was exhausted. He said that he'd played baseball the day before.

I talked to Paige two months ago. She said they were going to a restaurant the next week.

I talked to John in spring. He said that Alice had won an award the month before.

I haven't seen you since 2012, you said you were going to Europe that year. How was it?

We use *here* and *there* in a similar way to say when talking about places. *Here* and *there* are in relation to the person speaking.

Jack is watching the game **here**.

She said Jack was watching the game **there**.

here: where the person speaking is.

there: not where the person speaking is.
(we know or say where it is)

Practice

Tell your friend what Dianne and Eric told you last summer. There may be more than one answer.

I saw Dianne and Eric last summer...

1. Dianne: We went away on vacation last month. _____.
2. Eric: We came back last week. _____.
3. Dianne: I can help you plan your trip next month. _____.
4. Dianne: I got a new job last year. _____.
5. Dianne: I got a haircut yesterday. _____.
6. Eric: I ate a big sandwich for lunch today. _____.
7. Dianne: We're going to the cinema this Friday. _____.
8. Eric: I'll be really busy at work next week. _____.

think and know

We use other verbs such as *think* in the same way.

We talk about what we think about now.

I **think** he **buys** food.

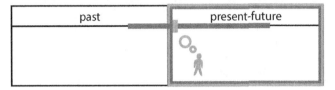

We talk about what we thought (in the past) about something (in the past).

I **thought** he **bought** food.

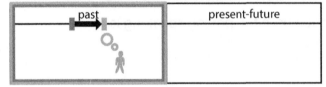

We can also use *had* + *-en* form to say what we thought about the past of the past.

I **thought** he **had bought** food.

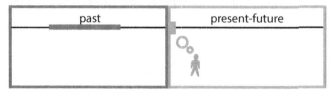

Past thought: he has bought food.
There was evidence to suggest this happened.

We talk about what we think about the past.

I **think** he **bought** food.

We talk about options and possibilities we considered in the past.

I **thought** he **would buy** food.

We use *would have* + *-en* form to talk about a result we predicted in the past. We are often surprised because what we predicted isn't what happened.

I **thought** he **would have bought** food.

Past thought: he will have bought food.
I expected the result: we have food, but he didn't buy it.

What we **know** is the **truth**. What we **think** is our **opinion**.

I **knew** it **would** work. The truth: it worked.
I **thought** it **would** work. My opinion: it may or may not have worked.

Practice

Say what the people think. There may be more than one answer.

Example: The beef is very good.
Joan thinks *the beef is very good* .

1. Germany will win.
   James thinks_____.

2. I'll be late.
   I think_____.

3. The beef was very good.
   Joan _____.

4. Before the game: Germany will win. They lost.
   James _____.

5. I'll be late.
   (I wasn't late) I _____.

22

Think and say 2
content clauses: reported speech

ask

People *ask* questions. We say what people asked.

We use *if* when there are a limited number of possible answers.
We use *if* when we talk about yes/no questions. There are two possible answers, *yes* and *no*.

Are you going to eat that fish?

He asked **if** you're going to eat that fish.

? • yes
• no

We use *if* when we talk about questions with *or*. The options listed are the only possible answers.

Would you like tea, coffee **or** juice?
She asked **if** I'd like tea, coffee or juice.

Subject	Verb		Subject	Verb	Object etc.
		"Do	you	play	baseball?"
He	asked	**if**	I	played	baseball.
He	asked	**if**	I	play	baseball.
		"Can	we	go	to a restaurant or a bar?"
She	asked	**if**	we	could go	to a restaurant or a bar.
She	asked	**if**	we	can go	to a restaurant or a bar.
		"Will	Alice	win	an award?"
John	asked	**if**	Alice	would win	an award.
John	asked	**if**	Alice	will win	an award.

Practice

You are talking to some people in French. Your friend doesn't understand French.
Tell him what he is being asked.

Example: Pierre: (Do you play the piano?) *Pierre asked if you played the piano* .
or *Pierre asked if you play the piano* .

1. Lola: (Are you from America?) _____.
2. Chloé: (Do you like France?) _____.
3. Hugo: (Are you hungry?) _____.
4. Pierre: (Can you teach me English?) _____.
5. Chloé: (Have you seen the Eiffel Tower?) _____.
6. Lola: (Are you coming shopping tomorrow?) _____.
7. Hugo: (Would you like to have some coffee?) _____.

We use **question words** when we ask for added information about a time, place, person, thing etc.

We use the question words *where*, *when*, *why*, and *how*.

Subject	Verb	Question word	Subject	Verb	Object etc.
He	asked	**"Where** do **where**	you I	play played	baseball?" baseball.
He	asked	**where**	I	play	baseball.
John	asked	**"Why** did **why**	Alice Alice	win won	an award?" an award.

We follow the same pattern when we ask about a subject or an object with *who* or *what*.

Subject	Verb	Question word	Subject	Verb	Object etc.
He	asked	**"What** sports do **what** sports	you I	like?" liked.	
He	asked	**what** sports	I	like.	
She	asked	**"What** day is **what** day	it?" it	 was.	
She	asked	**what** day	it	is.	
They	asked	**"Who** **who**	 	is was	the tallest?" the tallest.*
They	asked	**who**		is	the tallest.*
They	asked	**who**	the tallest	was.*	
They	asked	**who**	the tallest	is.*	

*We use *the tallest* as the subject or object. The meaning is the same. "Steve is the tallest" or "the tallest is Steve."

We often add a recipient. (See page 202.)

Subject	Verb	Recipient	Question word / if	Subject	Verb	Object etc.
He	asked	her	**"Where** did **where**	you she	go?" went.	
She	asked	the teacher	**"What** day is **what** day	it?" it	 was.	
John	asked	Alice	"Did **if**	you she	win won	an award?" an award.

Practice

You are talking to some people in French. Your friend doesn't understand French.
Tell him what he is being asked. You can add a recipient (you), but it isn't needed in this situation.

Example: Pierre: (Where do you live?) _Pierre asked (you) where you lived_ .
or _Pierre asked (you) where you live_ .

1. Lola: (What food do you like?) _____.
2. Chloé: (Where are you from?) _____.
3. Hugo: (What is your name?) _____.
4. Pierre: (When did you arrive?) _____.
5. Chloé: (How was your flight?) _____.
6. Lola: (Who are you traveling with?) _____.
7. Hugo: (How long will you be in France?) _____.

the meaning

When we tell people what was said the meaning is very important. We often choose to use more direct language rather than formal language so that the meaning is clear, even if the person spoke in more formal language.

More direct:

More formal/polite:

"**Can** I come in?" (Is it an option?)
She asked if she **could** come in.

"**May** I come in?" (Is it one of my options?)
She wants to know if she has permission.
She wants to know if it is an option
She asked if she **could** come in.

We don't need to use the same formal language when we tell people what someone said. We can use the same words or just express the meaning.

"**Would** you like tea or coffee?"
He asked if I **wanted** tea or coffee. Expressing the meaning.
He asked if I**'d like** tea or coffee. Using the same words.

When someone uses informal language (sometimes rude) we often use more formal or polite language to communicate the meaning of what they said.

"The air conditioner is **fucked**."
He said (that) the air conditioner was **broken**. Expressing the meaning without the swearing.

There are different ways of talking about the future. There are small differences but the basic meaning of any of these sentences fits the situation.

April 16: "I**'ll take** a vacation in June."
April 23: She said (that) she**'d take** a vacation in June.
April 23: She said (that) she **was taking** a vacation in June.
April 23: She said (that) she **was going to take** a vacation in June.
April 23: She said (that) she**'d be taking** a vacation in June.
April 23: She said (that) she**'ll take** a vacation in June.
April 23: She said (that) she**'s taking** a vacation in June.
April 23: She said (that) she**'s going to take** a vacation in June.
April 23: She said (that) she**'ll be taking** a vacation in June.

We can use different words that express the same meaning.

April 23: She said (that) she **was going on holiday** in June.

There are many more ways we can express this meaning. Common expressions in this situation include: *taking a vacation*, *taking a holiday*, *going on vacation* and *going on holiday*.

There are also different ways of talking about periods of time in the past.

"I **would often play** tennis when I was a child."
He said (that) he **would often play** tennis when he was a child.
He said (that) he **used to play** tennis when he was a child.
He said (that) he **often played** tennis when he was a child.

In some situations we use completely different verbs to make the meaning clear.

Must has no past form so we often use another expression that has a similar meaning such as *had to* or *needed to*.

"You **must** come home early today."
She told us we **had to** come home early that day.
She told us we **needed to** come home early that day.

Using *must* is also possible. We know we are talking about the past because of the context.

She told us we **must** come home early that day.

The meanings of *shall* and *should* often seem different, so we often use a expression (such as *want to*) that matches the meaning of what the person said.

"**Shall** we go to a restaurant?"
She asked me if I **wanted to** go to a restaurant.
She wanted to know what I thought was the right thing for us to do to make a decision.
She asked me if we **should** go to a restaurant.
This has a different meaning. She wanted my advice. Was it hypothetically the right thing to do?

"Shall we go to a restaurant?" is a more polite way of saying "Do you want to go to a restaurant?"

Speaking a second language isn't about substituting words from your first language into a new one, it is about understanding how to communicate in a new way. It is important to understand the meaning of what needs to be communicated and use words that express that meaning clearly.

Practice

Make sentences explaining what the people said, told you or asked you.
Example: "You must be home before 10:00." She said *I had to be home before 10:00*.

1. "May I have a drink of water, please?" He asked _____.
2. "Would you mind taking the dog outside?" She asked _____.
3. "I must buy her a present." He said _____.
4. "Can we go soon?" Sienna asked _____.
5. "Shall we go soon?" He asked _____.
6. "You must wear a tie." She said _____.
7. "I'm going to the park on Friday." You said _____.
8. "If it's not too much trouble, could I take the day off?" She asked _____.

185

telling people what to do

When we tell people what to do there is no subject.

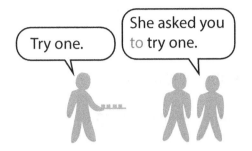

	Verb	Object etc.
	Try	one.

Subject	Verb	Recipient	*to*	Verb	Object etc.
She	asked	you	**to**	try	one.

When we say what someone was told to do, we add *to* to show things happening in sequence.
(See page 82.)
1. say/ask/tell
2. do (verb)

Subject	Verb	Recipient	Polite language	*to*	Verb	Object etc.
He	said		"Please	**to**	go." go.	
She	asked	the children	"Could you please	**to**	be be	quiet?" quiet.
John	told	Alice		**to**	"Win win	an award." an award.

We usually use polite language like "please" and "could you" when we ask people to do things.
When we say what people told us to do we use direct language so the meaning is clear.

When we make negative sentences we add not.

Subject	Verb	Recipient	Polite language	*not*	*to*	Verb	Object etc.
He	said		"Please	**don't** **not**	**to**	go." go."	
She	told	the children	"Don't	**not**	**to**	make make	a sound." a sound.
John	asked	Alice	"Could you	**not** **not**	**to**	make make	a speech?" a speech.

Practice

Make sentences explaining what the people said, told you or asked you.

Example: "Please try one." She asked me _to try one_____.

1. "Please open your textbooks to page 128". The teacher told us _____.
2. "Could you call Hannah?" Sienna said _____.
3. "Don't be late." He said _____.
4. "Please don't leave the door open" Leo told me _____.
5. "Could you please carry my bags?" She asked me _____.

186

about

We use *about* to show something is near a point.

It's **about** 10:00.

Not exactly, but near that point in time. It's really 9:58.

9:58   10:00

We also use *about* when we are not referring to the exact point someone makes when they speak. We often simplify what people say and tell people the general topic.

She talked **about** her family

She said a few main points.

her family

Subject	Verb	Recipient	*about*	Topic	Place/Time
She	talked		about	her family.	
He	spoke		about	his experience	in the jungle.
We	asked	the boss	about	holiday pay.	
They	told	us	about	the old days.	
I	think		about	her	all the time.

Practice

Complete the sentences. Use *about* for general topics. Leave the space blank when we are giving specific information.

Example: (Topic: her family) She talked *about her family*_____.

1. Tell me _____ your new job.
2. Could you tell me _____ the time?
3. We asked _____ how hot it was.
4. We asked _____ the weather.
5. She gave a presentation _____ the environment.
6. He always thinks _____ other people.
7. Hey, stop! What are you doing here? Who are you? Tell me _____ your name.

hopes and wishes

We use the present form for things that are **real**. We use the past form for things that are **hypothetical**.

We **hope** for things we want in the present-future. These things are possible.

I hope it **is** sunny.

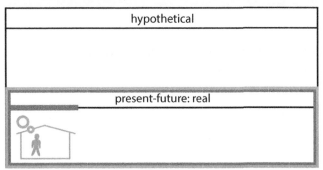

It is possible that it's sunny. I don't know, I haven't looked outside.

There's a real chance.

We **wish** for things we are imagining. We talk about them hypothetically.

I wish it **was** sunny.

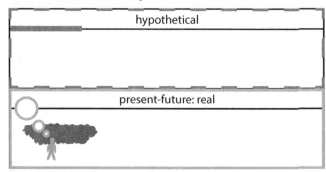

It isn't sunny.
Was is in the past tense because we are not talking about the real present-future.

We are talking hypothetically. (See page 111.)

Hopes and wishes often need a subject and verb to explain the details.

Subject	Verb	(that)	Subject	Verb	Object/Description	
He	**hopes**	(that)	she	looks	amazing.	He doesn't know how she looks yet.
She	**hopes**	(that)	she	is	home before 7:30.	She'll try, but may be late.
I	**wish**	(that)	he	was	happy.	He isn't happy.
I	**wish**	(that)	we	had	a full tank of gas.	We don't have a full tank of gas.

Practice

Complete the sentences with *hope* or *wish*.

1. I _____ I could fly.
2. I _____ they compromise.
3. Amanda _____ she was famous.
4. She _____ to be a singer.
5. They _____ they can afford it.
6. They _____ they could afford it.
7. Martin _____ he was young again.

188

23

Review of think and say
content clauses: reported speech

review of think and say

We say what people think or say in the present-future.

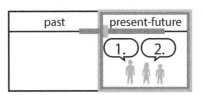

We say what is thought or said in the present-future, about the present-future.

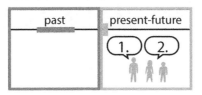

We say what is thought or said in the present-future, about the past...

... or a hypothetical situation.

we say what people thought or said in the past.

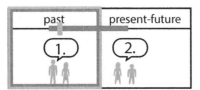

We say what was said in the past. We refer to the time it was said. (It may also be true in the present)

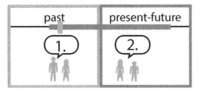

We say what was said in the past, and is still true in the present-future.

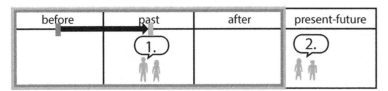

We can make it clear something happened before it was said in the past...

...or before a hypothetical present.

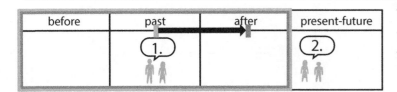

We can make it clear something was happening after it was said in the past.

Communicating the meaning is more important than using the same words.

We use words that communicate the meaning clearly.

There are different ways of talking about the past and future, the meaning is essentially the same.

examples

"I**'m** hungry."	He **says** (that) he**'s** hungry.
"I **like** tennis."	She **says** (that) she **likes** tennis.
"I**'ve finished** cleaning my room."	He **says** (that) he**'s finished** cleaning his room.
You **have** three sisters.	She **knows** (that) you **have** three sisters.
She **isn't working** tomorrow.	He **hopes** (that) she **isn't working** tomorrow.

"I **went** to Africa last month."	She **says** (that) she **went** to Africa last month.
You **learned** something today.	I **hope** (that) you **learned** something today.
You **were** in a hurry.	I **think** (that) you **were** in a hurry.

"I **would** go to Europe if I **could** get time off."	She **says** (that) she**'d** go to Europe if she **could** get time off.
	I **wish** (that) I **had** a new car.

"**Are** you ready?"	I **asked** if we **were** ready.
"I **went** to school yesterday."	He **said** (that) he **went** to school the day before.
"I**'ve been** to Antarctica."	She **said** (that) she**'d been** to Antarctica.
"**Can** we play golf on Wednesday?"	They **asked** if they **could** play golf on Wednesday.
We **have** time.	We **thought** (that) we **had** time.

"I**'ve been** to Antarctica."	She **said** (that) she**'s been** to Antarctica.
"The money **is** in the account."	They **said** (that) the money **is** in the account.
"They **live** near the river."	We **were told** (that) they **live** near the river.
(On Sunday) "We**'re playing** golf on Thursday."	(On Tuesday) She **said** (that) they**'re playing** golf on Thursday.
(4:00) "He **leaves** at 5:30."	(5:15) I **heard** (that) he **leaves** at 5:30.

"I **went** to Africa last month."	I **heard** (that) she**'d been** to Africa the month before.
"We **played** golf on Wednesday."	She **said** (that) they**'d played** golf on Wednesday.
"I **went** fishing yesterday."	He **said** (that) he**'d been fishing** the day before.

"I**'d go** if I had the money."	She **said** (that) she**'d have gone** if she had the money.
"I **could fix** it for you."	He **said** (that) he **could have fixed** it for us.

(On Sunday) "We**'re playing** golf on Thursday."	(On Friday) She **said** (that) they **were playing** golf yesterday.
(On a Sunday) "I**'m working** tomorrow.	(Next year) He **said** (that) he **was working** the following day.
(4:00) "He **leaves** at 5:30."	(5:45) I **heard** (that) you **were leaving** at 5:30.

"**Shall** we leave soon?"	He **asked** me if I **wanted to** leave.
"You **must** bring something to eat."	They **said** (that) we **had to** bring something to eat.
"**May** I **borrow** your pen, please?"	She **asked** if she **could borrow** my pen.
	She **asked** me **to lend** her my pen.

"When I **used to** live in Japan, I **would** often eat sushi."	He said he **would** often eat sushi when he **lived** in Japan.
	He said he often **ate** sushi when he **lived** in Japan.
	He said he **used to** eat sushi when he **lived** in Japan.
"I**'m going** to the picnic on the weekend."	She **said** she **was going** to the picnic on the weekend.
	She **said** she**'d go** to the picnic on the weekend.
	She **said** she **was going to go** to the picnic on the weekend.

quiz

Choose the best sentences.

1. Jackson said he wanted something to eat.
   Did Jackson say "I want something to eat"?
   (a) yes
   (b) no
   (c) maybe

2. A: (Tuesday) "We're having pasta for dinner."
   B: (Thursday)
   (a) He says they are having pasta for dinner.
   (b) He said they are having pasta for dinner.
   (c) He said they were having pasta for dinner.
   (d) any of the above

3. A: (1:00PM) "We're having curry for dinner."
   B: (2:00PM)
   (a) He says they are having curry for dinner.
   (b) He said they are having curry for dinner.
   (c) He said they were having curry for dinner.
   (d) any of the above

4. A: (1:00PM) "I'll be home at 6PM."
   B: (4:00PM)
   (a) She said she was home at 6PM.
   (b) She said she'd be home at 6PM.
   (c) She said she'll be home at 6PM.
   (d) either (b) or (c)

5. A: (1:00PM) "I'll be home at 6PM."
   B: (7:00PM) She's still not home, but...
   (a) She said she was home at 6PM.
   (b) She said she'd be home at 6PM.
   (c) She said she'll be home at 6PM.
   (d) either (b) or (c)

6. (a) I wish I have more time.
   (b) I wish I had more time.
   (c) (a) for future or (b) for past.

7. (a) I hope you have a great day.
   (b) I hope you had a great day.
   (c) (a) for future or (b) for past.

8. (a) You're on time! I hear you'll be late.
   (b) You're on time! I heard you'll be late.
   (c) You're on time! I heard you'd be late.

9. A: (May) "I went shopping yesterday."
   B: (November)
   (a) She said she went shopping yesterday.
   (b) She said she went shopping the day before.
   (c) She said that she'd been shopping the day before.
   (d) any of the above
   (e) either (b) or (c)

10. A: (3:07PM) "I live in Moscow."
    B: (3:08PM)
    (a) He says that he lives in Moscow.
    (b) He said that he lives in Moscow.
    (c) He said that he lived in Moscow.
    (d) any of the above
    (e) either (b) or (c)

11. A: Don't take the garbage out today. It's Tuesday.
    B:
    (a) My mistake, I think it is Wednesday.
    (b) My mistake, I thought it is Wednesday.
    (c) My mistake, I thought it was Wednesday.

12. A: (1:00PM) "Are you cooking dinner tonight?"
    B: (2:00PM)
    (a) She asked if I was cooking dinner tonight.
    (b) She asked if I was going to cook dinner.
    (c) either (a) or (b)

13. A: (Monday) "You must wear leather shoes tomorrow."
    B: (Thursday)
    (a) She said that we must wear leather shoes on Tuesday.
    (b) She said that we had to wear leather shoes on Tuesday.
    (c) She said that we needed to wear leather shoes on Tuesday.
    (d) any of the above

24

Where and when

prepositions of place, prepositions of time

adding a place

There are many words we can use to say **where** something is or happens.

We often simply refer to a place. (See page 4.)

Where do you work?
I work **at** the airport.

Where do you work?
I work **in** an office.

Where do you work?
I work **on** a boat.

Sometimes we might want to say where something is, based on where something else is.
In front of, *behind*, *above*, *below*, *over*, *under*, *apart* and *away* focus on **distance** and **direction**.

From me

A is in front of B.
(closer to me)

A is behind B.
(further from me)

From the center of the Earth

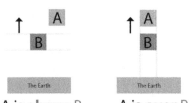

A is above B.   **A is over B.**
(further from Earth)

A is below B.   **A is under B.**
(closer to Earth)

From me

A is away.
(far from me, in
any direction)

distance from each other

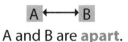

A and B are apart.

Below and *under* have similar meanings but they are used differently.

It is raining so I'm
standing **under**
an umbrella.

I'm in a building,
looking at the
street **below** me.

The same applies for *above* and *over*: I held the umbrella **over** her. We looked at the building **above**.

These words can be used to emphasize **distance**...

Subject	Verb	Distance	Direction
They	sat	two rows	**in front of** the band.
We	were	100 meters	**above** the valley.

...or just say the **direction** from one thing to the next.

They sat in front of the band.

We were above the valley.

We can use *away* to show **distance**...

The beach is **one kilometer** away (from here).

...or say something or someone is **not here**.

Sorry, he's away today. He's not here.

By, *beside*, *between*, *near* and *opposite* **express other relationships in space** (not distance).

We live by the mountains.
The mountains can be
used to locate our house.
(For more on *by* see page 208)

I put it beside the bed.
(beside = by the side of)
The side of the bed can
be used to locate it.

**It's between the bed and
the window.**

I live near the bank.
I live in the same general
area as the bank.

She sat opposite me.
I am on the other side of
the table.
We are facing each other.

We also use expressions with *to* and *from*.

from A   to B

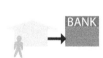

I live next to the bank.
In **sequence**.
The bank is next to my house.
Direction doesn't matter.

I live close to the bank.
My house is close to the
bank. It is not far.

She sat across from me.
I sat across **the table**
from her. (=opposite)

Practice

Look at the picture and complete the sentences. There may be more than one answer.

    A: Do you know who everyone is?
1. B: Hannah is sitting _____ the door.
2.   Patrick is sitting _____ the window.
3.   Phil is sitting _____ Patrick.
4.   Courtney is sitting _____ Hannah.
    A: When does Phil go on leave?
5. B: I'm not sure, check the calendar _____ Courtney.
    A: Have you seen my keys?
6. B: That could be them _____ the table,
    _____ Patrick and Phil.

When we talk about places we often talk about **movement**.
We use *from* and *to* to talk about origins and destinations.

I went **from** the bank **to** the supermarket.

We use *up* and *down* to talk about movement in relation to the Earth. We use *back* to talk about the **direction** of movement in relation to where the subject was before.

The plane flew **up**.

We went **down**.

back

They went **back**
(to where they were).

We use *in*, *out (of)*, *through*, *on*, *off*, *across* to talk about movement involving something else. If the listener knows what we are talking about, we don't need to say what the something else is.
We often come into contact with this thing.

I got **in** the car.

I walked **out** the door.

The payment went **through** *.

I got **on** the horse.

I stepped **off** the train.

We walked **across** the road.

*Payments go through a process. We don't say "the process" but we understand this is what happens.

We can add more information, such as a destination.

Subject	Verb	Direction	Destination
The plane	flew	up	to the clouds.
We	went	down the path	to the beach.
They	went	back	home.
I	walked	into	the garden.
I	walked	out of the house	to the garden.
The payment	went	through	to the bank.
I	got	onto	the horse.
We	walked	across the road	to the bakery.

We also use *up* and *down* to when we move **north** or **south**.

The plane flew up to Norway. (north)
We went down to Cape Town. (south)

Into (*in* + *to*) and *onto* (*on* + *to*) are so common that they have become one word.

We use *forwards*, *backwards* and *sideways* to talk about movement in relation to the subject.

We moved **forwards**.   The car is rolling **backwards**.   She stepped **sideways**.

We use *over*, *under*, *towards* and *past* to talk about movement in relation to something else.

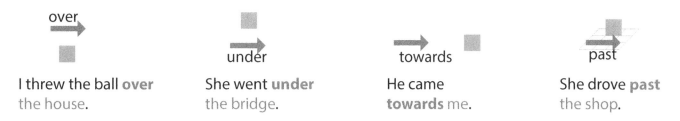

I threw the ball **over** the house.

She went **under** the bridge.

He came **towards** me.

She drove **past** the shop.

We use *where* to ask about **places**.

Where		Sub.	Verb	Place/Destination
Where	**do**	you	work?	
		I	work	at the bakery.
Where	**did**	you	go?	
		I	went	to the beach.

where

Practice

Make questions with *where*. Use the words in brackets. Circle the best word to compete the answer.

Example: A: <u>*Where do you live*</u>?
　　　　 B: I live (at)(in)(on) Toronto.

1. A: (my wallet) Where_____?
    B: It's (at)(behind)(over) **your bag.**
2. A: (Cheryl) Where_____?
    She's gone (backwards)(into)(with) **the supermarket.**
3. A: (Roger) Where_____?
    B: He eats lunch (at)(away)(between) **a park** (at)(away)(between) **the office and the train station.**
4. A: (tomorrow) Where_____?
    B: I'm studying (towards)(apart)(in) **the library.**
5. A: (yesterday) Where_____?
    B: I went on a tour (off)(through)(down) **Zurich.**
6. A: Where is the bathroom?
    B: Go (down)(near)(over) **the hall,** (back)(past)(under) **the bedrooms. It's** (at)(in)(on) **the end of the hall.**

adding a time

We use *when* to ask about **time**.

There are many words we can use to say when something happens.

We often simply refer to a time. (See page 6.)

When are you going?
I'm going **at** 4:00.

When are you going?
I'm going **in** September.

When are you going?
I'm going **on** Monday.

The words *ago*, *away* and *apart* are used with *be* to say the **distance** between fixed times.

ago
(in the past)

away
(in the future)

apart
(time between things)

Subject	Verb (*be*)	Time Distance	Direction
The party	was	a week	**ago**.
The show	is	just minutes	**away**.
Our birthdays	are	four days	**apart**.

I'm here for the party.

Party? That was a week **ago**!

We also use *ago* with other verbs. *Ago* says when something happened in the past in relation to now.

We went shopping two days **ago**.
I met her a week **ago**.

Before and *after* are used to show the **order** things happen.

before

after

Before and *after* can be used to say when by adding a **distance**...

Subject	Verb	Time Distance	Direction
I	left	two hours	**before** them.
We	stayed	a long time	**after** the meeting.

...or just say the **order** things happen.

I left before them. I left before they left.
We stayed after the meeting.

We also use *before* when we use *have* and the -en form referring to **before this time**.

A: Have you eaten at this restaurant **before**? B: No, I haven't been here **before**.

Some words express a relationship between points in time (for example: start/finish/now).

For is used to specify a length of time (a duration).

I was waiting **for** an hour.
(the duration:
from start to finish)

I've been waiting **for** an hour.
(the duration:
from start to now)

Since says when something started and *until/till* says when something finishes.

I've been waiting **since** 9:00.
(when I started: 9:00)

I'm working **until** 6PM. or: I'm working **till** 6PM.
(when I finish: 6PM)

We also use *since* to **emphasize** how much time has passed since an event, and *until/till* to **emphasize** how much time there is until an event. We add a **distance**. These sentences use *be*.

It's three years **since** I graduated.
≈ I graduated three years ago.

It's ten days **until** my birthday. or: It's ten days **till** my birthday.
≈ My birthday is ten days away.

We use *in* to say something finishes at a point in time after now. We use *by* to say something finishes before another point in time.

It'll be there **in** an hour.
(point in time from now)

I'll be home **by** 7PM.
I'll get home before 7PM; I'll be there at 7PM.

Ago is used to refer to the past and *in* is used to refer to the future in similar situations.

We use *ago* to express **distance** from the present-future.

I saw him three days **ago**.

We use *in* to express a **point** of time in the present-future.

I see him **in three days**.

Practice

Choose the best words to complete the sentences.

1. I'm at home. I'll be here (by) (until) 3PM.
2. She's moving to the city in January. I'm moving two months (ago) (before).
3. I'm still at work, but I'll be home (after) (until) 7 o'clock.
4. I played baseball (two days ago) (in two days).
5. I've played baseball (since) (until) I was three.
6. He played professional football (since) (until) he was 35.

We use *when* to ask about **times**.

when		Subject	Verb	Object/Description	Time
When	**do**	the Smiths	eat?		
		They	eat		in the afternoon.
When	**does**	Robert	have	breakfast?	
		He	has	breakfast	at 8AM.
When	**did**	Patricia	play	soccer?	
		She	played	soccer	on Friday.
When	**are**	you		free?	
		I	'm	free	on Friday.
When	**are**	you	working		this week?
		I	'm working		on Friday.

when

We don't need to say the words in gray. They have already been said so we can leave them out.

We use *how long* to ask about **periods of time**.

how long		Subject	Verb	Object/Description	Time
How long	**have**	the Smiths	lived	here?	
		They	've lived	here	for three years.
How long	**has**	Robert	been waiting?		
		He	's been waiting		since 10AM.
How long	**are**	you	working		today?
		I	'm working		till 5:30.

Practice

Make questions with *when* or *how long*. Use the words in brackets. Circle the best word to compete the answer.

Example: A: <u>When are you playing baseball   </u>?

      B: I'm playing baseball (at)(in)(on) Sunday.

1. A: (the meeting) _____?
    B: It's (at)(in)(on) **11:00.**
2. A: (the bus)_____?
    it leaves (at)(in)(on) **10 minutes.**
3. A: _____?
    B: I've played tennis (ago)(by)(since) **I was five.**
4. A: (Roger)_____?
    B: He eats lunch (after)(ago)(away) **12:30.**
5. A: _____?
    B: The best weather is (at)(in)(on) **August.**
6. A:_____?
    B: I went to Zurich **two weeks** (ago)(by)(since).

25

Who, what, why and how
indirect objects and prepositional phrases

adding a recipient

Some verbs suggest that a person **gets** or **receives** the object. This person is the recipient.
We add the recipient like this:

Subject	Verb	Recipient	Object	Place/Time	
We	gave	**Julie**	a present.		Julie got the present.
He	bought	**me**	lunch.		I got lunch.
I	teach	**kids**	English	on Mondays.	The kids get an English lesson.
They	sent	**us**	a letter.		We got a letter.

> These sentences also make sense if we leave the recipient out. Adding it adds more information.
> We are saying **who** or **what** gets it.

A person can be the recipient of their own action.

Subject	Verb	Recipient	Object	Place/Time	
We	gave	**ourselves**	a present.		We got the present.
He	bought	**himself**	lunch.		He got lunch.
I	teach	**myself**	English	on Mondays.	I get an English lesson.
They	sent	**themselves**	a letter.		They got a letter.

to: adding a destination

from A to B

When someone or something moves we add a destination with *to*. The destination can be a place, person, thing or event.

I went **to school**. (place)   I went **to the desk**. (thing)
I went **to the doctor**. (person)   I went **to a meeting**. (event)

The **object** moves to the destination.

Subject	Verb	Object	Destination	
I	took	my son	**to the doctor.**	My son moved (I did too).
I	sent	a letter	**to the office.**	The letter moved.

When there is no object the **subject** moves to the destination.

Subject	Verb	Object	Destination	
I	walked		**to the shops.**	I moved.

We can add *to* to show the object **moves** from the subject to the destination.

Subject	Verb	Object	Destination	Place/Time	
We	gave	a present	**to Julie.**		The present moved from us to Julie.
He	passed	the ball	**to me.**		The ball moved from him to me.
I	teach	English	**to kids**	on Mondays.	Knowledge moves from me to the kids.
They	sent	a package	**to us.**		The package moved from them to us.

These sentences make sense if we leave the *to destination* part out. Adding it adds more information. We are saying **where** it goes. We talk about something moving from A to B.

In some situations one way is more natural and makes more sense.

We use *to* and a destination to talk about **movement**.

We use a recipient to talk about someone **getting** something.

I need to open the door.

Sorry, I gave the keys **to Laura**.

Where the keys went.

She gave **me** a kiss.

What **I got**.

Often, both ways fit the same situation. We talk about **movement** or someone **getting** something.

He gave a present **to her** on her birthday.

The present went from him **to her**.

He gave **her** a present on her birthday.

He gave it. **She got** it.

Practice

Complete the sentences with the words in brackets and *to* when required.
There may be more than one answer. Leave one space blank.

Example: (her grandmother) She sent <u>*her grandmother*</u> a letter _____.
     or   (her grandmother) She sent _____ a letter <u>*to her grandmother*</u>.

1. (me) The boss gave _____ a raise _____.
2. (Africa) He sent _____ the package _____.
3. (the catcher) She threw _____ the ball _____.
4. (the committee) She announced _____ her decision _____.
5. (him) The meal cost _____ $100 _____.
6. (Wendy) A: Where is your skateboard? B: I sold _____ it _____.

When someone or something moves we add a source with *from*. The source can be a place, person, thing or event.

I come **from Australia**. (place)   Peaches come **from a tree**. (thing)
I got a prescription **from the doctor**. (person)   I have the notes **from the meeting**. (event)

When we expect the destination or source to be a **place** we ask with *where*.

where		Subject	Verb	Object	Destination/Source
Where	did	you	walk		to?
		I	walked		to **the shops**.
Where	did	you	get	the table?*	
		I	got	it	from a friend.

* If we don't know, we often assume it is from a place (probably a shop). If we expect it to be from a person, we ask: 'Who did you get the table from?'

When we expect the destination or source to be a **person** we ask with *who*.

who		Subject	Verb	Object	Destination/Source
Who	did	you	get	the present	**from**?
		I	got	it	from **Julie**.
Who	did	he	pass	the ball	**to**?
		He	passed	it	to **me**.

When we expect the destination or source to be a **thing**, we ask with *what*.

what		Subject	Verb	Object	Destination/Source
What	did	she	connect	the hose	**to**?
		She	connected	it	to **the tap**.

Practice

Complete the questions with *where*, *who* or *what* and *to* or *from* where needed. Leave some spaces blank.

Example: A: ___Who___ did you give the keys ___to___?
         B: I gave them to **Laura**.

1. A: _____ did you go on your vacation _____?
    B: We went to **Florida**.
2. A: _____ did she pass the ball _____?
    B: She passed it to **Sophia**.
3. A: _____ are you _____?
    B: I'm from **Ireland**.
4. A: _____ address should I send it _____?
    B: Send it to **14 Main Rd, Franklin**.
5. A: _____ do you go on Mondays _____?
    B: I go to **school**.

for: making connections

We use *for* to explain things by making connections.

We use *for* to explain **how long** things happen, showing the **length** of time connecting when something starts and finishes. (See page 199.)

I lived in England **for** four years.

start   finish

We also use *for* to connect an **action** with a **reason** why we do the action.

action   reason

Subject	Verb	Object/Description	Reason
We	**have**	food	**for dinner**
She	**bought**	a card	**for her mother.**
He	**got**	some socks	**for his birthday.**
I	**ran**		**for my life.**

why

Sometimes a *recipient*, *to* or *for* can be used in the same situation. The meaning is slightly different.

I sang **you** a song. Recipient: you. You got my gift of music.
I sang a song **to you**. Destination: The song went from me to you.
I sang a song **for you**. Reason: I sang it because I thought you'd like it.

Sometimes they have very different meanings.

I'll send **you** it. Recipient: you. **You** will receive it.
I'll send it **to you**. Destination: you. **You** will receive it.
I'll send it **for you**. Reason: you. You want it sent. I'll send it. **Someone else** will receive it.

Practice

Complete the sentences with the words in brackets. Use *for* or *to* when needed.
There may be more than one answer. Leave one space blank.

Example: (him) I booked _____ the flights *for him* .

1. (us) They cooked _____ dinner _____.
2. (you) I wrote _____ a song _____.
3. (me) This is really heavy, could you take _____ my bag _____, please?
4. (the car) Could you take _____ my bag _____, please?
5. (me) They opened _____ the door _____.
6. (her) I gave _____ a hug _____.
7. (my friends) I send _____ messages _____ on their birthdays.

Another reason for using *to* or *for*:

With longer expressions we use *to* and *for* to make it easier for the listener to follow.

They gave bonuses **to** staff who had been working there for more than 10 years.
The listener takes the important information into account while they receive more information.
They gave staff who had been working there for more than 10 years bonuses.
This is harder to follow.

We form questions about a recipient with *to* and *for*. This makes things clearer for the listener.

A: I gave her a hug.
B: Who did you give a hug **to**?
A: Arianna.

A: I bought him lunch.
B: Who did you buy lunch **for**?
A: Jack.

Practice

Complete the sentences with the words in brackets. Use *for* or *to* when needed. There may be more than one answer. Leave one space blank.

Example: (the athletes who completed the race) They presented _____ awards
to the athletes who completed the race .

1. (the guests who attended our wedding) We gave _____ the cake _____.
2. (him) I ordered _____ a coffee _____.
3. (the people at the party) We ordered _____ a pizza _____.
4. (My brothers, sisters, aunts and uncles) I cooked _____ dinner _____.
5. (only my closest friends) I tell _____ my secrets _____.
6. (you) I'm baking _____ a cake _____.
7. (you) I've left _____ some pizza _____ in the fridge.
8. (them) That awesome shot won _____ the game _____.

Other ways to add a reason

We can also add a reason with *to* and a **verb** to describe the next thing to happen in sequence. (See page 82.)

I bought some water **to drink**.

Or with *because* and another **subject**, **verb** and **object** stating why.

I bought some water **because I was thirsty**.

We can say the reason first. We use *so* to refer what has previously been understood. The listener has understood the reason because the speaker has just said it.

I was thirsty so I bought some water.

We use *why* to ask for a **reason**.

We can answer using *for* to connect an action with a reason.

Why		Subject	Verb	Object	Reason
Why	did	she	buy	a card?	
		She	bought	it	**for her mother.**
Why	did	he	get	some socks?	
		He	got	them	**for his birthday.**

We can also say why with *to* and a verb, *because* or *so*.

Why did you buy that chocolate?
I bought it **for** my girlfriend. (*for* + person/thing)
I bought it **to** give to my girlfriend. (*to* + verb)
I bought it **because** my girlfriend likes it. (*because* + statement)
My girlfriend likes it **so** I bought it. (statement + *so*)

We can also ask with *who* or *what*.

Who/What		Subject	Verb	Object	Reason
Who	did	she	buy	a card	**for?**
		She	bought	it	for **her mother.**
What	did	he	get	some socks	**for?***
		He	got	them	for **his birthday.**

* *What...for* can be used instead of *why* when speaking casually.

Practice

Complete the questions with *why, who...for* or *what..for*. Complete the answers with *for, to, so* or *because*. There may be more than one answer.

1. A: _____ are you going running?
   B: I go running _____ I like staying fit.
2. A: _____ are you preparing _____?
   B: I'm preparing _____ the festival.
3. A: _____ does Anthony work overtime?
   B: He works overtime _____ get more money.
4. A: _____ didn't you go out yesterday?
   B: It rained a lot _____ we didn't go out.
5. A: _____ have you opened a savings account?
   B: I've opened a savings account _____ save money _____ college.

by: adding a method

We use *by* for what is between two points. We use *by* to say **how** things happen.

We use *by* to say how we locate something. (See page 195.)

We live **by** the mountains.
The mountains can be used to locate our house.
How do you find our house? Find the mountains.

We use *by* to show what we used to reach our destination. We are talking about the middle part between the origin and destination. We are saying **how** we reach our destination.

We went **by** car.

We went **by** road.

We use *by* to show how we complete a task. We are talking about the middle part between taking on the task and completing the task. We are saying **how** we achieve our goal.

I paid **by** credit card.
We say what thing was used.

I sold more ice cream **by** lowering the price.
We use a verb in the -ing form to describe the action taken.

Subject	Verb	Object/Destination	Method	
I	**contact**	him	**by phone.**	Method of **contact**: phone
She	**traveled**	to New Orleans	**by plane.**	Method of **travel**: plane
He	**saved**	money	**by going out less.**	Method of **saving**: going out less
I	**held**	her	**by the hand.**	Method: **holding** her hand

We do NOT use *a*, *the* or *plurals* with **methods**. We speak about the method generally.

We also use *by* to show **who** completed a task. We are saying how it happened, **someone** did something. (See page 91.)

It was painted **by** a famous artist.

with: adding a part

We use *with* to say something is a **part** of something or something additional.

I went shopping **with** my sister.
We went shopping. (We = me + my sister)
She was part of the experience.

I opened the bottle **with** a bottle opener.
The combination (me + bottle opener)
opened the bottle.

Subject	Verb	Object	Part	What does it?
We	eat	noodles	**with a fork.**	We + fork.
She	bought	a dress	**with her birthday money.**	She + birthday money.
He	plays	golf	**with his friends.**	He + his friends.

With and *by* provide different information. Sometimes they can both be used in the same situation. When we use *with*, we say which one or ones (using *a/an*, *the*, *my* or *plurals* etc.)

By tells us the **method**.
We say how the **action** is completed.

  I **made** it **by hand**.
  Focus on the **method**.
  Method: **hand**

With tells us additional **parts** of a noun.
(usually the **subject** or **object**)

  I made it **with my own two hands**.
  Me + my hands made it.
  Important part: **my hands**

We use *without* to make it clear something is **not part** of the subject.

  My sister wasn't feeling well so I went **without** her.

Practice
Complete the sentences with *by*, *with* or *without*.

1. He goes to work _____ train.
2. They played soccer _____ Shirley last week.
3. I paid _____ credit card.
4. I paid _____ a credit card.
5. I grabbed him _____ his arm.
6. Sally is busy. I'm going swimming _____ her.
7. She played _____ her hair.
8. She plays the guitar _____ ear.
9. She plays the guitar _____ a pick.
10. He's fixing the chair _____ glue.
11. I picked up the mouse _____ my fingers.
12. I picked up the mouse _____ its tail.

209

We use *how* to ask for a **description** of something.

How was it? *I want you to describe it.*

We ask for descriptions of **methods**. We can answer using *by* describing the method used to complete the task.

How did you get there? *(get - asking about how the goal (arrival) was achieved)*
We went there **by car.** *(go - describing moving along the path to the destination)*

We can say how something happens with *with*. We describe what is used. This thing is an important **part** of how it happens.

The door was locked. How did you open it?
I opened it **with the key.**

We can also describe how things happen by stating the **action** we take to complete the task.

How did you get here so quickly?
I ran.

how		Subject	Verb	Object etc.	Process/Part
How	**does**	Andrew	get	home?	
	He	goes	home	by bus.
How	**did**	Michelle	cut	the paper?	
	She	cut	the paper	with scissors.

We often use *who* and *what* to ask about people and things.

who/what		Subject	Verb	Object etc.	Process/Part
Who	**did**	you	go		with?
	I	went		with my cousin.
What	**did**	she	cut	the paper	with?
	She	cut	the paper	with scissors.

Practice

Complete the sentences with *how, who* or *what*.

1. A: _____ does Melissa pay for her groceries?
   B: She pays by credit card.
2. A: _____ did you cut the bread with?
   B: I couldn't find the bread knife so I used my pocket knife.
3. A: _____ was it written by?
   B: Shakespeare.
4. A: _____ are you getting home tonight?
   B: Mum is picking me up.
5. A: _____ did you have dinner with?
   B: Natalie.

26

Describing nouns
modifiers

of

We add *of* to say what something is made of, contains or is part of.

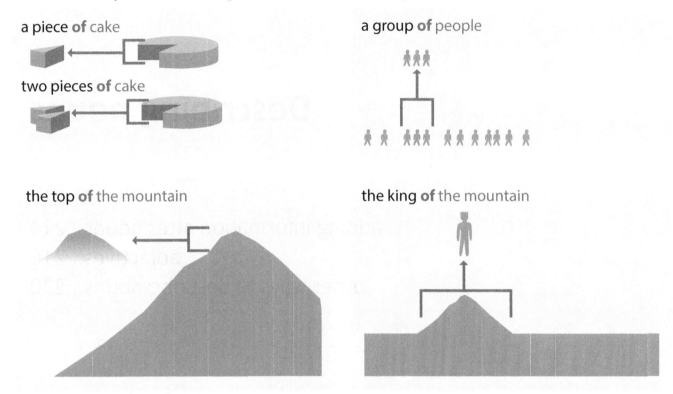

a piece **of** cake

two pieces **of** cake

a group **of** people

the top **of** the mountain

the king **of** the mountain

We also add *of* to describe the proportion or size of something.

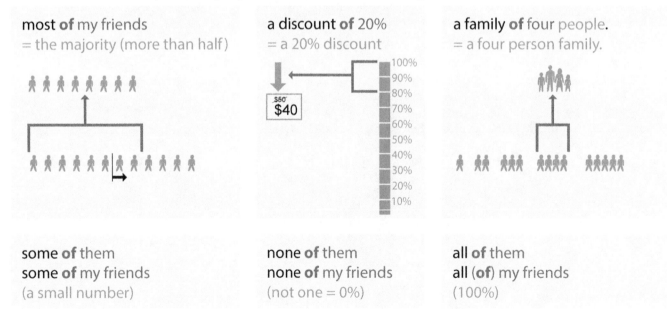

most of my friends
= the majority (more than half)

some of them
some of my friends
(a small number)

a discount of 20%
= a 20% discount

none of them
none of my friends
(not one = 0%)

a family of four people.
= a four person family.

all of them
all (of) my friends
(100%)

We can use *all* with or without *of*.
We use *all* with *of*. We think about each person or thing in the group. (100% = every part)
We use *all* without *of*. We think of the group as a whole. (100% = the whole group)

We use *of* to add information to nouns.
(subjects, objects, destinations, reasons, quantities, processes, times and places)

Subject	Verb	Object	Place/Time/Reason etc.
A group of people	meet		here on Wednesdays to discuss language.
I	ate	**two pieces of cake.**	
They	climbed		to t**he top of the mountain.**
He	bought	a gift	for **the king of the mountain.**
The team	won		by **a margin of 10 points.**
The news	spread		by **word of mouth.**
We	went	camping	with **a family of four.**
She	woke		in **the middle of the night.**
I	waited		on **the corner of 52nd and Broadway.**

Of and *'s* can often be used in the same situation.

The <u>name</u> **of** the driver is Sam.
The emphasis is on <u>name</u>. (what)

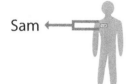

The <u>driver's</u> name is Sam.
The emphasis is on <u>driver's</u>. (whose)

We sometimes use *of*, we sometimes use *'s*.

Queen Elizabeth II is **the <u>Queen</u> of England.**
In most situations, what she is (the Queen) is more important than whose queen she is (England's). She is **<u>the</u>** one and only queen.

A <u>friend</u> of John's is coming to visit.
We use *a*. The person is **one** of **many** friends. It could be anyone.
The emphasis is on <u>friend</u>. (what)

John's friend is coming to visit.
This is more specific. We expect the listener to know who we are talking about.
The emphasis is on <u>John's</u>. (whose)

He's **John's brother**.
We talk about family connections. Whose brother is important.

Practice

Choose the best words to complete the sentences.

1. **Could I have** (a slice of cheese) (cheese's slice), **please?**
2. **Who is** (the President of the United States) (the United States' President)**?**
3. **Who is** (a sister of Maria's) (Maria's sister)**?**

adding information after nouns

We use words such as *in*, *on*, *at*, *to* and *with* to add information to nouns too.

The man on the left likes football.
(saying which man: where he is)

I'd like **a ham sandwich with** cheese.
(adding a part: ham sandwich + cheese)
≈ I'd like a ham and cheese sandwich.

Subject	Verb	Object/Description	Place/Time/Reason etc.
A friend from high school	works		there.
The box under my bed	is	full of old clothes.	
We	have	**lessons for children.**	
They	climbed		to **the hut on the mountain.**
I	sent	a gift	to **my cousin in Europe.**
We	went	camping	with **a family with two children.**

We can also add *to* and a destination or goal (a noun or a verb) to a noun.

The road to the lake is that way.
This is **the place to be**.

We often add information to more than one noun in the sentence.

I asked **the man in the shop** if they had **any books about gardening**.
The **man** is in the shop. I want **books** about gardening.

We can continue to add information to the same noun or another noun. We use our common sense to tell what the added information is referring to.

The boy near the window with black hair is my nephew.
The **boy** is near the window. The **boy** has black hair. The **boy** is my nephew.
The boy near the window with blue curtains is my nephew.
The **boy** is near the window. The **window** has blue curtains. The boy is my nephew.

Sometimes what the extra information is referring to is not clear.

Subject	Verb	Object	
		main noun	Part
I	saw	a man	with binoculars.

Subject	Verb	Object	Part
I	saw	a man	with binoculars.

I saw **a man** **with** binoculars.
I saw a man. The man had binoculars.

I saw a man **with** binoculars.
I used binoculars and saw a man.

Sometimes the only way to be sure is to ask the speaker to make it clear.
"Did you have the binoculars or did the man have the binoculars?"

In most situations common sense makes it obvious.

Anna took a photo of a monkey **with** my phone.
Anna had my phone.

Anna took a photo of a monkey **with** a long tail.
The monkey had a long tail.

Anna took a photo of a monkey **with** my phone.
The monkey had my phone. This is less likely.

Anna took a photo of a monkey **with** a long tail.
No. This is ridiculous.

Practice

Choose the best words to complete the sentences.

Example: The bag (near)(of)(with) the door is mine.

1. The president (for)(of)(with) the company has decided to retire.
2. I bought a cup (in)(from)(of) coffee (near)(of)(with) the change (in)(from)(of) lunch.
3. Some (in)(from)(of) my coworkers go home at 4:20.
4. The keys are (in)(from)(of) the bag (of)(to)(under) the table (near)(of)(with) the window.
5. The meat (in)(for)(of) dinner is (in)(for)(of) the fridge.

adjectives

Some words are only used to **describe** nouns. These words are called adjectives. We often put them before nouns. There are many things we use adjectives to describe.

Other is the most common adjective in the English language.

Other = not this one.
The: the listener knows which one.

There are only two bananas here. We are not talking about the one we first talked about.

Another = an + other.
An: We are talking about one of the other bananas.

There are more bananas here.

There are lots of things we can describe with adjectives.

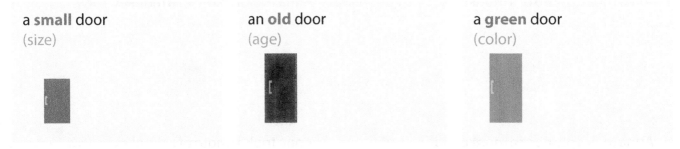

a **small** door
(size)

an **old** door
(age)

a **green** door
(color)

We describe any noun in the sentence: a noun in the subject, object, time, place, reason etc.

Subject	Verb	Object	Place/Time/Reason etc.
A small group	meets		here on Wednesdays to discuss language.
I	ate	**two big sandwiches.**	
They	climbed		to **the top of the high mountain**.
He	bought	a gift	for **his old friend**.
The team	trained		for **a long time**.
We	live		in **a beautiful village**.

We use adjectives to describe the subject of the sentence, often after *be*.

Subject	Verb	Description
He	is	**thirsty.**
They	look	**happy.**

216

Adjectives tell us how something is different from other things. Nouns tells us what something is.

This is a **big banana**.

big (adjective): how it is different from other bananas - not all bananas are this big.
banana (noun): what it is.

We sometimes use more than one adjective.
The adjectives we use first are the ones that give the most **obvious** or **important differences**.

This is a **big ripe banana**.

When you see it, the most obvious thing it is **big**. It is also **ripe**.

Adjectives that come later help describe **what** something is.

A **23-year-old Canadian woman** won the marathon.
They sat at the **small old wooden table**.
Can I have the **other little red and yellow ball**?

The order depends on what is important and needs emphasizing.

I have a **big important job** for you. We emphasize the fact that it is big.
I focus on the **important little details**. We emphasize the fact that they are important.

Practice

Complete the sentences using the adjectives in brackets. Which order do you think is best?

Example: He was wearing a __dirty__ __white__ __cotton__ shirt. (cotton, white, dirty)

1. I want to buy a _____ _____ _____ sofa. (large, leather, black)
2. They live in a/an _____ _____ house. (big, expensive)
3. Can I have _____ _____ slice of cake please? (thick, another)
4. They cooked us a _____ _____ _____ banquet. (7-course, delicious, Vietnamese)
5. She seems like a/an _____ _____ woman. (intelligent, young)
6. The group has just released a/an _____ _____ album. (new, amazing)
7. That little boy took the _____ _____ boy's toy car. (little, other)

We use *how* to ask for a **description** of something.

How was your driving test?
It was difficult, but I passed.

Adjectives are used to describe nouns. We also use *how* with an adjective to ask about scale. We ask where it lies between two points.

How big is an ant?
Not very. It's small.

How tall is a giraffe?
Very tall. About 6m tall.

How hot is it?
It's 26°C.

How long is the show?
It's 2 hours long.

how	Adjective		Subject	Verb	Object/Description
How	**old**	**is**	your grandmother?		
			She	's	88.
How	**long**	**is**	the Amazon River?		
			It	's	6437km long.
How	**tall**	**do**	you	have to be to ride	the roller coaster?
			You	have to be	at least 120cm tall.

how + adjective

We can describe nouns by talking about their **scale**.

Subject	Verb	Object		
			Description	Main noun
I	had	a	thirty minute	nap.
We	saw	three	seven meter	crocodiles.

(one nap, thirty minutes long)
(three crocodiles, seven meters long)

We count the main noun: **a nap** and **crocodiles**. We use *a/an* or add *s*.

We don't use *s* with general descriptions, even if we are talking about more than one minute or meter. Words that come before a main noun ending in *s* tell us who it belongs to.

I saw an American car. The **car** is American.
I saw an American's car. The **owner** of the car is American.

Adjectives are useful when saying **which one**. We say how it is different.

which	Object		Subject	Verb	Object etc.
Which	**cup**	**would**	you	like?	
			I	'd like	a red one, please.
Which	**bag**	**is**	yours?		
			Mine	is	the leather one.

which

We also use *how* to ask for a quantity.

How many bananas do you eat?
I eat 2 bananas every day.

none   a lot

We can count bananas.

How much is it?
It's $10.

none   a lot

When we say *how much* and don't say what we are referring to money.
To count money we need a currency, in this example: dollars.

how	*much/many*	Object		Subject	Verb	Object/Description etc.
How	**much**	**bread**	**do**	you	eat?	
				I	eat	a lot of bread.
				I	eat	six slices of bread a day.
				I	don't eat	bread.
How	**many**	**sisters**	**does**	Jeff	have?	
				He	has	a lot of sisters.
				He	has	five sisters.
				He	doesn't have	any sisters.
						None.

Practice

Complete the sentences with *how* or *which* (use the expressions: *how long, which one*, etc).

1. A: _____ do you have to be to vote?
    B: 18.
2. A: _____ centimeters are in a foot?
    B: About 30 I think.
3. A: _____ was the concert?
    B: It was great.
4. A: _____ are these shoes?
    B: They're $50.
5. A: _____ is Lake Baikal?
    B: It's 1642m deep.
6. A: _____ should I buy?
    B: That one.
7. A: _____ water does Dominick drink?
    B: Eight glasses a day.
8. A: _____ is a game of cricket?
    B: Five days.
9. A: _____ dollars can I get for £100?

other ways to describe nouns

We add other words before nouns to describe what, when, where, why or how something is used or what it is a part of. These words are often other nouns.

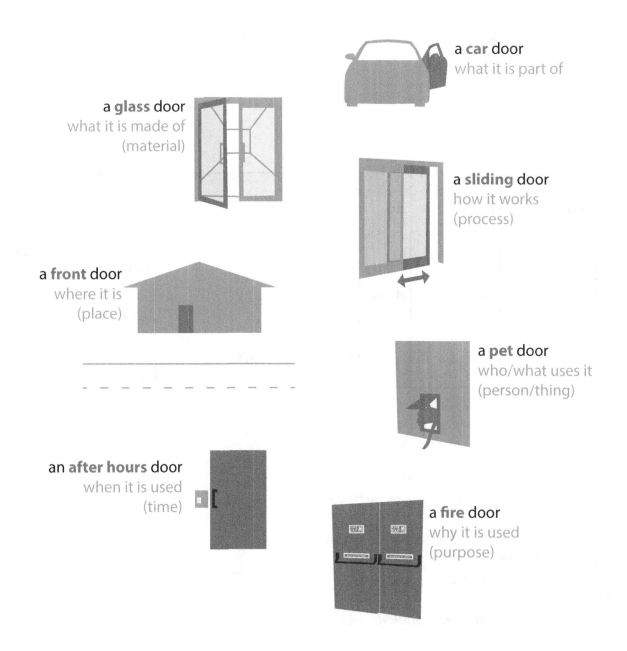

a car door
what it is part of

a glass door
what it is made of
(material)

a sliding door
how it works
(process)

a front door
where it is
(place)

a pet door
who/what uses it
(person/thing)

an after hours door
when it is used
(time)

a fire door
why it is used
(purpose)

We use our common sense to understand if we are talking about a part, material, process, etc. For example: a glass door is made of glass but a fire door is not made of fire.

There are some things that can be described several ways. It depends on what we are focusing on.

The car door is broken.
(what **kind** of door)
(simplest and most common)

The door of the car is broken.
(what the door is **part of**)

That car's door is broken.
(which car it belongs to)

Sometimes these expressions have very different meanings.

This is my mother's **picture**.

The picture **belongs** to my mother.
= This picture is my mother's.
(emphasizing **whose** picture it is)

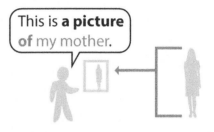

This is **a picture** of my mother.

The picture **contains** an image of my mother.
(emphasizing **what** the picture is of)

This is **a teacup**.
It is a cup. Its **purpose** is holding tea. It is empty.

This is **a cup** of tea.
It is a cup. It **contains** tea.

Nouns are sometimes used together so often that they become one word. (tea + cup = teacup)

Practice

Complete the sentences using the words in brackets with *of*, *'s* or by itself. There may be more than one answer. Leave one space blank.

Example: (the car) I left my bag in the _____ back seat *of the car*.

1. (Oliver) This looks like _____ bag _____.
2. (picture) They wrote a _____ book _____ for kids.
3. I'm thirsty. (water) Could I have a _____ glass _____, please?
4. (the pool) They swam to the _____ end _____.
5. (the company) She's _____ president _____.
6. (photo) Would you like to see my _____ album _____?

Note: the order of adjectives

The order of adjectives depends on culture and the way people think. There isn't one correct order to use.

The expressions *big beautiful (something)* and *beautiful big (something)* are both commonly used. It depends on which one we want to emphasize.

Culture and thinking changes over time. Many modern day Americans think "bigger is better", this is reflected in language used in the United States. Americans tend to say *big beautiful*.

Source: American English corpus - Google Books Ngram

In the UK, both expressions are common, but recent trends show that *beautiful big* is used more often.

Source: British English corpus - Google Books Ngram

The general pattern that is often taught is:
opinion - size - age - shape - color - origin - material - purpose. (or something similar)
This is generally true. We generally think that the things to the left are important characteristics. However, adjectives don't always follow this pattern. It is up to you and what you think is important.

Tip: If you are not sure about which wording seems more natural Google Books Ngram Viewer is a great way to check. It shows how frequently phrases have occurred in books over time. books.google.com/ngrams/

27

Adverbs

front, mid and end position

saying where, when and how

We can say *where*, *when* and *how* with just **one word**, an **adverb** (for example: *home*, *tomorrow*, *automatically*). We use **adverbs** in the same way we use expressions with *at*, *in*, *on*, *to*, *for*, *with*, *by* etc.

wh-		Subject	Verb	Place/Time/Description
Where	did	you	go?	
		I	went	**overseas.**
		I	went	to Africa.
When	is	the game?		
		It	is	**tomorrow.**
		It	is	on Wednesday.
How	does	the door	open?	
		It	opens	**automatically.**
		It	opens	by itself.

These **adverbs** describe **where** things happen. They have **general** meanings.

Subject	Verb	Object	Where
He	went		**home.**
There	is	a shop	**nearby.**
She	took	her bag	**upstairs.**
I	'll see	you	**around.**
The plane	flew		**up.**

We also use *at*, *in*, *on*, *to*, *for*, *with*, *by* etc. in these situations for **specific** information.

He traveled **to** Africa.
There's a shop **on** this street.
She took her bag **to** her room.
I'll see you **in** class.
The plane flew **into** the sky.

These **adverbs** describe **when** things happen.

Subject	Verb	Object/Place	When
He	plays	tennis	**sometimes.**
They	exercise		**regularly.**
She	went	to work	**early.**
I	'll see	you	**again.**

He plays tennis **on** Mondays.
They exercise **at** 5PM.
She went to work **at** 6AM.
I'll see you **in** July.

These **adverbs** describe **how** things happen.

Subject	Verb	Object/Place	How
She	plays	tennis	**well.**
He	solved	the problem	**simply.**
We	went	to the park	**together.**
The bus	stopped		**suddenly.**

adding information to verbs

We use **adjectives** to add information to **nouns**.

Subject	Verb	Object
She	drives	a **normal** car.
He	spoke	with a **soft** voice.
The **lucky** man	won	the lottery.

We use **adverbs** to add information to things that are not nouns. We add information to **verbs**.

Subject	Adverb + Verb	Object
She	**normally** drives	a car.
He	**softly** spoke.	
He	**luckily** found	the ticket.

There is often more than one way to think about things. The pairs of sentences below have the same basic meaning, so either one can be used in the same situation. Some adverbs can be used **before** the verb, or for added information at the **end** of the sentence.

The bus **suddenly** stopped. (**what** happened: *suddenly* describes *stop*)
The bus stopped **suddenly**. (**how**: *suddenly* describes **how** the bus stopped)
I **sometimes** play tennis. (**what** happens: I sometimes play)
I play tennis **sometimes**. (**when** I play: from time to time)

Adverbs that give an **opinion** go at the end. We are not simply saying what happens, we are saying **how** we think it happens.

She plays tennis **well**. (**how** she plays: what I think)
He sang the song **perfectly**. (**how** he sang: what I think)
That'll do **nicely**. (**how** it will do: what I think)

We put the adverb before verbs to say how **factual** something is or how **likely** it is to be **true**.

He **definitely** did it. (**what** happened: this is factual information based on evidence)
I'll **probably** go shopping tomorrow. (**what** is likely based on my plans)
It's **certainly** a good idea. (**what** it is: there is no question about it - it's a fact)
I **almost** lost my phone. (**what** was close to happening. In fact, it didn't happen)
I **just** finished in time. (**what** was close to not happening. In fact, it did happen)

Practice
Complete the sentences. Leave one space blank. There may be more than one answer.

Example: (suddenly) The bus _suddenly_ stopped _____ .
          or (suddenly) The bus _____ stopped _suddenly_ .

1. (here) We _____ sleep _____.
2. (quickly) He _____ picked up his bag _____.
3. (yesterday) I _____ went running _____.
4. (late) They _____ worked _____.
5. (poorly) The team _____ played _____.
6. (nearly) We've _____ finished the page _____.
7. (definitely) I can _____ help you _____.

225

linking and emphasis

We move added information about time to the start of the sentence to emphasize it. We are thinking about **when** we do particular things.

We're going to the zoo **tomorrow**. When is added at the end.
Tomorrow we're going to the zoo. There is more emphasis on **when**.
We're going to the museum **on Monday**. When is added at the end.
On Monday we're going to the museum. There is more emphasis on **when**.

We start sentences with adverbs to help put the sentence in perspective for the listener. We sometimes connect the sentence to what the listener knows or what was previously said.

Adverb	Subject	Verb	Object	Time
Personally,	I	like	watching tennis.	
However,	I	've never played	tennis.	
Maybe	I	'll try	it	tomorrow.

We often use a comma (,) or a pause when speaking to separate the adverb from the rest of the sentence. We often use the adverb to give perspective, pause, then continue.

We can also use *personally* before the verb because we are saying what I do.

I **personally** like tennis. (what I like)

We move *when* or *how* information to the start of the sentence for emphasis.

Suddenly, the bus stopped. (emphasis on **how**)
The bus stopped **suddenly**. (how the bus stopped)
The bus **suddenly** stopped. (what happened)
Sometimes I play tennis. (emphasis on **when**)
I play tennis **sometimes**. (when I play: from time to time)
I **sometimes** play tennis. (what happens: I sometimes play)

Practice

Choose a position for the words in brackets. Leave the other spaces blank.
Which do you think is best? There may be more than one answer.

1. (yesterday morning) _____ I _____ was _____ half asleep _____ . The doorbell rang.
2. (slowly) _____ I _____ crawled out of bed _____ and went to the door. It was the postman.
3. (suddenly) While I was talking to him, _____ the door _____ blew closed _____ behind me.
4. (unfortunately) _____ I was _____ locked out of the house _____, in my pajamas.
5. (luckily) I went around the back and _____ a window was _____ left open _____ .

> The sentences above are also good without adverbs. Adverbs used in this way provide additional information. Use them only when you feel they are needed.

start, middle or end?

We put adverbs in different parts of sentences for different reasons.

Now I like it. Saying when. At the start to emphasize that I didn't like it before. (most common)
I like it **now**. Saying when. (also very common)
I **now** like it. Information (that this is current) is added to the verb. (more formal)

The place the adverb is in the sentence often depends on the meaning of the verb. The same adverb is often added in different places depending on how the speaker is thinking.

He'll do it **soon**. Saying **when** he will do it.
He'll **soon** forget it. Saying **what** he will **do** (the adverb gives more information about the verb - soon forget, never forget etc.).

NOTE: 'He'll soon do it' and 'He'll forget it soon' are both possible but not as common.

Sometimes the position of an adverb can change the meaning.

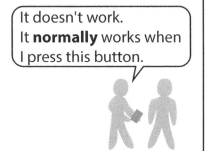

(**what** normally/usually happens)   (**how**: in a normal way - as expected)
Working like that is normal.   It **works** now.
But, it **doesn't work** now.

We can also say:

Normally, it works when I press this button.
(normally = when everything is normal)

Practice

Complete the sentences. Leave one space blank.

1. (naturally) She didn't have a c-section, _____ she gave birth _____.
2. (naturally) She was at the end of the pregnancy, so _____ she gave birth _____.
3. (clearly) Please speak up. We _____ can't hear you _____ at the back.
4. (clearly) Tap him on his shoulder to get his attention. He _____ can't hear you _____.
5. (normally) We didn't know they were famous so we _____ treated them _____.
6. (normally) People _____ treat them special _____.
7. (simply) We _____ told them _____ what we needed and they gave it to us.
8. (simply) What a great solution, how did you _____ do it so _____?

saying how often

When we say how often something happens we usually put the adverb **before** the verb.

Subject	Adverb + Verb	Object
I	**always** do	the dishes.
I	**usually** do	the dishes.
I	**often** do	the dishes.
I	**sometimes** do	the dishes.
I	**rarely** do	the dishes.
I	**never** do	the dishes.

Adds information to the verb: **do** the dishes.

We also use *usually*, *often* and *sometimes* to say **when** something happens. These adverbs are used for added information at the **end** of the sentence.
We use *sometime* to talk about something that will or may happen in the future.

Subject	Verb	Object	When
I	do	the dishes	**usually**.
I	do	the dishes	**often**.
I	do	the dishes	**sometimes**.
I	'll do	the dishes	**sometime**.

Saying when: many times or at one time.

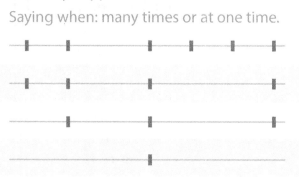

We put *usually*, *often*, *sometimes* and *sometime* **first** for emphasis.

When	Subject	Verb	Object
Usually	I	do	the dishes.
Often	I	do	the dishes.
Sometimes	I	do	the dishes.
Sometime	I	'll do	the dishes.

Saying when: many times or at one time.

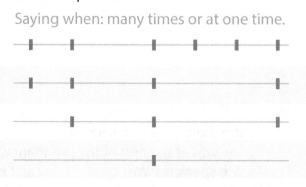

Putting *sometimes* **first** is very common, but we often use it in the middle or end of a sentence too. The meaning is essentially the same. They are just different ways of thinking and constructing sentences. It is very common to use *one day* or *someday* instead of *sometime*.

We usually use *always* before the verb.

Subject	Adverb + Verb	Object
I	will **always** love	you.

It is also possible to use *always* to say **when** (meaning forever), but only for things that are permanent.

Subject	Verb	Object	When
I	will love	you	**always**.

Love is considered permanent and we add *always* to make the sentence stronger.

I will **always** love you. (**what** will happen)
I will love you **always**. (**when** = always/forever)

Emphasizing *always* at the start of the sentence is not common. We use *always* in the middle or at the end of the sentence to emphasize *love*.

We also use *always* with the -ing form.

Life is good. I'm **always** going out and meeting with friends.
It seems like this is what I am doing at any given time.

We sometimes don't think it's right that it always happens.

He's **always** going out and meeting with friends. He should focus on his studies!
It seems like this is what he is doing at any given time—and I've had enough of it.

Never says something **doesn't happen**. It doesn't say when, so we don't put *never* at the start or end of the sentence.

He **never** goes out. ≈ He **doesn't** go out. (*never* is stronger, *doesn't* is softer)

Practice

Complete the sentences. Leave two spaces blank. There may be more than one answer.

A: What do you do on the weekend?
1. B: Lots of things. (usually) _____ I _____ go to the park _____.
2. (often) _____ I _____ go to a local restaurant _____.
3. (always) _____ They/they _____ have good food _____.
4. (never) _____ I _____ have to pay for it _____.
5. (always) _____ My/my girlfriend _____ pays _____.
6. (sometimes) _____ We/we _____ get ice cream for dessert _____.

negative sentences

When we make negative sentences, we put *not* before or after the adverb in different situations.

We use *always* when things happen every time. We use *don't always* when things do **not** happen **every time**.

I **don't always** do the dishes.
Not every time: there are times when I do and times when I don't.

We use *sometimes* when things happen more than once. We use *sometimes don't* when there is **more than one time** something does **not** happen.

≈   I **sometimes don't** do the dishes.
There are times when it doesn't happen.

We use *often* and *usually* in either way. We say *don't often* or *often don't*.

Often is used when things happen many times.

We use *don't often* when things do **not** happen **many times** (but they sometimes happen).

We **don't often** have parties.
It doesn't happen much, but there are times when it does happen.

We use *often don't* when there are **many times** things do **not** happen.

I **often don't** have enough time to go to the supermarket after work.
I want to, but it is often not possible.

Usually is also used when things happen many times. These things happen almost every time.

We use *don't usually* when things do **not** happen **many times**. They rarely happen.

I **don't usually** eat at restaurants.
It generally doesn't happen, but there are times when it does happen.

We use *usually don't* when there are **many times** things do **not** happen. (almost every time)

I **usually don't** go to that restaurant because it's expensive.
I have a choice. I usually choose not to.

There are situations when *don't usually* and *usually don't* both fit. You can say it either way.

I **don't usually** like seafood, but that was delicious!
I only like it sometimes, very rarely.

≈   I **usually don't** like seafood, but that was delicious!
There are many times I don't like it.

Practice

Complete the sentences. Leave one space blank. Which word order do you think is best?

1. I work really long hours. (usually) I _____ don't _____ get home in time for dinner.
2. (often) I _____ don't _____ get home until 11PM.
3. (often) We _____ don't _____ have visitors, but my cousin is staying with us this week.
4. (sometimes) We are really busy with her so I _____ don't _____ have time to check my email before work.
5. (always) We _____ don't _____ have our meals together, but we're having dinner together on Friday.
6. (usually) I _____ don't _____ go out on Fridays but it's a special occasion.

Some adverbs (such as *probably*, *certainly* and *definitely*) are useful when talking about options and possibilities (with *will/would*, *can/could* and *should*).

In positive sentences, we usually put the adverb after the first verb. We use *probably* when we decide that out of many options or possibilities, this one is likely.

I'll probably get a dog.

- a: (a) I get a cat.
- b: (b) I get a dog.
- c: (c) I don't get anything.

I'm thinking about my options. (There may be other options too.)

We put the adverb (*probably*) before the first verb (*will* or *won't*). We put <u>stress</u> on the <u>first verb</u> and emphasize what is likely to **happen** or **not happen**.

I probably <u>will</u> get a dog.

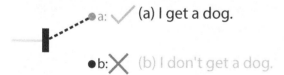

- a: (a) I get a dog.
- b: (b) I don't get a dog.

I probably <u>won't</u> get a dog.

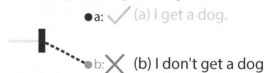

- a: (a) I get a dog.
- b: (b) I don't get a dog.

When there is no word to stress, we add and stress *do*. We focus on what does or doesn't happen.

She **probably <u>does</u>** like him.

She **probably <u>doesn't</u>** like him.

We use *do* before the adverb to emphasize every time, many times or more than one time.

He <u>does</u> **always** do the dishes.
I <u>do</u> **usually** like seafood.
We <u>do</u> **often** have parties.
Amazing things <u>do</u> **sometimes** happen.

We use *do* after the adverb to emphasize what happens.

He **always** <u>does</u> do the dishes.
I **usually** <u>do</u> like seafood.
We **often** <u>do</u> have parties.
Amazing things **sometimes** <u>do</u> happen.

more than one verb

When we use more than one verb, the first verb tells us if a sentence is positive or negative (with not). We often put adverbs after the first verb and before the other verbs.

| Subject | Verb | | | Time |
	First Verb	Adverb	Other Verbs	
She	is	**definitely**	working	now.
She	will	**probably**	be working	now.
She	has	**apparently**	been working	all day.
She	will	**actually**	have been working	all day.

We put adverbs before the first verb to focus on the positive or negative.

| Subject | Verb | | | Place/Time |
	Adverb	First Verb	Other Verbs	
She	**definitely**	was	working	there last month.
She	**probably**	would	be working	somewhere else now.
She	**apparently**	hasn't	been working	all week.
She	**actually**	won't	have been working	all day.

Adverbs are used before different verbs for different reasons. It depends on what we are focusing on when we are thinking and speaking. The difference in meaning in the sentences below is subtle.

She **actually** won't have been working all day. Focus on **not** working all day.
She won't **actually** have been working all day. Focus on what she**'s been doing**.
She won't have **actually** been working all day. Focus on what she **was doing**.

We focus on different verbs depending on how we are thinking at the time. The difference in meaning in the sentences below is subtle. The top sentence is more common.

The population has been **slowly** increasing over the last 10 years. Focus on the speed of **change**.
The population has **slowly** been increasing over the last 10 years. (no focus)

Practice

Complete the sentences. Leave one space blank. There may be more than one answer.

A: Do you think you'll come to the barbecue on Sunday?
1. B: (probably) I've been thinking about it, but I _____ won't _____ go.
2. A: Just come. (definitely) You _____ 'll/will _____ enjoy it.
3. B: (honestly) Sorry, I _____ can't _____ make it this time.
   A: That's ok. How have you been anyway?
4. B: Good. (quickly) I _____ 've/have _____ been _____ going through all my notes to revise for the exam tomorrow. It is pretty difficult.
5. (probably) I _____ should _____ have _____ started earlier.

one verb: be

Be is often used by itself. It carries little meaning on its own and joins the subject to a description, time or place etc. We often put adverbs after *be* the same as if it was the first verb when there is more than one verb.

Subject	Verb			Description/Time/Place
	be	Adverb	Other Verbs	etc.
It	is	**definitely**		finished.
The meeting	was	**actually**		at 10:15.
The meeting	wasn't	**actually**		at 10:15.
They	are	**usually**		on holiday.
They	aren't	**usually**		on holiday.
I	am	**never**		home.

We put adverbs before *be* to focus on the positive or negative.

Subject	Verb			Description/Time/Place
	Adverb	*be*	Other Verbs	etc.
That	**definitely**	is		him.
That	**definitely**	isn't		him.
The meeting	**actually**	was		at 10:15.
The meeting	**actually**	wasn't		at 10:15.
They	**usually**	are		on holiday.
They	**usually**	aren't		on holiday.
I	**never**	am		home.

We add emphasis by stressing *be*. (This is the same as with do. See page 231)

That **definitely** <u>is</u> him.   That <u>is</u> **definitely** him.

Practice

Complete the sentences. Leave one space blank. There may be more than one answer.

1. A: (always) Steve _____ 's/is _____ late.
    B: He might be stuck in traffic.
2. C: (probably) He _____ 's/is _____ stuck in traffic.
3. (often) The traffic _____ 's/is _____ really bad around here.
4. D: (definitely) He messaged me earlier. He _____ 'll/will _____ be _____ here soon.
5. Steve: Hi everyone! Nice to hear you all talking about me. (actually) I _____ was _____ stuck in traffic. There was an accident.
6. (usually) By the way, I _____ 'm/am _____ on time.

233

adverbs and adjectives

Many adjectives can be turned into adverbs by adding *-ly*.

normal → *normally*   certain → *certainly*   happy → *happily*
soft → *softly*   usual → *usually*   sad → *sadly*
lucky → *luckily*   natural → *naturally*   perfect → *perfectly*
regular → *regularly*   simple → *simply*   beautiful → *beautifully*

Subject	Verb	Object/Place
She	drives	a **slow** car.
Bright stars	shine	in the night sky.
He	wears	**cheap** clothes.

Subject	Verb	Object	How
She	drives		**slowly**.
The stars	are shining		**brightly**.
He	got	his clothes	**cheaply**.

We also use the **adjective** form at the end of sentences. We describe the main noun of the sentence at the time it happens. We are describing a thing rather than the way of doing something.

Subject	Verb	Object	Description
She	drives		**slow**.
The stars	are shining		**bright**.
He	got	his clothes	**cheap**.

When she drives, she is slow.
The stars are shining now, they are bright.
When he got his clothes, they were cheap.

The meaning is essentially the same in the examples above. Sometimes these forms are used in different situations and mean different things.

We arrived **late**. When we arrived, we **were** late.
Have you seen any good movies **lately**? Lately tells us **when.** lately ≈ recently.
Please keep the path **clear**. I want the path to **be** clear.
Please speak **clearly**. This is **how** I want you to speak.

Some adjectives don't have an *-ly* adverb form. We use the adjective form at the end of sentences.

She drives **fast**. When she drives, she is fast.

Practice

Complete the sentences. Choose the best form. There may be more than one answer.

1. It went really (fast)(fastly).
2. Please play (safe) (safely).
3. Come (quick) (quickly)! Help!
4. We (hard) (hardly) ever work.
5. We're working (hard) (hardly).
6. We've (near) (nearly) finished.
7. We'll stay home and take it (easy) (easily).
8. I passed the test (easy) (easily).
9. Seafood should be eaten (fresh) (freshly).
10. Add some (fresh) (freshly) ground pepper.

a lot / any more

We use *a lot of* (before a noun) to describe a large amount.

Subject	Verb	Object
I	drink	**a lot** of coffee.

We use *a lot of* when we talk about one time.

I drank **a lot** of coffee at breakfast yesterday.
(one time: a large amount)

We use *a lot of* to talk about a large number.

I like **a lot of** sports.
(a large number: I like many sports)

We use *a lot* to add information about when: it happens often.

Subject	Verb	Object	When
I	drink	coffee	**a lot**.

When we say we do something *a lot*, we are saying that we do it many times.

I drank coffee **a lot** last year.
(many times)

With things that are considered permanent, we add *a lot* to make the sentence stronger.

I like sports **a lot**.
(how much: to what degree)

Any more and *anymore* are often used in questions and negative sentences.

We use *any more* (before a noun) to say we have reached the limit: the maximum amount.

Subject	Verb	Object
I	can't eat	**any more** cake.

Would you like **any more** cake?
I'm full. I can't eat **any more** cake.

We use *anymore* to add information about when: from that time on.

Subject	Verb	Object	When
I	can't eat	cake	**anymore**.

The doctor said I can't eat cake **anymore**.

Practice

Complete the sentences. Leave one space blank. There may be more than one answer.

1. (any more/ anymore) I've been vacuuming all morning. Please try to keep the house clean. I don't want to do _____ vacuuming _____.
2. (a lot of/a lot) What do you think about candidate A? I like _____ his policies _____, but I don't agree with all of them.
3. (a lot of/a lot) How about candidate B? I like _____ her _____. I'll definitely vote for her.
4. (any more/ anymore) I'm so tired. I can't keep my eyes _____ open _____.
5. (any more/ anymore) The door is fully open. It can't be _____ open _____.
6. (a lot of/a lot) We love hiking. We go to _____ the mountains _____—every month.
7. (a lot of/a lot) We love hiking. We go to _____ the mountains _____—different ones.

28

Stronger descriptions
intensifiers and mitigators

very/really

We use *very* to make basic descriptions stronger.

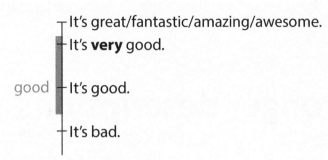

We use *really* to give words more emphasis.

We emphasize **descriptions** and make them stronger.

That dog is **really** big. = That dog is **very** big.
Really or *very* can be used in this situation.
Really comes from *real*. What we are describing is real, not imaginary.

We also use *really* to give **verbs** and **strong descriptions** more emphasis.

I **really** enjoyed it.	It's **really** great.	It's **really** very simple.
Enjoyed is a **verb**.	*Great* is a **strong description**.	*Very simple* is a **strong description** because it uses *very*.

We use *really* to make different parts of the sentence stronger.

You are **really beautiful**. Comparing: more beautiful than other beautiful people.
You **really are** beautiful. Saying the truth: Your beauty **is** real. I'm not making it up.
You **really are really beautiful**. We can even use *really* twice. However, once is usually enough.

not very/not really

Very or *really* often have a similar meaning in positive sentences, but in negative sentences, *very* and *really* have different meanings.

When we say something is *not good*, we are saying it is *bad*.

We use *not very* to make softer negative descriptions. Something that is *not very good* is *ok* or *bad*.

We use *not really* when something is **not true**.

The dog **isn't really** big.
I lied. I'm just small.

We also use *not really* to say no in a **softer** way.

A: Do you like olives?
B: No, **I don't**.
This can be a little strong.

A: Do you like olives?
B: No, **not really**.
This is softer.

We say *really don't* to emphasize the fact that we **don't** do something.

A: Here have some olives.
B: No, thank you. I **really don't** like them.
This is very strong. We are emphasizing **don't**.

Practice

Complete the sentences with *really* or *very*. There may be more than one answer. When can we use either one?

1. The movie was _____ fantastic.
2. It's _____ hot today.
3. I don't _____ like dogs.
4. We _____ had a great time.
5. Yesterday morning was cold, but it wasn't _____ cold this morning.
6. He drives _____ slowly.

fairly/pretty/quite/rather

We also add *fairly*, *pretty*, *quite* or *rather*. When we use these words **intonation** is very important. They don't have strong meanings so we use <u>word stress</u> to make descriptions stronger or weaker.

When we <u>stress</u> a word the vowel sound (a,e,i,o,u) becomes clearer, longer and has a higher pitch. We de-stress other words by making the vowel sound less clear, shorter and lower pitch.

It's pretty <u>good</u>.   It's quite <u>good</u>.   *Good* is <u>stressed</u> for more goodness.

good

It's <u>pretty</u> good.   It's <u>quite</u> good.   *Good* is de-stressed for less goodness.

good

- It's great/fantastic/amazing/awesome.
- It's very good. It's really good.
- It's **fairly** <u>good</u>. It's **pretty** <u>good</u>. It's **quite** <u>good</u>. It's **rather** <u>good</u>.
- It's good.
- It's **<u>fairly</u>** good. It's **<u>pretty</u>** good. It's **<u>quite</u>** good. It's **<u>rather</u>** good.
- It's bad.

Which one should I use?

It doesn't matter if you use *fairly*, *pretty*, *quite* or *rather*. It is personal preference. *Pretty* is considered more informal.

It's not what you say, but **how** you say it.

Why do we use these words?

These words are also used in other situations.

Something that is *fair* is **reasonable**, or ok.

What do you think about her decision?
I think it's **fair**.
(reasonable, balanced, even, ok)

It's **fairly** good. It is actually **good!** I didn't expect it to be good, but to be fair, it is good.
It's **fairly** good. It isn't very good, but it is ok. It is fair to say it is good.

Something that is *pretty* stands out from other things.
Pretty is very shallow in meaning, we are only talking about what is **obvious**.

He thinks the woman in the middle is **pretty**.
She stands out because of her looks.

It's **pretty** good. It is **good** and stands out more than other good things.
It's **pretty** good. The **obvious part** is good, I'm not sure about the rest.

We use *quite* to refer to the **whole** thing.

How was the party?
It was **quite** good.
(as a whole: good people, music, food etc.)

It's **quite** good. It is **good** as a whole.
It's **quite** good. Some aspects are less than good, but when you consider it as a **whole** it is good.

We also use *quite* with nouns.

That's **quite** an achievement. Considering all parts, it is a great achievement.

Rather is used to **compare** something to another thing. We talk about what we like more.

I'd **rather** not go. ('d = would)
I think not going is a better option than going.

It's **rather** good. It is **good**, compared to other similar things.
It's **rather** good. **Compared to some things**, it's good, but not really what I'd call good.

241

such/so

We use *such* to say something is a perfect example of what we are talking about.

That is such a big dog.
It is what we understand *a big dog* to be. This dog fits the definition of *big dog* perfectly.

We use *so* to connect something with what has previously been understood.
We use *so* before descriptions.

That dog is so big.
It is what we understand *big* to be, for a dog. This dog fits the definition of *big* perfectly.

(It is **big**, not small.)

Using *so* or *such* is stronger than using *very* or *really*.

good ⎰ It's great/fantastic/amazing/awesome.
       It's **so** good. It's **such** a good sandwich.
       It's very good. It's really good.
       It's good.
       It's bad.

There are many ways we describe things.

Subject	Verb	Object/Description
It	's	**so hot.**
It	's	**such a hot day.**
It	's	**very hot.**
It	's	**a very hot day.**
It	's	**really hot.**
It	's	**a really hot day.**

We use <u>word stress</u> to make descriptions stronger.

Practice

Make these sentences stronger using *so* or *such*.

Example: We had ___*such*___ a great time.

1. You're lucky to have _____ good friends.
2. He is _____ generous.
3. I've been waiting _____ long.
4. My grandfather is _____ old.
5. She is _____ a comedian.
6. Have you ever heard _____ an amazing singer?
7. We have _____ much to talk about.

enough/too

We use *enough* to say we have reached a good level. We use *too* to say something is excessive.

I've had **enough** to eat.

I've reached my limit.
I don't want to eat any more.

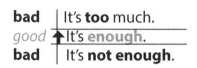

That's
not enough.

That's
enough.

That's
too much.

Too is so strong that it is **negative**.

We played our best but the other team was **too** good.

It was bad for us - we couldn't win.

I wanted to buy some new shoes but they were **too** expensive.

The price was so high it was bad. I couldn't buy the shoes.

bad ↑ It's **too** good.
   - It's great/fantastic/awesome.
   - It's so good.
good - It's very good/really good.
   - It's good.
bad ┼ It's bad.

We use *not enough* when something is below a certain level.

We didn't play well **enough**.

If we had played above a certain level we would have won.

I wanted to buy some new shoes but I didn't have **enough** money.

It was bad for me. If I had more money I would have bought them.

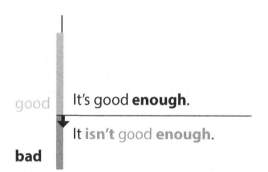

good   It's good **enough**.

        It **isn't** good **enough**.

bad

Practice

Circle the correct answers.

Example: Do you have a really big box? This box (is too big) (is big enough) (isn't big enough).

1. I have to be back at work at 2:00, so we have (too much) (enough) time for lunch.
2. I wanted to buy some coffee, but the line was (too long) (long enough) so I went home.
3. He can't stand up. He's had (too much)(enough) to drink.
4. It's 40°C. It's (too hot)(not hot enough) to go out.
5. My bag is really heavy, I brought (too much) (enough) stuff.
6. We (brought too much) (brought enough) (didn't bring enough) food. We're all still very hungry.

not that/not so/not such/not too

That refers to something which is not at the same place and time as the speaker. We use *that* to refer to what we thought in the past.

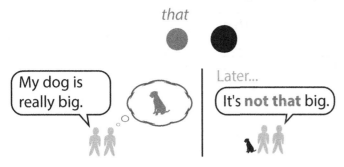

We use *so* to connect something with what has previously been understood. *Not so big* and *not that big* are similar expressions that can be used in the same situation. We say something isn't as big as we thought it would be.

I thought it would be bigger
It's not **so** big. = It's not **that** big.

We use *such* in the same way as *so*, but say what the thing is.

Too has a negative meaning. When we use *not* with *too* it becomes **positive**.

A: How was your lunch?
B: **Not too** bad. = It was ok/good.

A: Would you like some more?
B: Yes, ok. **Not too** much though. = Just a good amount.

29

Comparing
comparatives and superlatives

-er than

We add -er to adjectives to compare things to other things.

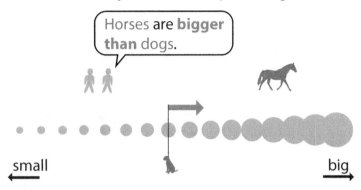

Horses are **bigger than** dogs.

small ← → big

Subject	Verb	Description (comparing)		
		Description	*than*	Thing
It	's	cold**er**	than	ice.
She	looks	old**er**	than	you.
We	ran	fast**er**	than	usual.

We don't add -er to longer words, we put *more* first. These are words with two syllables or more. We also add *more* with adverbs ending in -ly.

Subject	Verb	Description (comparing)			
		Amount	Description	*than*	Thing
It	's	**more**	delicious	than	apple pie.
He	looks	**more**	handsome	than	I thought.
She	finished	**more**	quickly	than	before.*

*We also use the adjective form in this situation: She finished **quicker** than before. (See page 234.)

However, for adjectives ending in -y we change the *y* to *i* and add -er. (even if they have two or more syllables)

Subject	Verb	Description (comparing)		
		Description	*than*	Thing
These towels	are	dri**er**	than	those ones.
He	looks	happi**er**	than	a bodybuilder directing traffic.
English	is	easi**er**	than	I thought.

When we compare **good** things, we use *better*. When we compare **bad** things we use *worse*.

Subject	Verb	Description (comparing)			
		Description	*than*	Thing	
This month's sales	are	**worse**	than	last month's.	(bad)
It	's	**better**	than	we expected.	(good)

We can also describe the object of the sentence.

Subject	Verb	Object (comparing)			
		Description	Object	*than*	Thing
I	have	smaller	feet	than	my sister.
She	drives	fancier	cars	than	me.
He	cooks	better	curry	than	pasta.

We use different words when comparing amounts.
We leave out the words in gray when they are obvious in the situation.

Subject	Verb	Description (comparing)				
		Amount	Thing	*than*	Thing	
I	've got	**more**	rice	than	I wanted.	(much)
They	bought	**more**	apples	than	me.	(many)
We	're spending	**less**	money	than	we expected.	(little)
There	are	**fewer**	(sheep)	than	300 sheep on our farm.*	(few)

*We don't say *sheep* twice. We usually add it after the number.

We can leave out the *than...* part when we are comparing something to what usually happens or how it is now or was before.

I would be there **sooner** than I will actually be there if the traffic wasn't so bad.
It usually takes three days but we are very busy this week so it might take **longer** than usual.
Your little girl is getting **bigger** than she was before.
It costs **more** than it did before/than we thought.

We add *much*, *a lot* or *way* to make these comparisons stronger. Which word you use is personal preference. *A lot* and *way* are more casual.

It's **much** more expensive than I thought. It's **a lot** better than I thought. I'm **way** happier now.

Practice

Complete the sentences with the correct form of the words in brackets. Use *more* when needed.
Example: Russia is _colder_____ (cold) than Thailand.

1. She's _____ (tall) than me.
2. I have _____ (long) hair than her.
3. Watching grass grow is _____ (exciting) than the movie I just watched.
4. Baseball is _____ (popular) in America than Europe.
5. We are _____ (busy) this month than we were last month.
6. Is that the price? It's much _____ (expensive) than it was yesterday.
7. A: Can I have some more coffee, please?
   B: Ok.
   (person A pours a small amount)
   B: Have _____ than that if you like.
8. A: What do you think?
   B: That looks much _____ (good).

as... as...

We use *as* to say that something about two things is the same.

She is as tall as her brother.
She and her brother are the same height. They are equally tall.

We sometimes exaggerate a little.

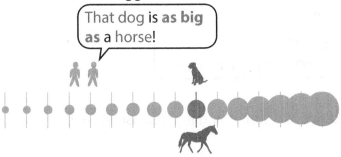

That dog is **as big as** a horse!

We compare measurable descriptions, including times and quantities.

Subject	Verb	Comparison (Description, Time, Amount etc.)					
		Amount	*as*	Description	*as*	Thing/Subject, Verb etc.	
It	's		**as**	cold	**as**	ice.	
I	came		**as**	soon	**as**	I could.	(time)
This soup	costs	half	**as**	much	**as**	it did before.	(quantity)

When we compare things we can add an **amount**.

This soup costs **half** as much as it did before. (before = $48, now = $24)
Your luggage is **twice** as heavy as mine. (your luggage = 40Kg, my luggage = 20Kg)

We use *as long as* to show that I will keep my promise for the length of time my conditions are met.

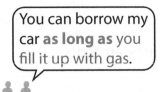

You can borrow my car **as long as** you fill it up with gas.

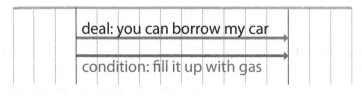

deal: you can borrow my car

condition: fill it up with gas

You can go out **as long as** you're back by 10:00.
I'll go **as long as** it doesn't rain.

As long as is often used in casual speech. We use *provided (that)* formal situations.

You may go out **provided** that you are back by 10:00.

We use words like *soon*, *fast*, *quick* and *long* for time.

Subject	Verb	Object etc.	Time				
				as	Description	*as*	Thing/Subject, Verb etc.
I	'll be	there		as	**soon**	as	possible.
	Stay		for	as	**long**	as	you like.

Much, *many*, *few* and *little* may add information to an object. They tell us the **quantity**.

Subject	Verb	Object					
			as	Description	Thing	*as*	Thing/Subject, Verb etc.
You	should eat		as	**much**	fruit	as	possible.
I	took		as	**little**	luggage	as	I could.
	Take		as	**many**	cookies	as	you like.

We don't need to say obvious things. These things are obvious because of the situation.

I took **as little** luggage **as** I could take.
Take **as many** cookies **as** you like.

We may add a **number** to give a **quantity** with *much*, *many*, *few* and *little*. We do this for **emphasis**.

There are **as few as** 300 Sumatran tigers left in the wild. (emphasis: this is a small number)
As much as 10Kg of chocolate was eaten at the party. (emphasis: this is a large amount)

As much can also be used to add a time. It tells us it happens **often**.

Subject	Verb	Object	Time				
				as	Description	*as*	Thing/Subject, Verb etc.
You	should eat	fruit		as	**much**	as	possible.
I	study	English		as	**often**	as	I can.

Practice

Complete the sentences with the expressions in the box on the right.

Example: A: Please come right away!
B: Ok. I'll be there __*as soon as*__ I can.

1. That's so expensive! It costs _____ it did yesterday!
2. A: Can I have some more coffee, please?
   B: Sure. Have _____ you like.
3. A: Can I stay here for another week?
   B: Sure. Stay _____ you like.
4. A: Can you turn on the air conditioner? It's _____ a sauna in here!
5. A: What does 'travel light' mean?
   B: It means you take _____ possible.
6. A: Mom, can I go to my friends house this afternoon?
   B: Ok, _____ you do your homework first.
7. A: How many tomatoes can I have?
   B: _____ you can carry.

> twice as much as
> as many as
> as little as
> as hot as
> as much as
> as soon as
> as long as
> as long as

249

the -est

We use *the -est* to compare things to **all** other things in a category.

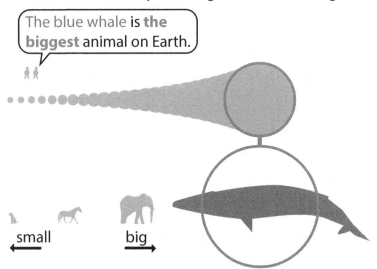

The blue whale is **the biggest** animal on Earth.

small ← big →

No animal on Earth is bigger than the blue whale.

Subject	Verb	Description (comparing to all others)	
		Description	Category
This morning	was	**the** cold**est**	morning this year.
My grandmother	is	**the** old**est**	person in our family.
We	ran	**the** fast**est**	on the day.

Subject	Verb	Description (comparing)	
		Description	Category
These towels	are	**the** dri**est**	on the washing line.
He	is	**the** happi**est**	person I know.
The C chord	is	**the** easi**est**	chord to play on the ukulele.

Subject	Verb	Description (comparing)		
		Amount	Description/Object	Category
We	ate	**the most**	delicious	ice cream in town.
I	ate	**the most**	ice cream	out of all the people I was with.
He	is	**the most**	handsome	guy I know.
She	is	**the most**	intelligent	student in the class.

Subject	Verb	Description (comparing to all others)		
		Description	Category	
This month's sales	are	**the worst**	we've ever had.	(bad, worse, worst)
It	's	**the best**	thing I've eaten.	(good, better, best)

not as... as...

We use *not as* to compare things to other things.

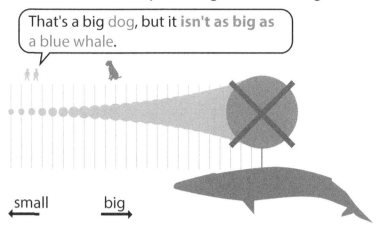

That's a big dog, but it **isn't as big as** a blue whale.

small ←   big →

A blue whale is bigger than the dog.

Subject	Verb	Comparison (Description, Time, Amount etc.)			
		as	Description	*as*	Thing/Subject, Verb etc.
It	is**n't**	**as**	cold	**as**	it was this morning.
The Internet	's **not**	**as**	fast	**as**	it should be.
This soup	does**n't** cost	**as**	much	**as**	it did before.

Subject	Verb	Comparison (Description, Time, Amount etc.)				
		as	Description	Thing	*as*	Thing/Subject, Verb etc.
I	did**n't** get	**as**	**many**	apples	**as**	I wanted.
He	does**n't** earn	**as**	**much**	money	**as**	me.

Practice

Complete the sentences with the correct form of the words in brackets. Use *most* when needed.

Example: A: I ate __*the most*__ ice cream.

       B: No you didn't. You did__*n't eat as much as*__ (not eat much) I did.

1. The Nile is _____ (long) river in the world.
2. The Amazon River is _____ (not long) the Nile, but it is _____ (large) river in the world, in terms of water flow.
3. My wife is _____ (amazing) woman I've ever met.
4. This is _____ (good) restaurant in the city.
5. It was_____ (not good) I thought it would be.
6. I scored _____ points. Daniel did_____ (not score many points) I did.
7. Horses are_____ (not fast) cheetahs. Cheetahs are _____ (fast) animals on land.

251

like

In previous sections we have used *like* as a verb.
When we like something, we are happy with that person or thing.

He likes his father.
Describing what he thinks:
He is happy having his father in his life.

He doesn't like his father.
Describing what he thinks:
He is happy not having his father in his life.

Subject	Verb	Object
He	**likes**	his father.
She	**doesn't like**	coffee.

We also use *like* in another way. When we compare things we often use *like* to say things are **similar**. *Not like* is often used to say things are **different**.

He's like his father.
Describing him:
He and his father are similar.

He isn't like his father.
Describing him:
He and his father are different.

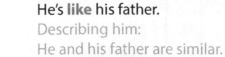

the same · **similar** · **different**

Subject	Verb	Object	*like*
He	's		like his father.
She	plays	the piano	like her mother.

We use *alike* when the things we are comparing are the subject.

Subject	Verb	Object	*alike*
He and his father	are		alike.

Sometimes things that seem unrelated at first are actually similar in some way.

"Minds are **like** parachutes, they only function when open." - Thomas Dewar

We use *be*(*am/are/is*) to describe something.

> She **is** a hard worker.
> He **is** a footballer.

We use *like* with verbs describing senses. We sense that these things are similar. The description might fit, but we are not 100% certain.

> She **seems like** a hard worker. I think she could be a hard worker, but I am not certain.
> It **feels like** it's going to rain. I don't know if it will rain, but I have the feeling.
> He **looks like** a footballer. He could be a footballer based on how he looks, but I'm not certain.
> It **sounds like** a good movie. I think it could be a good movie based on what people are saying. I'm not certain, I haven't seen it.

We can use any verbs describing senses in this way including *seem*, *look*, *sound*, *feel*, *taste* and *smell*.

We use *feel like* when we have a feeling that leads us to doing something.

Subject	Verb (*feel*)	*like*
He	**feels**	**like dancing.**
She	**feels**	**like** drinking **a cup of tea.**

> She **feels like** a cup of tea. We don't need to say 'drinking'. It is obvious that she'll drink it.
> I **feel like** a sandwich. We don't need to say 'eating'. It is obvious that I'll eat it.

Practice

Complete the sentences with the correct form of *like*, *look like*, *sound like* or *feel like*.

Example: A: Here is a photo of Peter's son.
　　　　 B: Yeah, He *looks like* his father.

1. A: Would you like to get a coffee?
   B: That _____ a good idea.
2. Those clouds are really dark. It _____ it'll rain.
3. A: What is your favorite food?
   B: I _____ noodles.
4. A: What would you like to eat?
   B: I _____ noodles.

like/as

Sometimes expressions with *like* or *as* can be used in the same situation.

We use *as* to say things are **the same**.

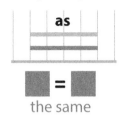
the same

We use *like* to say things are **similar**.

similar

Sam was late, **as** we expected. What we expected and what happened were the **same**.
Sam was late, **like** we expected. The events unfolded in a **similar** way to what we expected.

We use *such as* to give examples. We can also use *like*.

Water sports **such as** surfing, swimming and scuba diving, are popular in Australia.
The **same** sports listed are examples of popular water sports in Australia.
Water sports **like** surfing, swimming and scuba diving, are popular in Australia.
Sports **similar** to and including the sports listed are popular water sports in Australia.

We use *as... as...* to say things are the same in some way. We also use *like* to say things are similar. However, using *like* may have a different meaning.

That dog is **as big as** a horse. The dog and a horse are the **same** size (**both big**).
That dog is big **like** a horse. That dog and a horse are **similar**. They are **both big**.
She's **as tall as** her brother. They are the **same** height. (Example: she is 150cm, he is also 150cm. In this example, she and her brother are **not tall**. We compare them to each other).
She's tall **like** her brother. They are **similar**; they are **both tall**. (For example: She is 180cm - tall for a woman, her brother is 190cm - tall for a man. They are tall compared to most people.)

We use *as if* to say things are the same in some way in predictions and hypothetical situations. We also use *like* in these situations. We are speaking indirectly to express our opinion gently.

It looks **as if** it's going to rain. It looks the **same** as how it would look if it was going to rain.
It looks **like** it's going to rain. It looks **similar** to how it would look if it was going to rain.

Which should I use?
Expressions with *as* are more common in formal and written English.
Like is considered more informal and often used in spoken English.

Practice

Complete the sentences with *like* or an expression with *as*. There may be more than one answer.

1. It looks _____ you've had a great day.
2. We often eat seafood _____ shellfish, crab and shrimp.
3. It's a hot day today, _____ the weather report said.
4. Take as much time _____ you like.

30

Review of adding information

adjectives, adverbs, recipients and prepositional phrases

review of adding information

We add a recipient to say who gets something.

Subject	Verb	Recipient	Object

We add information about *where*, *when*, *why*, *how*, *who* and *what* to the end of the sentence.

Subject	Verb	Object	Added information

We use:
in, *on*, *at*, *above*, *next to*, etc. for places.
in, *on*, *at*, *before*, *after*, *ago* etc. for times.
to for a destination.
for to make a connection, often a reason.
by for a process (between start and goal).
with for an additional part.

We add similar information with **adverbs**, saying where, when and how.

We add information to the start of the sentence.

Added information	Subject	Verb	Object

We emphasize important information.

We add perspective for what follows.

We add adverbs before verbs for more information on **what** happens. We add **factual** information.

Adverb + Verb

We say how often something happens.

We say how factual something is.

We also add information to a noun. The noun may be in the subject, object or other added information.

Adjective + Noun

We add adjectives to describe the noun.

We add other words to describe the noun.

Noun	Added information

We can add information after a noun.

We also add information to a description.

Added information	Description

We use *very*, *really*, *so* and *too* to make the description stronger.

We use word stress with *fairly*, *pretty*, *rather* and *quite* to make descriptions stronger or weaker.

We use *not* with *very*, *really*, *so*, *that* and *too* to make the description weaker.

We use adjectives and adverbs to make comparisons.

$$\blacksquare \stackrel{?}{=} \blacksquare$$

We add *-er* or *more* when comparing two or more things.

We add *the -est* to compare something to all others.

We use *as...as* to say things are the same or not.

examples

I gave **them** a present.
I teach **her** English.

I bought **my wife** some flowers.
They cost **me** $20.

That shot won **them** the game.
We sent **the kids** a package.

We sat **in** the garden.
I'll see you **in** an hour.
I went **to** the supermarket.
We went **for** a drink.
We went **by** train.
We went **with** our friends.

We went **through** the forest.
I got there a few minutes **before** you.
I sent a letter **to** Tokyo.
We're having pasta **for** dinner.
It was painted **by** da Vinci.
Come now or I'll leave **without** you.

They live **near** a train station.
I've been reading **for** an hour.
I gave a present **to** my mother.
I picked some flowers **for** my mother.
Get more energy **by** exercising more.
I dug a hole **with** the shovel.

I went for a drink **yesterday**.
We went **home**.

The team played **well**.
The weather changed **suddenly**.

We go hiking **sometimes**.
She opened it **carefully**.

Yesterday I went for a drink.
On Monday I went to school.

Slowly she began to speak.
Suddenly the weather changed.

Sometimes we go hiking.
Someday I'll go there.

Apparently, this is the place.
Unfortunately, we may be late.

At first, we thought we were on time.
However, we may be late.

Maybe he will come.
Actually, he might not make it.

I **sometimes** walk to work.
We **always** enjoy life.

I **sometimes** don't have time.
I don't **always** have time.

We **often** go to the park after school.
I'm **usually** home.

It'll **probably** rain.
It'll **definitely** be good.

We **almost** ran out of gas.
I've **just** finished the report.

It **actually** happens.
It was **certainly** a great day.

I have a **black** bag.
I gave it to an **old** woman.

She's a **happy little** girl.
Can I have **another** drink?

It's a **beautiful** day.
Japanese food is delicious.

My black bag is my **school** bag.
The **ceiling** fan is broken.

Can I have a **plastic** cup, please?
Where's the **baby** bottle?

I want to get a new **laundry** sink.
Are you watching the **Brazil** game?

The man **with** brown hair is my uncle.
The shoes **by** the door are mine.

I got a free drink **with** my meal.
That book **on** the table is very good.

The house **opposite** ours is for sale.
Put it with the drinks **for** the party.

The show was **really** good.
It's **very** big.

I was **so** happy.
We were **too** late. The bus had left.

The new computer will be **very** fast.
We're having a **really** productive day.

The show was **pretty** good.
It's **quite** big.

I was **rather** pleased.
It's all **quite** exciting.

The new computer will be **pretty** fast.
We're having a **fairly** productive day.

The show **wasn't very** good.
It's **not that** big.

I'm **not too** happy about it.
It **wasn't so** hard after all.

The new computer **won't** be **that** fast.
She **doesn't really** like salad.

The show was **better** than we expected.
I'm **older** than my brothers.

We walked **faster** than last time.
It's **more humid** in the summer.

The show was **the best**.
I'm **the shortest** in my family.

We climbed **the highest** mountain in the world.
This is **the safest** car we have ever designed.

The show was **as good as** the other one.
I'm **not as tall as** my brother.

We climbed **as high as** the clouds.
This car isn't **as safe as** the old model.

257

quiz

Choose the best sentences.

1. (a) I bought it for you.
   (b) I bought it to you.
   (c) I bought it by you.

2. (a) I sent Russia the letter.
   (b) I sent the letter to Russia.
   (c) either (a) or (b)

3. (a) Alex gave me this bag.
   (b) Alex gave this bag to me.
   (c) either (a) or (b)

4. (a) Her story gave me courage.
   (b) Her story gave courage to me.
   (c) either (a) or (b)

5. (a) We went by car.
   (b) We went with car.
   (c) either (a) or (b)

6. Would you like a drink?
   (a) Could I have a juice glass please?
   (b) Could I have a glass of juice please?
   (c) either (a) or (b)

7. (a) It's an old story.
   (b) It's a story old.
   (c) either (a) or (b)

8. (a) Well it works.
   (b) It well works.
   (c) It works well.
   (d) any of the above

9. (a) Probably it'll rain.
   (b) It'll probably rain.
   (c) It'll rain probably.
   (d) any of the above

10. (a) Sometimes I go hiking.
    (b) I sometimes go hiking.
    (c) I go hiking sometimes.
    (d) any of the above

11. Which sentence is more natural?
    (a) We always don't work on Saturdays.
    (b) We don't always work on Saturdays.

12. Which sentence is more natural?
    (a) I sometimes don't get home until 8.
    (b) I don't sometimes get home until 8.

13. (a) I'm very hungry.
    (b) I'm really hungry.
    (c) either (a) or (b)

14. (a) I very like it.
    (b) I really like it.
    (c) either (a) or (b)

15. (a) I don't really like it.
    (b) I really don't like it.
    (c) both are good, (a) is stronger
    (d) both are good, (b) is stronger

16. Which sentence is more natural?
    (a) This one is more better than that one.
    (b) This one is more expensive than that one.

17. (a) It's fairly good.
    (b) It's pretty good.
    (c) It's quite good.
    (d) It's rather good.
    (e) any of the above

18. A B
    (a) A is bigger than B.
    (b) A is as big as B.
    (c) A isn't as big as B.

19. A B
    (a) A is bigger than B.
    (b) A is as big as B.
    (c) A isn't as big as B.

20. A B
    (a) A is bigger than B.
    (b) A is as big as B.
    (c) A isn't as big as B.

31

Talking about time
adverbial clauses

when

We add information with *when* to give details about the **point in time** we are referring to.
These details are based on the time of something else.

We use *when* to describe something that happens immediately after something else.
We talk about a time in the **past** or **future**.

I fixed the computer **when** I got to work.

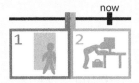

We use *fixed* (past form). It happened at a time in the past.

I'll fix the computer **when** I get to work.

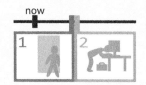

We use *will fix*. There are options in the future. This is when I choose to do it.

Subject	Verb	Object etc.	Time			
			when	Subject	Verb	Object/Place etc.
He	screamed		**when**	he	saw	the spider.
She	smiled		**when**	she	heard	the news.
I	'll call	you	**when**	I	find	the keys.
We	're going to leave		**when**	he	gets	here.

We also use *when* with general statements.
We add general information about the time we are referring to.

I fixed the computer **when** you were at work.

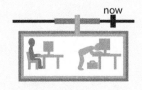

I'll fix the computer **when** you are at work.

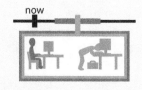

Subject	Verb	Object etc.	Time			
			when	Subject	Verb	Object/Place etc.
He	played	soccer	**when**	he	was	10.
She	swam	a lot	**when**	it	was	warm.
I	'll eat	sushi every day	**when**	I	live	in Japan .
We	're going to live	near the beach	**when**	we	're	retired.

We use *when* to say a longer action or event is **not finished** at the **point in time** something else happens. (See page 63.)

I was fixing the computer **when** you got to work.

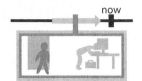

I'll be fixing the computer **when** you get to work.

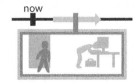

Subject	Verb	Object etc.	Time			
			when	Subject	Verb	Object/Place etc.
She	was talking	on the phone	**when**	I	saw	her.
He	was waiting	for a bus	**when**	he	heard	the news.
I	'll be waiting	at the station	**when**	you	arrive.	
We	're going to be traveling	around Africa	**when**	you	're	in France.

Practice

Make one sentence using *when*. We don't need to say the actual times.

Example: I'll be waiting at the station at 10:10. You arrive at 10:10.
<u>*I'll be waiting at the station when you arrive*</u>.

1. I lived in London in 2001. I was 23 in 2001.
    _____.

2. I went skiing a lot in February. I was on vacation in February.
    _____.

3. I'll go out for dinner every night next week. I'm in Spain next week.
    _____.

4. I can call you at 9:00. I arrive at 9:00.
    _____.

5. I was playing tennis from 11:00 to 12:00 yesterday. I saw Joe at 11:20 yesterday.
    _____.

6. I'll be working from 9:00 to 5:00 tomorrow. The game is on from 3:15 to 4:30.
    _____.

while

We use *while* for actions or events that happen between the **start** and **end** of something else.

I fixed the computer **while** you worked.

I'll fix the computer **while** you work.

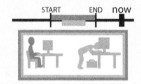

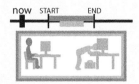

Subject	Verb	Object etc.	Time			
			while	Subject	Verb	Object/Place etc.
I	carried	her bag	**while**	she	talked	on the phone
He	listened	to music	**while**	he	waited	for the bus.
You	'll arrive		**while**	I	'm	at work.
You	're going to be	here	**while**	we	're	in Africa

We can use *be* and the -ing form in either part or both parts if we like.
We use the -ing form to emphasize actions happening.

I was fixing the computer **while** you were working.
I'll be fixing the computer **while** you're working.

I was fixing the computer **while** you worked.
I'll be fixing the computer **while** you work.

I fixed the computer **while** you were working.
I'll fix the computer **while** you're working.

In some situations, either *while* or *when* can be used. The meaning is essentially the same. This happens when we make it clear the action is not finished at the time by using *-ing*.

I saw her **while** she was talking on the phone. While: between the start and end of the activity.
I saw her **when** she was talking on the phone. When: I saw her. I say what she was doing at that point in time.

We sometimes leave out words when they aren't really needed.

Subject	Verb	Object etc.	Time			
			while	Subject	Verb	Object/Place etc.
He	heard	the news	**while**	he	was waiting	for the bus.

He heard the news while waiting for the bus.

While and *when* often give sentences different meanings.

I'll clean the table **while** you wash the dishes.
While: between the start and end - I'll clean the table, at the time you'll be washing the dishes.
I'll clean the table **when** you wash the dishes.
When: immediately after - I'm waiting for you to start washing the dishes, then I'll clean the table.

Practice

Make one sentence using *when* or *while*. You don't need to say the actual times.
There may be more than one answer.

Example: She talked on her phone. During that time I carried her bag.
I carried her bag while she talked on her phone .

1. I waited to see the doctor. During that time I read a magazine.

    _____.

2. We made a lot of friends last week. We were on holiday last week.

    _____.

3. I liked video games in 2001. I was a child in 2001.

    _____.

as

We use *as* when something happens **at the same time** something else happens.

I got to the bus stop **as** the bus was leaving.

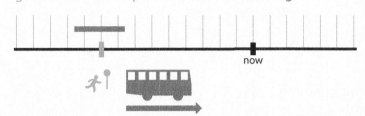

Subject	Verb	Object etc.	Time			
			as	Subject	Verb	Object/Place etc.
She	said	"hello"	**as**	she	entered	the room.
He	farted		**as**	he	stood up.	
People	get	wiser	**as**	they	get	older.
The cost	will go	up	**as**	sales	increase.	

The longer action comes after *as*.
We are specifying the time. The action happens at the time of the longer action or event.

As and *while* have different meanings.

Take each day **as** it comes.

The day comes, you take it **at that time**.

Get it **while** it's hot!

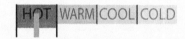

It will be hot for **a period of time**.
After that period it will be considered warm, cool, then cold.

Sometimes either *as* or *while* can fit the same situation.

We danced **as** the band played.

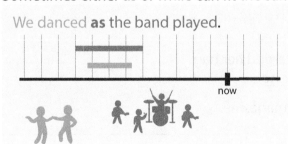

We danced and the band played **at the same time**.

We danced **while** the band played.

We danced for **a period of time**, between the start and end of the band's performance.

Practice

Make one sentence using *as*. These things happened at the same time.

Example: She entered the room. At that time she said "hello".
She said "hello" as she entered the room _____.

1. I left work at 5:37 yesterday. I saw Joe at 5:37 yesterday.
   _____.

2. Sea levels will rise. Islands will go underwater.
   _____.

3. Take the clothes off the washing line. Put them in the basket at that time.
   _____.

Compare when, *while* and *as*.

when	*while*	*as*
We add information about a **point** in time.	We add information about a **period** of time. (between the start and end)	We add information about something that happens at the **same** time.

Practice

Complete the sentences with *when, while* or *as*. There may be more than one answer.

Example: You'll arrive _while_ I'm at work.   *(or when)*

1. You arrive at 6:00. I leave at 6:00. I won't really see you because I'll leave ___ you arrive.
2. We're waiting for you in the parking lot. We'll give you more information _____ you get here.
3. I fell asleep _____ they were talking about politics.
4. Leo ran _____ he saw the dog.
5. We sat and looked out to sea _____ the sun went down.
6. Grace liked drawing _____ she was a child.
7. It's sunny now. Let's go out _____ the weather is good.

before, after, since and until

Before, *after*, *since*, *until/till* can be followed by a time or event.

I'll be there **before** 6:00.
I'll be there **before** the parade.

I've been waiting **since** 9:00.
I've been waiting **since** lunch.

START   NOW   FINISH

I'll leave **after** 11:00.
I'll leave **after** the meeting.

I work **until** 6PM. or: I work **till** 6PM.
I work **until** close. or: I work **till** close.

START   FINISH

We can also add the event using a subject and verb (and object etc.).

Subject	Verb	Object etc.	Time	Subject	Verb	Object/place etc.
She	took off	her shoes	**before**	she	entered	the room.
You	'll arrive		**after**	I	leave	for work.
I	've eaten	sushi every day	**since**	I	moved	to Japan.
We	're going to live	here	**until**	we	retire.	

32

A sentence in a sentence
relative clauses

explaining which one

We sometimes add a subject and verb (and object etc.) to add information to a noun. We do this if either the speaker or listener doesn't know the name of the person or thing we are talking about or we choose not to use the name. We connect it to what we know.

The shop (that) I bought my shoes at **is having a sale.**
(I bought my shoes at a shop. + That shop is having a sale.)

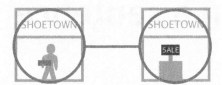

We use *the* because the listener knows which shop. The added information tells them.

It can be a group of people or things.

The people **that** got lost **will be late.**
(Some people got lost. + Those people will be late.)

We always use *that* when the main noun and the subject of the added information are the same.

The people **that** got lost **will be late.** If we don't use *that* and say 'The people got lost' we think the sentence ends there. It has a subject, verb and object. 'The people that got lost' is a subject, the listener expects a verb to follow.

Subject Main Noun	*that*	Subject	Verb	Object	Place/Time etc.	Verb	Object/Place/ Time etc.
The shop	(that)	I	bought	my shoes	at *	is having	a sale.
The people	**that**	*	got		lost	will be	late.

* If this subject, verb and object, etc. was a separate sentence the main noun would fit here.

🔴 *this*   We use *this* to talk about something in our current time and place.

⚫ ⬤ *that*   We use *that* to talk about something in another time or place. We use *that* to add needed information about a noun by adding a subject and verb.
It is usually obviously at a different time or place so *that* is often optional.

We can talk about **part** of a group of people or things.

Some people **that** like music **like singing.**
(Some people like music. + Some of these people like singing.)

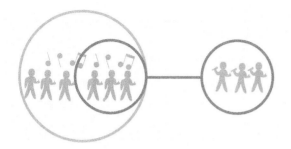

A woman (that) I work with **rides a motorcycle.**
(I work with some women. + One of these women rides a motorcycle.)

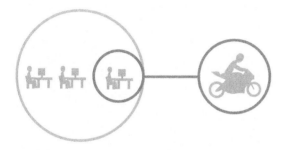

We use *a* because I work with more than one woman. I'm not specifically saying which one.

Subject						Verb	Object/Place/
Main Noun	*that*	Subject	Verb	Object	Place/Time etc.		Time etc.
Some people	**that**	*	like	music		like	singing.
A woman	(that)	I	work		with *	rides	a motorcycle.

We can add information to the subject or object of the sentence.

| Subject | | | | | | Verb | Object/Place/ |
Main Noun	*that*	Subject	Verb	Object	Place/Time etc.		Time etc.
The shop	(that)	I	bought	my shoes	at *	is having	a sale.
The friend	(that)	I	gave	the cake	to *	lives	in that house.
A woman	**that**	*	works		in our office	rides	a motorcycle.

| Subject | Verb | Object | | | | | | |
		Main Noun	*that*	Subject	Verb	Object	Place/Time etc.
1981	was	the year	(that)	I	was born		(in) *.
These	are	the shoes	(that)	I	bought	*	yesterday.
I	play	a sport	**that**	*	requires	skill.	

Practice

Make one sentence. There may be more than one answer.

Example: I bought my shoes at a shop. The shop is having a sale.
The shop *(that) I bought my shoes at is having a sale*   .

1. My friend plays the drums. He plays in a band.
    My friend _____.
2. This is the ring. I gave it to my wife.
    This is the ring _____.
3. I was in another country in June. I was in Russia.
    Russia is the country _____.
4. The team won yesterday. They played really well.
    The team _____.

when, where, which, who

We can also complete these sentences with *when*, *where*, *which* or *who*.

Subject						Verb	Object/Place/Time etc.
Main Noun	*wh-*	Subject	Verb	Object	Place/Time etc.		
The shop	**where**	I	bought	my shoes	*	is having	a sale.
The friend	**who**#	I	gave	the cake	to *	lives	in that house.
A woman	**who**	*	works		in our office	rides	a motorcycle.

#In formal English we use *whom* instead of *who* when we refer to someone other than the subject.

Subject	Verb	Object						
		Main Noun	*wh-*	Subject	Verb	Object	Place/Time etc.	
1981	was	the year	**when**	I	was born		*.	
These	are	the shoes	**which**	I	bought	*	yesterday.	
I	play	a sport	**which**	*	requires	skill.		

When and *where* are for times and places. A time or place includes words like *in*, *on* and *at*.
That refers to a thing. It doesn't include *at*, so *at* is often left by itself at the end of the sentence.

    The shop (that) I bought my shoes **at** * . (* = the shoe shop, a thing)
    The shop where I bought my shoes *. (*= at the shoe shop, a place)

This is the same as when we use these words in questions.

    What shop did you buy your shoes **at**? The shoe shop.
    Where did you buy your shoes? **At** the shoe shop.

Practice

Make one sentence without using the name. There may be more than one answer.

Example: Which shop is having a sale? The shoe shop. I bought my shoes at the shoe shop.
The shop *(that) I bought my shoes at*_____.
The shop *where I bought my shoes*_____.

1. Which park do you want to go to? Nelson Park. We went there last time.
   The park _____.
2. Which team won? Manchester United. Manchester United wears red.
   The team _____.
3. Which person got the job? Claire. Claire came to the interview on time.
   The one _____.

describing things in two ways

We can put a comma (,), or pause when speaking, and describe something again. The words between the commas provide more information. Our intonation changes when we say the words between the commas. We use a lower pitch to make it clear that this is added information.

We sometimes want to give more information about the subject.

Subject		Verb	Object/Place/Time etc.
1	2		
Shoetown,	a shop in the city,	is having	a sale.
A friend of mine,	Trevor,	lives	in that house.
Emily,	an office worker,	rides	a motorcycle.

A friend of mine, Trevor, lives in that house.

We sometimes want to give more information about the object.

Subject	Verb	Object/Place/Time etc.		
			1	2
I	was born	in	1981,	a good year.
This	is		Angela,	my aunt.
I	play		golf,	a sport.

This is Angela, my aunt.

We describe a noun with a subject and verb to give more information. (See page 268.)

Subject			Subject	Verb	Object/Place/Time etc.	Verb	Object/Place/Time etc.
1	2	*that*					
Shoetown,	the shop	(that)	I	bought	my shoes at *,	is having	a sale.
Trevor,	the friend	(that)	I	gave	the cake to *,	lives	in that house.
Emily,	a woman	that	*	works	in our office,	rides	a motorcycle.

The same thing can be said in two sentences.

Shoetown is having a sale. Shoetown is the shop (that) I bought my shoes at.
Trevor lives in that house. Trevor is the friend (that) I gave the cake to.
Emily rides a motorcycle. Emily is the woman that works in that office.

Subject	Verb	Object			Subject	Verb	Object/Place/Time etc.
		1	2	*that*			
These	are	my new shoes,	shoes	(that)	I	bought	* yesterday.
I	play	golf,	a sport	that	*	requires	skill.

These are my new shoes. These are the shoes (that) I bought yesterday.
I play golf. Golf is a sport that requires skill.

simplifying

The listener often knows what we are talking about because we have already said using another word. We often don't say the place, the person etc. (2) when it is obvious.

Subject			Subject	Verb	Object/Place/Time etc.	Verb	Object/Place/Time etc.
1	2	wh-					
Shoetown,	the place	where	I	bought	my shoes *,	is having	a sale.
Trevor,	the friend	who	I	gave	the cake to *,	lives	in that house.
Emily,	the woman	who	*	works	in our office,	rides	a motorcycle.

Subject	Verb	Object				Subject	Verb	Object/Place/Time etc.
		1	2	wh-				
These	are	my new shoes,	shoes	which	I		bought	* yesterday.
I	play	golf,	a sport	which	*		requires	skill.

Subject			Subject	Verb	Object/Place/Time etc.	Verb	Object/Place/Time etc.
1	2	that					
Shoetown,	the place	that	I	bought	my shoes at *,	is having	a sale.
Trevor,	the friend	that	I	gave	the cake to *,	lives	in that house.
Emily,	a woman	that	*	works	in our office,	rides	a motorcycle.

Subject	Verb	Object				Subject	Verb	Object/Place/Time etc.
		1	2	wh-				
These	are	my new shoes,	shoes	that	I		bought	* yesterday.
I	play	golf,	a sport	that	*		requires	skill.

We use *that* in these sentences to make it clear that this is extra information.

Practice

Make one sentence. The important sentence is in **bold**. The other sentence provides additional information.

Example: **Trevor lives in that house**. I gave the cake to Trevor.

_Trevor, (the person) who I gave the cake to, lives in that house_____.

_Trevor, (the person) that I gave the cake to, lives in that house_____.

Trevor lives in that house. **I gave the cake to Trevor.**

_I gave the cake to Trevor, (a person) who lives in that house_____.

1. **The cheetah is the fastest animal on land**. It can reach speeds of up to 120Km/h.

    _____.

2. Soda is high in sugar. **Soda is unhealthy.**

    _____.

3. **My brother lives in Sydney.** He is a dentist.

    _____.

4. I met Elizabeth this morning. **She likes skiing.**

    _____.

273

-ing and -en

Be is the most common verb in English. It often has an important role and tells us if we are talking about the present-future or not. When we add information with the -ing or -en form, *be* isn't needed, another verb provides the important information so we can leave *be* out.

Subject					Verb	Object/Place/Time etc.
Main Noun	*that*	Subject	Verb	Object/Place/Time etc.		
The people	that	*	are playing	football in the park	look	happy.
The employees	that	*	are chosen	for the new project	will be given	a raise.

The people playing football in the park look happy.
Some people are playing football in the park. They look happy.
The employees chosen for the new project will be given a raise.
Some employees will be chosen for a new project. They will be given a raise.

Subject	Verb	Object/Place/Time etc.				
		Main Noun	*that*	Subject	Verb	Object/Place/Time etc.
I	talked	to the man	that	*	was watering	the garden.
These	are	the players	that	*	are suspended	for 50 games.

I talked to the man watering the garden.
A man was watering the garden. I talked to him.
These are the players suspended for 50 games.
Some players are suspended for 50 games. These are the players.

Practice

Make one sentence. Make them as simple as possible.

Example: Some people are playing football in the park. They look happy.
The people playing football in the park look happy   .

1. A woman is playing the piano. She is very good.
    _____.

2. Someone will be elected president. This person will have a lot of responsibility.
    _____.

3. I gave them a letter. The letter was written by my boss.
    _____.

4. Some of my friends are living in the city. They really enjoy it.
    _____.

what

Expressions such as *the thing(s) that...* don't provide much information.
We can use one word (*what*) to provide the same information. (what = the thing that)
We use these sentences to change emphasis.

Subject				Verb	Object/Place/Time etc.
what	Subject	Verb	Object/Place/Time etc.		
What	you	need	*	is	a cold drink.
What	I	do	*	helps	people.

What you need is a cold drink. Emphasizing the thing you need. ≈ You need a cold drink.
What I do helps people. Emphasizing the thing I do. ≈ I help people.

We use *when*, *where*, *who*, *why* and *how* in the same way. (when = the time that, where = the place that, who = the person that, why = the reason that, how = the way that)

Subject	Verb	Object/time/place etc.			
		wh-	Subject	Verb	Object/Place/Time etc.
I	heard	what	he	said	*.
I	saw	what	*	made	the noise.
I	asked	when	she'll	arrive	*.
This	is	where	we	got	married *.
She	doesn't know	who	you	like	*.
She	knows	who	*	likes	you.
I	'd like to know	why	the bus	was	late *.
I	've forgotten	how	I	did	it *.

I heard what he said. I heard the thing that he said.
I saw what made the noise. I saw the thing that made the noise.
I asked when she'll arrive. I asked the time that she'll arrive.
This is where we got married. This is the place that we got married.
She doesn't know who you like. She doesn't know which person you like.
She knows who likes you. She knows which person likes you.
I'd like to know why the bus was late. I'd like to know the reason that the bus was late.
I've forgotten how I did it. I've forgotten the way that I did it.

Practice

Simplify these sentences using *what, when, where, who, why* or *how*.

Example: I heard the thing that he said. *I heard what he said* _____.

1. I remember which person you are. _____.
2. I don't know which place she went. _____.
3. He told me the reason he was late. _____.
4. I remember the time that the rain started. _____.
5. They explained the way that it works. _____.

275

polite questions

We use these sentence patterns as questions too. These questions can be about what we know, see, hear, etc.

	Subject	Verb	Object/Place/Time etc.			
			wh-	Subject	Verb	Object/Place/Time etc.
Did	you	hear	what	he	said	*?
Did	you	see	what	*	made	the noise?
Does	she	know	who	you	like	*?
Does	she	know	who	*	likes	you?
Is	this		where	you	got	married *?
Did	you	ask	when	she'll	arrive	*?
Have	you	forgotten	how	you	did	it *?
Do	you	know	why	the bus	was	late *?

We often use this sentence pattern to ask questions. These questions are very useful, starting with expressions like *do you know* or *could you tell me* makes them more polite. We use *if* when there are a limited number of possible answers, for example: yes/no questions.

	Subject	Verb	Recipient	Object/Place/Time etc.			
				wh- or if	Subject	Verb	Object/Time etc.
Do	you	know		what time	the bus	leaves	*?
Could	you	tell	me	what	the exchange rate	is	*?
Do	you	know		who	*	is selling	the tickets?
Could	you	tell	me	where	the restaurant	is	*?
Could	you	tell	me	when	they	open	*?
Do	you	know		why	the bus	was	late *?
Do	you	know		if	there	's	a toilet near here?

We can also use *can* instead of *could*, but *could* is more polite. (See page 114.)

Practice

Make these questions polite.

Example: Where is the restaurant? (could) <u>*Could you tell me where the restaurant is*</u> ?

1. Where does he live? (know) _____?
2. When is the meeting? (know) _____?
3. How old is she? (know) _____?
4. What is the time? (could) _____?
5. Is there an ATM near here? (know) _____?
6. How do you get to the supermarket? (could) _____?
7. Who does that bag belong to? (could) _____?

33

Other sentence patterns
bare infinitives and word order

make it happen

We add verbs to a sentence with *to*. These things happen in **sequence**. (See page 82.)
Both verbs relate to the subject. The verb after *to* is the subject's goal.

| Subject | Verb 1 | | | Verb 2 | Object etc. |
	Verb	Ob.	*to*	(goal)	
We	**have**		**to**	**buy**	food.
They	**need**		**to**	**work**	tomorrow.
We	**asked**	**her**	**to**	**come**	early.
I	**want**	**you**	**to**	**dance.**	

1. **We** have to. 2. **We** buy food.
1. **They** need to. 2. **They** work tomorrow.
1. **We** asked. 2. **Our goal:** she comes early.
1. **I** want it. 2. **My goal:** you dance.

now   to goal

We are talking about things happening in sequence.

We sometimes add verbs to a sentence without *to*. In sentences with *let*, *make* and *help* the **first** verb refers to what the **subject** does, the second verb refers to the **object**'s does.

Subject	Verb	Object	Verb	Object etc.
Examples	help	**me**	understand.	
I	let	**her**	come	in.
Singing	makes	**us**	feel	good.
I	made	**him**	do	the dishes.

Examples help me. I understand.
I let her. **She** came in.
Singing makes us. **We** feel good.
I made him. **He** does the dishes.

With *help*, the subject and object often have the same goal, so we can think about it either way; with or without *to*. There isn't really any difference. Either sentence can be used.

Examples help me understand. **Examples** help me. I understand.
Examples help me to understand. **Examples** help me. This is **their goal;** it is why they were made.
I helped him move the sofa. I helped him. **He** (and I) did it.
I helped him to move the sofa. I helped him. Moving the sofa is **our goal**. He and I did it.

Let and *allow* are used in similar situations, but are used differently because of their meanings.

We let her come in. We didn't stop her. **She** did it.
We allowed her **to** come in. We gave her permission to. **Our goal:** control who comes in.
Let me introduce myself. You don't stop me. **I** do it.
Allow me **to** introduce myself. You grant me permission. **Your goal:** control the situation. (formal)

Sentences often start with *let's* meaning *let us*.

Let's get a coffee. (Let us get a coffee.) May nothing stop us.
Let's move on to the next page. (Let us move on to the next page.) May nothing stop us.

Make can be used in lots of situations.

is NOT (object) | **is (object)**

make (object)

There **isn't** a sandwich.   She **makes** a sandwich.   There **is** a sandwich.

I'm **making** breakfast tomorrow.
He **made** a donation.
She likes **making** new friends.
We **made** a reservation.
They **make** the bed every morning. The bed is not as they want it. They make it. It is how they want it.

Make is a simple verb that can be used instead of:
construct, create, manufacture, prepare, produce, arrange, invent etc.

We also use *make it* when we successfully go somewhere but we don't have much **time** or **energy**.

The bus is late but you can still **make it** to school on time. There isn't much time.
They paddled really hard and just **made it** across the river. They didn't have much more energy.

We also use *make* with an object and and another verb (as on the previous page). The second verb refers to what the object does.

(person/thing) does NOT (verb) | **(person/thing) does (verb)**

make (person/thing)(verb)

It **doesn't** work.   I **make** it work.   It works.

Singing **makes** me feel good.
She **made** the TV work.
The machine is **making** the table shake.
Gas **makes** the car go.
I'll **make** him do the dishes.

When we use *was made* (*be + -en form*), the subject does the action, so we use *to*.

He was made **to** do the dishes. He was made to. He did the dishes.

We also use *to* with *ask* and *tell*. We focus on what the subject says. We don't know if the person does the action or not.

I'll ask them **to** open the window. They may or may not open it. It's their decision.
I told her **to** come in. She may or may not have come in.

Practice

Complete the sentences with *to* where needed. Leave other spaces blank. There may be more than one answer.

1. He asked me _____ buy milk.
2. He was made _____ feel like he didn't matter.
3. I helped them _____ clean the house.
4. My boss makes me _____ work overtime.
5. I told her _____ be here on time.
6. Let's _____ go home.

get it done

We use *have* to refer to a part of something, or **something additional**

I **have** a cat.

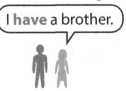
I **have** a brother.

I **have** a bicycle.

We also use *have* when **someone additional** does something.
The subject **arranges** the object to do something.

Subject	Verb	Object	Verb	Object etc.
She	had	him	**take**	her photo.
He	has	someone	**cut**	his hair.

She arranged it. **He** took her photo.
He arranges it. **Someone** cuts his hair.

We often don't say who did it. We simply say what happens to the object, **affecting** the subject.

Subject	Verb	Object	Verb	Object etc.
She	had	her photo	**taken.**	
He	has	his hair	**cut.**	

She was affected. **Her photo** was taken.
He is affected. **His hair** is cut.

> We use the -en form to shift focus. We describe what happens to the object.

We use *get* when things change. (We don't have someone do it, then we have someone do it.)
We say what causes this change. (The subject **causes** someone to do something.)

Subject	Verb	Object	*to*	Verb	Object etc.
She	got	him	**to**	**take**	her photo.
He	gets	someone	**to**	**cut**	his hair.

She caused it. **Her goal:** photo. He did it.
He causes it. **His goal:** cut hair.

> We use *to*. The second verb is the subject's goal. Someone additional does it.

We often don't say who did it. We simply say what happens to the object, **caused** by the subject.

Subject	Verb	Object	Verb	Object etc.
She	got	her photo	**taken.**	
He	gets	his hair	**cut.**	

She caused it. **Her goal:** photo.
He causes it. **His goal:** cut hair.

We can often use *have* or *get* in the same situations. With *get* the subject causes the action.
Have is less direct and therefore more formal. With *have* the subject may not actually do anything.

She **had** her photo taken. She may or may not have asked someone. (formal/informal)
She **got** her photo taken. She asked someone to do it. (informal)

In some situations *have* and *get* have different meanings.

She **had** her bike stolen. She did not ask for this to happen. It **affected** her.
She **got** her bike stolen. She did something that **caused** it. She should have been more careful.
His boss **had** him promoted. His supervisor **arranged** it. *Got* also fits: the boss caused it.
His exceptional work on the project **got** him promoted. His exceptional work **caused** it.

experience it

When we say what we see, hear, feel etc. we don't use *to* before the second verb.
The **first** verb refers to what the **subject** does, the second verb refers to what the **object** does.

S.	Verb	Object	Verb	Object etc.	
We	saw	your mom	**rescue**	a dog.	We saw your mom. **She** rescued a dog.
I	'm watching	the rain	**come**	down.	I'm watching the rain. **It** is coming down.
You	will hear	someone	**knock**	at the door.	You will hear someone. **They** will knock.

We can also use the *-ing* form in these situations to emphasize something happening.

We saw your mom **rescuing** a dog. We saw your mom. **She** was rescuing a dog (not finished).

Why do we say *look at* and *listen to*?

As we can see above, *see*, *watch* and *hear* are followed by an object. We say **what we experience**.

Look and *listen* aren't followed by an object. When we are awake, we are always looking and listening. It is **what we do**.

We look **at** things. Our eyes move around and we focus on one thing at a time. We can only see what we are looking at.

We listen **to** things. There are many sounds around us all the time. The thing we listen to is the thing we give our attention to.

Subject	Verb	Place
He	looked	**at the sculpture.**

He can only see what he is looking at.
He can't see what is behind him.

Subject	Verb	Destination
I	'm listening	**to music.**

I can hear a dog, someone talking and someone working; but I'm not listening to those things.

We may add a verb after the place or destination. This refers to what the **place** or **destination** does.

Look at her **go**! I look at her. She goes. (fast!)
We listened to him **talk** about his time abroad. We listened to him. He talked.

Practice

Complete the sentences with *to* or *at* where needed. Leave other spaces blank.

1. I look _____ the tide times before I go _____ fishing.
2. I listen _____ the news _____ keep up to date with current events.
3. I watched _____ my daughter _____ open her birthday presents.
4. I watched _____ a documentary _____ learn about history.
5. I heard _____ you _____ got a new car.
6. Look _____ him _____ dance!
7. I saw _____ her _____ give him a present.

here you are

We move *here* and *there* to the start of the sentence to focus on **where**.

> Oh...**You**'re **here**....
> I thought you were coming
> next week...

Emphasis on *you*.
You is new information.

> I thought you were coming
> next week...
> but **here** you **are**...

Emphasis on *here*.
We don't focus on *you*;
we already said *you*.

Some expressions are better in some situations depending on what we are focusing on.

Subject	Verb	Place
It	is	here.

Has my package arrived yet?
Yes, **it**'s here.

Emphasis on **it** (the package). We want to know about the package, is it here or not?

Place	Subject	Verb
Here	it	is.

Could you help me look for my pen?
Yes... **here** it is!

Emphasis on **here**. We want to know **where**. Where is it?

When we give something to someone, we talk about what **is here**.

The thing we are giving is here. We can say '**Here** it **is**'— referring to the thing we are giving.

> Can I see your ID, please?

> Yes, **here** it **is**.

The person receiving the object is also **here**. It is more polite to refer to the person, so we usually say '**Here** you **are**'.

> Can I see your ID, please?

> Yes, **here** you **are**.

Sometimes the thing we are giving is important. The end of a sentence is also a strong position so we put it there.

> Can I see your ID, please?

> Yes, **here** is
> **my passport**.

We also use the expressions 'there you are' or 'here you go' etc. in these situations.

We also put important information last for emphasis.

Place	Subject	Verb
Here	it	**is.**

Could you help me look for my pen?
Yes... **here** it **is**!

It is not important because we already know what it refers to (the pen). *Is* is more important.

Place	Verb	Person/Thing
Here	is	**your pencil**.

Could you help me look for my pen?
Yes... **here** is **your pencil**...

Your pencil is important because it is new information.

here comes the end

We also focus on **where** when we talk about things coming and going.

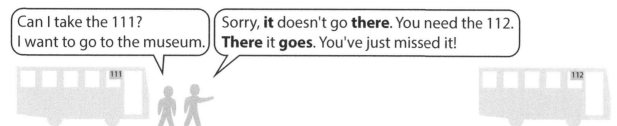

Can I take the 111?
I want to go to the museum.

Sorry, **it** doesn't go **there**. You need the 112.
There it **goes**. You've just missed it!

Subject	Verb	Place
It	goes	**there.**
The bus	goes	**to the museum.**

I want to go to the museum.
Take this bus. **It** goes **there**.
What it is and **where** generally it goes.

Place	Subject	Verb
There	it	**goes.**

Does the 112 stop here?
Yes... **there** it **goes**. You've just missed it!
Where it is and **movement**.

These sentences are also useful in this situation.

Place	Verb	Person/Thing
There	goes	**the bus.**

Hurry up, we're late!
Oh no, **there** goes **the bus**!
Where it is and **what** it is.

Subject	Verb
The bus	is **leaving**.

Let's go. **The bus** is **leaving** soon.
What it is and what it is **doing**.

We also use other words to say where.

Place	Subject	Verb
There	it	**goes.**
Up	you	**come.**
In	she	**comes.**
Off	you	**go.**

Practice

Complete the sentences. Put the words in the best order. There may be more than one answer.

1. I'm looking for my shoes. (they)(there)(are) _____.
2. Can I borrow your car? (the keys)(are)(here) Sure, _____.
3. Can I borrow your car? (the keys)(are)(in the drawer) Sure, _____.
4. The beat in this song is awesome! (comes)(here)(it)_____!
5. This song is awesome! (comes)(here)(the best part) _____!
6. We're ready for our journey. (go)(we)(away) And _____!

283

34

Review of adding more
clauses

review of adding more

We can add another subject and verb (and object etc.) to say when something happens.

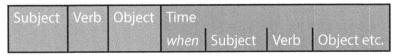

Subject	Verb	Object	Time			
			when	Subject	Verb	Object etc.

When, *while* and *as* are used in the same way, with different meanings.

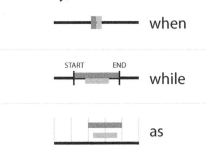

We add another subject and verb (and object etc.) **after** a noun to add information about the noun.

Subject					Verb	Object etc.
Noun	*(that)*	Subject	Verb	Object etc.		

We use *who, which, where* and *when* in a similar way.

We add a verb with *to* when both verbs relate to the subject.

Subject	Verb 1			Verb 2	Object
	Verb	Object	*to*	(goal)	

We use *to* to say the subject's goal.

When the first verb relates to what the subject does and the second verb relates to what the object does, we add the verb without *to*.

Subject	Verb	Object	Verb	Object etc.

The subject-verb-object order is very common. However we sometimes change the order to emphasize different words. Different orders have different uses.

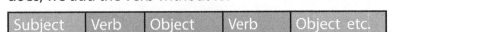

Subject	Verb	Place		or	Place	Subject	Verb		or	Place	Verb	Person/Thing

examples

I'll cook dinner **when** I get home.
I lived in England **when** I was young.
What did she say **when** you gave it to her?

When I get home, I'll cook dinner.
When I was young, I lived in England.
When you gave it to her, what did she say?

He went out **while** I was on the phone.
We were reading books **while** we were waiting.

While I was on the phone, he went out.
While we were waiting, we were reading books.

We watched **as** it happened.
It got louder **as** it came closer.

As it happened, we watched.
As it came closer, it got louder.

The people **that** got here first took the good seats.
This is my friend **that** plays the guitar.

The people **who** got here first took the good seats.
This is my friend **who** plays the guitar.

The donations (that) we received are for the homeless.
It was a day **that** would never be forgotten.

The donations **which** we received are for the homeless.
It was a day **which** would never be forgotten.

The town (that) he was born in is over there.
The bank is in the street (that) the park is in.

The town **where** he was born in is over there.
The bank is in the street **where** the park is.

It was sunny on the day (that) she arrived.
The year (that) everything changed was 2016.

It was sunny on the day **when** she arrived.
The year **when** everything changed was 2016.

I want **to** help.
I want you **to** help.
I got her **to** open the door for me.

Do I need **to** bring anything?
Do you need me **to** bring anything?
What did you get him **to** do?

I wouldn't like **to** sing.
I wouldn't like you **to** sing.
I didn't get him **to** do anything.

It makes **me** happy.
I saw **him walk** the dog.
I had **someone open** the door for me.
I had **my nails done**.
I got **my nails done**.

She let **them leave** early.
I watched **her climb** the tree.
What did you have **him do**?
What did you have **done**?
What did you get **done**?

They helped **me fix** the car.
We should listen **to him sing**.
I didn't have **him do anything**.
I didn't **have anything done**.
I didn't **get anything done**.

I go **off**.
The balloon went **up**.
She comes **in**.
Jackson is **there**.

Off I **go**.
Up the balloon **went**.
In she **comes**.
There Jackson **is**.

Off goes **the car**.
Up went **the balloon**.
In comes **Zoe**.
There's Jackson.

quiz

Choose the best sentences.

1. (a) We went home when it started raining.
   (b) We went home while it started raining.
   (c) either (a) or (b)

2. (a) I did the shopping when she was at work.
   (b) I did the shopping while she was at work.
   (c) either (a) or (b)

3. (a) As I got in the car, the sun came out.
   (b) When I got in the car, the sun came out.
   (c) either (a) or (b)

4. (a) We left before the rain started.
   (b) We left until the rain started.
   (c) either (a) or (b)

5. (a) I'll be here until 6.
   (b) I'll be here since 6.
   (c) either (a) or (b)

6. (a) The lady that works here is my aunt.
   (b) The lady works here is my aunt.
   (c) either (a) or (b)

7. (a) The lady that I live with is my aunt.
   (b) The lady I live with is my aunt.
   (c) either (a) or (b)

8. (a) The man that I live with is my uncle.
   (b) The man who I live with is my uncle.
   (c) either (a) or (b)

9. (a) This is the place where we saw the bear.
   (b) This is the place what we saw the bear.
   (c) This is the place we saw the bear.
   (d) either (a) or (c)
   (e) either (b) or (c)

10. (a) The ostrich, which is the largest bird in the world, is found in Africa.
    (b) The ostrich which is the largest bird in the world is found in Africa.
    (c) either (a) or (b).

11. (a) Matt, the friend who lives in the city, is having a party tonight.
    (b) Matt, who lives in the city, is having a party tonight.
    (c) either (a) or (b)

12. Which is more natural?
    (a) Did you hear what happened?
    (b) Did you hear about the thing that happened?

13. (a) She helped save the injured koala.
    (b) She helped to save the injured koala.
    (c) either (a) or (b)

14. (a) The teacher made her do it again.
    (b) The teacher made her to do it again.
    (c) either (a) or (b)

15. (a) We had the carpet cleaned.
    (b) We got the carpet cleaned.
    (c) either (a) or (b)

16. (a) They had him perform for the class.
    (b) They got him perform for the class.
    (c) either (a) or (b)

17. The train should be here soon...
    (a) It comes here!
    (b) here it comes!
    (c) either (a) or (b)

18. We're finished. Let's celebrate!
    (a) Let's = Let is
    (b) Let's = Let us

Two tenses

core concepts

Many English grammar books suggest the English language has three tenses. This is false. English is a two tense language.

"And even at the level of the broad framework of grammatical principles, we have frequently found that pronouncements unchallenged for 200 years are in fact flagrantly false." - Rodney Huddleston and Geoffrey K. Pullum (2005), *A Student's Introduction to English Grammar*, Cambridge University Press.

Huddleston and Pullum go on to explain that English has two primary tenses.

Why is English traditionally classified as having three tenses?

Latin has three tenses. People looked at Latin grammar (which has verbs inflected for past, present and future) and assigned the same categories to English. Current linguistic theory clearly states that English has two tenses, however, many grammar books for students are still written based on the traditional (and incorrect) classification. *Real Grammar* is consistent with current linguistic theory, explaining English grammar based on English. It is crucial that students are given the correct framework for the language they are studying.

"[W]e have no more business with a *future tense* in our language, than we have with the whole system of Latin moods and tenses" - Joseph Priestley (1772), *The Rudiments of English Grammar (3rd Edition)*.

no future tense

Real Grammar describes English as having **two tenses**: the present tense (referring to the present-future), and the past tense (NOT referring to the present-future). Many grammar books say English has three tenses: past, present and future. It doesn't. Recognizing that English only has two tenses helps students understand English on a deeper level and avoid many common errors.

The first verb of every English sentence indicates tense and is in either the present form (present-future) or past form (not present-future).

Some people claim that the so called 'future tense' is not constructed with verb inflection, but with the 'future tense marker' *will*. There are two main reasons why this is confusing for students:

1. *Will* is used for the present

Will is actually in the present form (its past form is *would*), so it is used to talk about the present-future. It is better not to use the term 'future tenses' because the so called 'future simple', 'future perfect' and 'future progressive', are often used to talk about the present.

He's been working really hard so he**'ll be** hungry. (future simple: description in the present)
My daughter is very helpful. She**'ll** always **pick** up garbage and put it in the trash. (future simple: general statement referring to what she does—generally in the present-future, as well as the past)
They **will have arrived** by now. (future perfect: result of action in the present)
She**'ll be sleeping** now. (future progressive: unfinished action in the present)

2. Using *will* is not the simplest way of talking about the future

We can simplify the idea of past, present and future into three consecutive days: yesterday, today (now) and tomorrow. When we ask someone about these days we usually ask in the following way:

PAST	PRESENT	FUTURE
What did you do yesterday?	What are you doing (now)?	What are you doing tomorrow?

Everyone agrees that the past and present questions above are what we use, but there are many ways of talking about the future. Some people may claim the future question is 'What will you do tomorrow?' or 'What are you going to do tomorrow?' (considering *will* and *be going to* as future tense markers). While these sentences are grammatically correct and useful, they are NOT talking about the future in the simplest way possible. The most common way is 'What are you doing tomorrow?' Students need to understand that this is how we usually talk about the future, clearly and simply. The stuff about *will* being a future tense marker is just confusing.

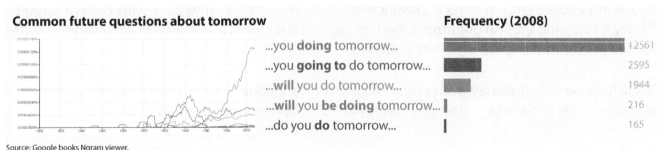

Common future questions about tomorrow

Frequency (2008)

...you **doing** tomorrow...	12561
...you **going to** do tomorrow...	2595
...**will** you do tomorrow...	1944
...**will** you **be doing** tomorrow...	216
...do you **do** tomorrow...	165

Source: Google books Ngram viewer.
The words 'what' and 'are' have been omitted from this search as Ngrams has a five word maximum. All uses of these collections of words are used for asking about the future.
The results for "What are you doing tomorrow" and "you doing tomorrow" are almost identical. Numbers indicate frequency (percentage × 10⁻¹⁰)

This book looks at these different ways of talking about the future, what they mean, and why they are used.

What about *will*?

Will is very useful when talking about the future, but it is important that we don't confuse this with the true meaning of the word. *Will* is a modal verb. We use modal verbs when we consider options and possibilities. Any of these modal verbs can be used when we talk about the future.

It'**ll** rain tomorrow.
It **may** rain tomorrow.
It **might** rain tomorrow.
It **should** rain tomorrow.
It **could** rain tomorrow.

I'**ll** buy some cheese.
I **may** buy some cheese.
I **might** buy some cheese.
I **can** buy some cheese.
I **could** buy some cheese.

I **must** buy some cheese.
I **shall** buy some cheese.
I **should** buy some cheese.
* different modal verbs fit
different situations.

Will doesn't indicate future time. *Will* is used when we consider **options** or **possibilities** and make a decision or prediction about the future or the present.

We talk about what is certain without a modal verb.

PAST	PRESENT	FUTURE	certain:
It rained yesterday.	It's raining (now).		
I saw it.	I see it.		**rain**

We consider possibilities and make a prediction using *will*. We don't know for certain.

PAST	PRESENT	FUTURE	possibilities:
	It will be raining (now).	It will rain tomorrow.	
	I can't see the weather.	I don't know for certain.	prediction: no rain
	I make a prediction.	I make a prediction.	**rain**

We consider our options and make a decision.

I need cheese... I'**ll** get some from the supermarket after work.
I consider when and how to get the cheese and make a decision.

How do we know if we are talking about the present or the future?

The words we use only convey some of the meaning. We get a lot of meaning from context.

I'm not drinking. I'm driving.
(present)   (future)

She'll be asleep. I'll wait.
(present)   (future)

We often know what is happening in the present, when something is not happening in the present we know that it is happening in the future.

As we can see above, we talk about the future in the same way we talk about the present. English has no future tense. *Will* is used to talk about options and possibilities, and this may be useful when talking about the future or the present. It is important to understand how the simple concept of modality and the two English tenses work together to express a wide range of ideas.

For further reading about English not having a future tense, see: Rodney Huddleston and Geoffrey K. Pullum (2002), *The Cambridge Grammar of the English Language* , Cambridge University Press, 208–212.

294

Tense, aspect and modality

core concepts

The verb is the heart of the sentence. Here are the core concepts of English verbs:

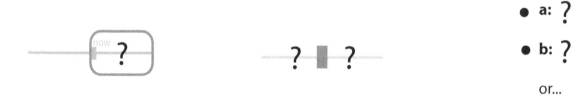

tense:
time reference (when):
present-future or not.
(present form/past form)
Required information

aspect:
how an action, event or state
relates to the flow of time.
(-ing form/-en form)
Additional information

modality:
consideration of
options or possibilities.
(modal verbs)
Additional information

The diagrams on the following pages show how tense and aspect combine to create a wide range of sentence patterns. We also look at how the core concept of modality relates to how we use modal verbs (can/could, will/would, shall/should, may/might and must). The third diagram looks at quasi-modality and how quasi-modal verbs relate to modal verbs.

These pages reflect traditional analyses of grammar, broken down into core concepts that are easier for students to understand.

tense and aspect

Here are the core concepts of the English system of tense and aspect and how they are combined.

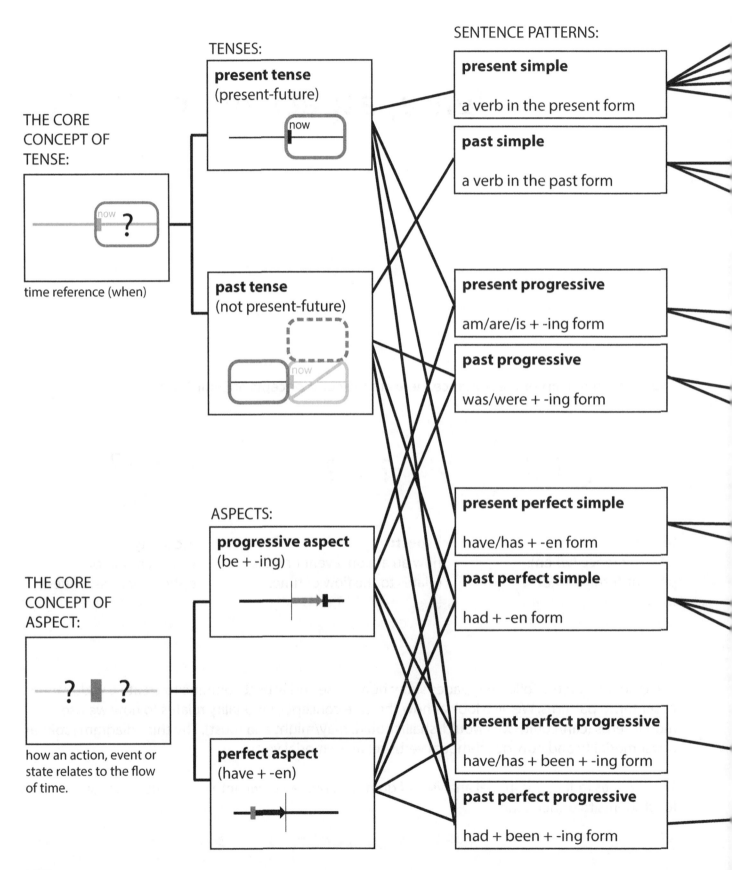

THE CORE
CONCEPT OF
TENSE:

time reference (when)

TENSES:

present tense
(present-future)

now

past tense
(not present-future)

now

ASPECTS:

progressive aspect
(be + -ing)

THE CORE
CONCEPT OF
ASPECT:

how an action, event or
state relates to the flow
of time.

perfect aspect
(have + -en)

SENTENCE PATTERNS:

present simple

a verb in the present form

past simple

a verb in the past form

present progressive

am/are/is + -ing form

past progressive

was/were + -ing form

present perfect simple

have/has + -en form

past perfect simple

had + -en form

present perfect progressive

have/has + been + -ing form

past perfect progressive

had + been + -ing form

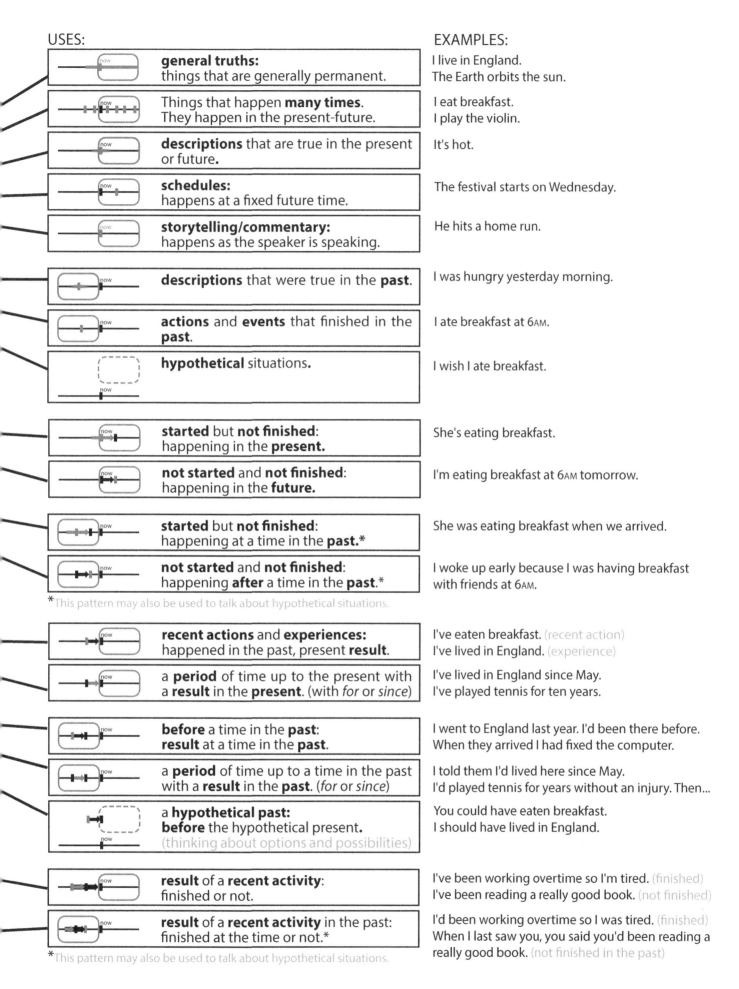

USES:

		EXAMPLES:
	general truths: things that are generally permanent.	I live in England. The Earth orbits the sun.
	Things that happen **many times.** They happen in the present-future.	I eat breakfast. I play the violin.
	descriptions that are true in the present or future.	It's hot.
	schedules: happens at a fixed future time.	The festival starts on Wednesday.
	storytelling/commentary: happens as the speaker is speaking.	He hits a home run.
	descriptions that were true in the **past.**	I was hungry yesterday morning.
	actions and **events** that finished in the **past.**	I ate breakfast at 6AM.
	hypothetical situations.	I wish I ate breakfast.
	started but **not finished:** happening in the **present.**	She's eating breakfast.
	not started and **not finished:** happening in the **future.**	I'm eating breakfast at 6AM tomorrow.
	started but **not finished:** happening at a time in the **past.***	She was eating breakfast when we arrived.
	not started and **not finished:** happening **after** a time in the **past.***	I woke up early because I was having breakfast with friends at 6AM.

*This pattern may also be used to talk about hypothetical situations.

	recent actions and **experiences:** happened in the past, present **result.**	I've eaten breakfast. (recent action) I've lived in England. (experience)
	a **period** of time up to the present with a **result** in the **present.** (with *for* or *since*)	I've lived in England since May. I've played tennis for ten years.
	before a time in the **past:** **result** at a time in the **past.**	I went to England last year. I'd been there before. When they arrived I had fixed the computer.
	a **period** of time up to a time in the past with a **result** in the **past.** (*for* or *since*)	I told them I'd lived here since May. I'd played tennis for years without an injury. Then...
	a **hypothetical past:** **before** the hypothetical present. (thinking about options and possibilities)	You could have eaten breakfast. I should have lived in England.
	result of a **recent activity:** finished or not.	I've been working overtime so I'm tired. (finished) I've been reading a really good book. (not finished)
	result of a **recent activity** in the past: finished at the time or not.*	I'd been working overtime so I was tired. (finished) When I last saw you, you said you'd been reading a really good book. (not finished in the past)

*This pattern may also be used to talk about hypothetical situations.

297

modal verbs

Here is the big picture of the English modal system showing how and why modal verbs are used in various ways.

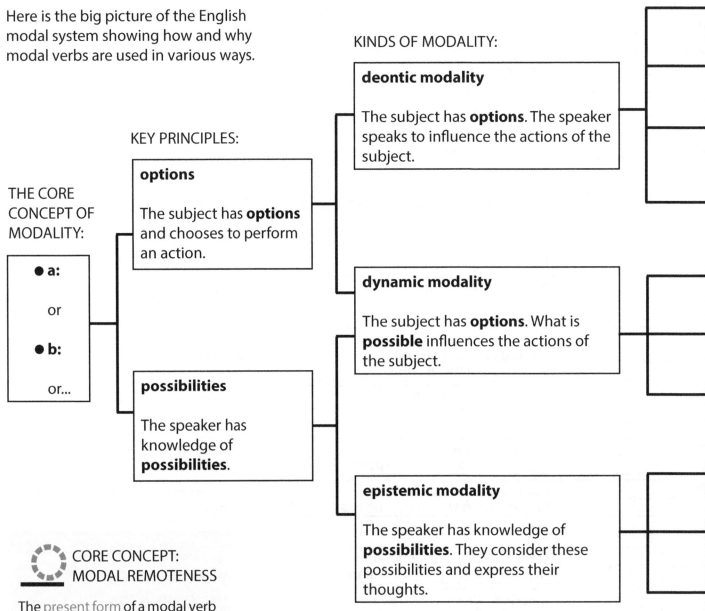

THE CORE CONCEPT OF MODALITY:

- a:

  or

- b:

  or...

KEY PRINCIPLES:

options

The subject has **options** and chooses to perform an action.

possibilities

The speaker has knowledge of **possibilities**.

KINDS OF MODALITY:

deontic modality

The subject has **options**. The speaker speaks to influence the actions of the subject.

dynamic modality

The subject has **options**. What is **possible** influences the actions of the subject.

epistemic modality

The speaker has knowledge of **possibilities**. They consider these possibilities and express their thoughts.

CORE CONCEPT: MODAL REMOTENESS

The present form of a modal verb is used when actualization in the present-future is a real option or possibility.

The past form of a modal verb is used for hypothetical or unreal situations. We speak as though these things will not actually happen in the present-future.

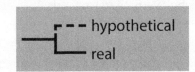

- - - hypothetical
——— real

CORE MEANINGS OF MODAL VERBS:

 can/could

We use *can/could* to say something is an option or a possibility. Nothing is stopping it from being one.

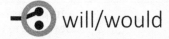 will/would

We use *will/would* to say what we decide or predict.

FUNCTIONS:	PURPOSES:	MODALS USED:	EXAMPLES:
creating options	**permission**	can may	You can/may borrow it. You can't/may not borrow it.
highlighting options	**suggestion**	could might	You could/might try to leave early.
selecting options	**advice**	should#	You should try talking to him.
	order	will shall**	You will/shall come here at once. You will not/shall not talk back. ** *Will* is much more common than *shall*.
eliminating options	**obligation**	had better should# must	I must/had better/should go. You mustn't/had better not/shouldn't be late. * *Should* may be interpreted as advice if said softly or obligation if said strongly.
highlighting possible options	**ability**	can/could*	Can you drive? I can drive. I can't drive. Could you drive when you were eighteen?
eliminating possible options	**requirement**	must	Whales must surface to breathe.
selecting possible options	**decision**	will/would* shall**	Will you go home soon? I'll go home soon. I won't go home soon. Shall we go home soon? * Past forms may be used for past times. ** *Shall* is mainly used in questions when making decisions.
highlighting possibilities	**uncertainty**	may/might could	That may/might be him. That may not/might not be him.
eliminating possibilities	**deductions**	must can't	That must be her. (deducing: eliminating other possibilities) That can't be her. (eliminating this possibility)
selecting possibilities	**predictions**	should will	She should be ready by now. Will she be ready? She'll be ready by now. She won't be ready yet.

 shall/should

 may/might

 must

We use *shall/should* to say something is the right thing to do.

We use *may/might* to say something is an option or possibility, but not the only one.

We use *must* to say there is only one reasonable option or possibility.

Had better is an idiomatic expression that is used to fill the gap in the modal system left by *must* not having a past form.

299

quasi-modal verbs

Quasi-modal verbs end in *to*. They can be used in place of a modal verb.

KINDS OF QUASI-MODALITY:

deontic quasi-modality

The speaker states the **option** that has been **chosen**.

dynamic quasi-modality

What the subject does has been predetermined based on **options** relating to what is **possible**.

epistemic quasi-modality

We have made a **conclusion**. Only one thing is **possible** based on current or past events.

THE CORE CONCEPT OF QUASI-MODALITY:

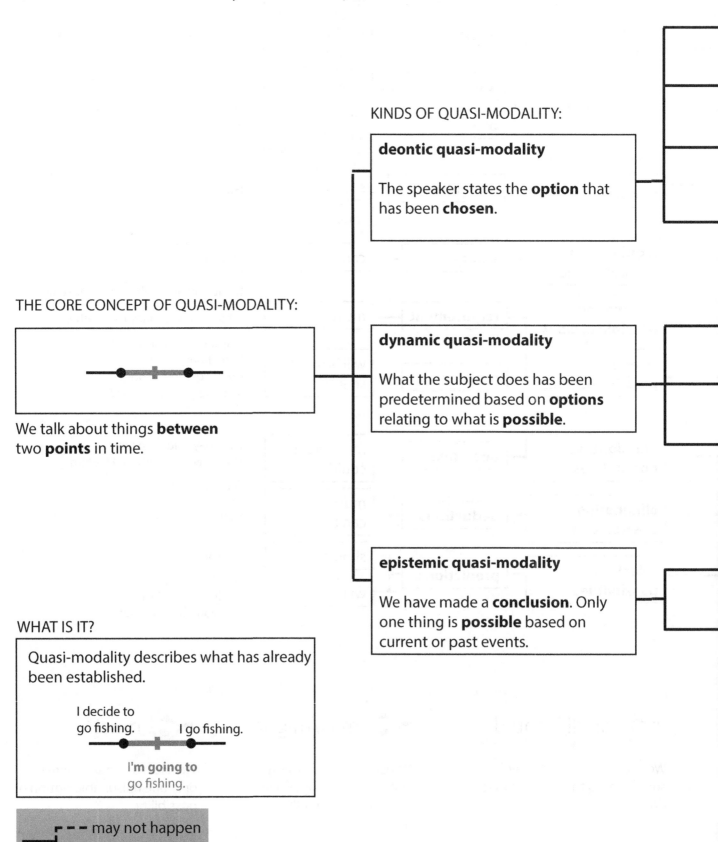

We talk about things **between** two **points** in time.

WHAT IS IT?

Quasi-modality describes what has already been established.

I decide to go fishing.

I go fishing.

I'm going to go fishing.

- - - may not happen

—— will happen

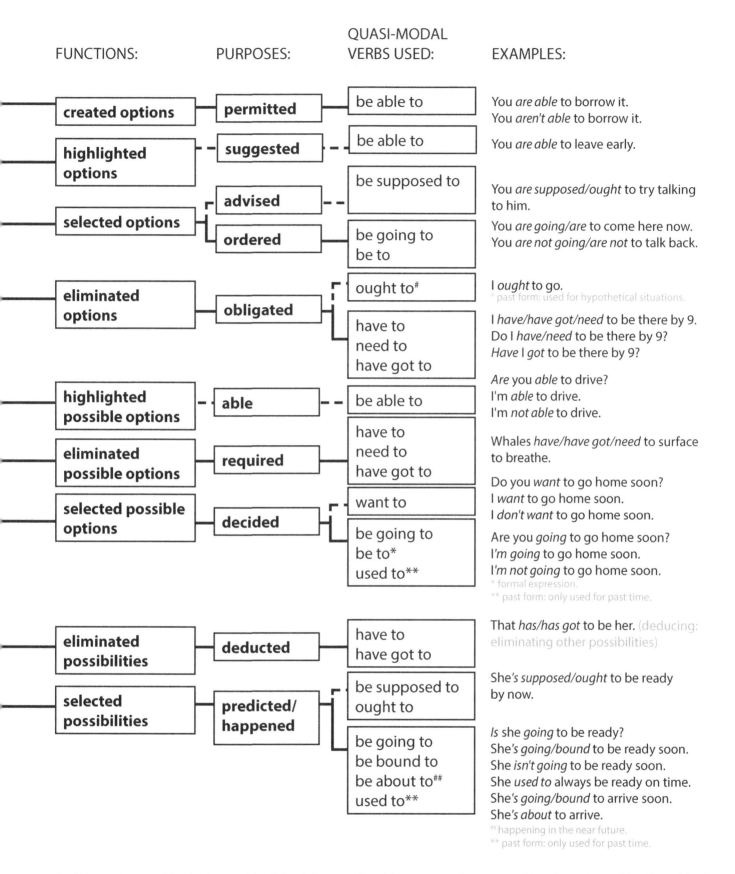

FUNCTIONS:	PURPOSES:	QUASI-MODAL VERBS USED:	EXAMPLES:
created options	**permitted**	be able to	You *are able* to borrow it. You *aren't able* to borrow it.
highlighted options	**suggested**	be able to	You *are able* to leave early.
selected options	**advised**	be supposed to	You *are supposed/ought* to try talking to him.
	ordered	be going to be to	You *are going/are* to come here now. You *are not going/are not* to talk back.
eliminated options	**obligated**	ought to#	I *ought* to go. # past form: used for hypothetical situations.
		have to need to have got to	I *have/have got/need* to be there by 9. Do I *have/need* to be there by 9? *Have* I *got* to be there by 9?
highlighted possible options	**able**	be able to	*Are* you *able* to drive? I'm *able* to drive. I'm *not able* to drive.
eliminated possible options	**required**	have to need to have got to	Whales *have/have got/need* to surface to breathe.
selected possible options	**decided**	want to	Do you *want* to go home soon? I *want* to go home soon. I *don't want* to go home soon.
		be going to be to* used to**	Are you *going* to go home soon? I*'m going* to go home soon. I*'m not going* to go home soon. * formal expression. ** past form: only used for past time.
eliminated possibilities	**deducted**	have to have got to	That *has/has got* to be her. (deducing: eliminating other possibilities)
selected possibilities	**predicted/ happened**	be supposed to ought to	She's *supposed/ought* to be ready by now.
		be going to be bound to be about to## used to**	*Is* she *going* to be ready? She's *going/bound* to be ready soon. She *isn't going* to be ready soon. She *used to* always be ready on time. She's *going/bound* to arrive soon. She's *about* to arrive. ## happening in the near future. ** past form: only used for past time.

Ought is sometimes considered to be a modal verb. It only has a past form. It has no present form so many things that are impossible with modal verbs are also impossible with *ought*. 'I didn't ought to...' 'I will ought to...' etc. These structures require the present form to be used, so they are not possible with *ought* which doesn't have a present form.

Ought has been classified here as a quasi-modal as it relates to the core concept of quasi modality but not the core concept of modality. The interesting thing about *ought* is that it is a past form that is used to express hypothetical situations. Other quasi-modals are generally used for present-future and past (but not hypothetical).

Answers and index

answers

There is not one correct answer to every problem. Language is used for communication; we share our thoughts with others. We say things in different ways depending on how we are thinking. It is not about being right or wrong.

In this book, we sometimes give more than one answer. Answers are given to check that the language you use communicates what you are thinking.

This answer section often gives the short form of basic verbs ('s, 'll, 'd etc.), but the full word (is/has, will or would/had) is always acceptable too. We often use the short forms when our speech is flowing. We sometimes use the full words for emphasis or to slow things down and give us time to think.

Basic building blocks

1: Constructing Basic Sentences

Page 2: word order
We play golf.
I eat fish.
I like cheese.

Page 3: do
Do you like seafood? No, I don't.
Do you drive? Yes, I do.
Do you do karate? No, I don't.

Page 3: don't
I don't like seafood.
I don't drive.
I don't do karate.

Page 5: adding a place
Either *at* or *in* can be used in either situation, but we usually think about it the following way.
1. Owen and Charlotte plan to meet at the shopping mall. Owen arrives and calls Charlotte.
   Owen: I've just arrived. Where are you?
   Charlotte: I'm <u>in</u> the supermarket.
   Owen wants to know where to go to meet her. Charlotte thinks of the supermarket as a building with walls and uses *in*.
2. Owen is at home and decides to call Charlotte.
   Owen: Where are you?
   Charlotte: I'm <u>at</u> the supermarket.
   Owen wants a general idea of where she is. Charlotte thinks of the general point in space, and uses *at*.

1. I live <u>in</u> Chicago.
2. I live <u>in</u> an apartment.
3. I live <u>on</u> the 6th floor.
4. I live <u>in</u> room 608.
5. I'm <u>in</u> Mexico.
6. We often say I'm <u>at</u> the beach when thinking of the beach as a point in space.

We can also think of a beach as a surface and say I'm <u>on</u> the beach. If the listener is close to us, I'm <u>on</u> the beach is more common as this extra information helps them find us.

7. I'm <u>on</u> the sand.

Page 7: adding a time
1. I start work <u>at</u> 9AM.
2. I finish work early <u>on</u> Fridays.
3. I finish <u>at</u> 4PM.
4. I have a holiday <u>in</u> January.
5. I go back to work <u>on</u> January 18th.
6. I play golf <u>on</u> Sundays.

Page 9: where and when
1. <u>Where do you swim?</u>
   At the beach.
2. <u>When do they have dinner?</u>
   At 7PM.
3. <u>Where do you read books?</u>
   On the bus.
4. <u>Where do you live?</u>
   In Canada.
5. <u>When do you finish work?</u>
   At 5:30.
6. <u>When do you travel?</u>
   In spring.

2: Basic Verbs

Page 13: have (and be)
1. I'<u>m</u> Tom.
2. I'<u>m</u> Scottish.
3. I <u>have</u> brown hair.
4. I <u>have</u> blue eyes.
5. I <u>have</u> a nice smile.
6. I'<u>m</u> tall.
7. I'<u>m</u> a police officer.

1. I'<u>m</u> big.
2. I <u>have</u> big ears.
3. I'<u>m</u> heavy.
4. I <u>have</u> four legs.
5. I <u>have</u> a tail.
6. I'<u>m</u> gray.
7. I'<u>m</u> an elephant.

Page 14: be (am/are/is)
1. She'<u>s</u> American.
2. He'<u>s</u> English.
3. I'<u>m</u> Korean.
4. It'<u>s</u> a bird.
5. You'<u>re</u> Canadian.
6. They'<u>re</u> bus drivers.
7. We'<u>re</u> taxi drivers.
8. I'<u>m</u> happy.

Page 15: be (am/are/is)
1. <u>Is</u> she American?
2. <u>Do</u> you run?
3. <u>Do</u> you like chicken?
4. <u>Are</u> you at work?
5. <u>Are</u> they hungry?
6. <u>Do</u> they like hamburgers?
7. <u>Is</u> he young?
8. <u>Am</u> I awake?

1. She <u>isn't</u> American.

or She'<u>s not</u> American.
2. He <u>isn't</u> English.
   or He'<u>s not</u> English.
3. I'<u>m not</u> Korean.
4. It <u>isn't</u> a bird.
   or It'<u>s not</u> a bird.
5. You <u>aren't</u> Canadian.
   or You'<u>re not</u> Canadian.
6. They <u>aren't</u> bus drivers.
   or They'<u>re not</u> bus drivers.
7. We <u>aren't</u> taxi drivers.
   or We'<u>re not</u> taxi drivers.
8. I'<u>m not</u> happy.
   NOTE: Saying *am not*, *are not* or *is not* is possible but stronger.

Page 16: adding s to verbs
1. He likes fish.
2. She mixes cement.
3. We drink milk.
4. She plays tennis.
5. I have a car.
6. He has black hair.
7. She goes to work.

Page 17: adding s to verbs
Does he like seafood?
Does he shower?
Does she do karate?

She doesn't like seafood.
We don't shower.
He doesn't do karate.

1. <u>Does</u> she <u>eat</u> beef?
2. He <u>eats</u> beef.
3. We <u>don't play</u> golf.
4. <u>Do</u> you <u>play</u> golf?
5. <u>Does</u> he <u>play</u> golf?
6. <u>Do</u> you <u>live</u> in Brazil?
7. <u>Does</u> she <u>live</u> in Brazil?
8. <u>Do</u> they <u>live</u> in Brazil?
9. She <u>doesn't smoke</u>.
10. He <u>doesn't drink</u>.
11. They <u>don't live</u> in Miami.
12. He <u>likes</u> tennis.

Page 18: who and what
1. What <u>sports do you like?</u>
   I like soccer and tennis.
2. Who <u>plays tennis on Saturdays?</u>
   Victoria does.
3. What <u>music do you like?</u>
   I like rock, blues and pop music.
4. What <u>food do you like?</u>
   I like Italian food.
5. Who <u>wants chocolate ice-cream?</u>
   Me!
6. What <u>time do you have breakfast?</u>
   I have breakfast at 6:20.
7. What <u>books do you read?</u>
   I read mysteries.

3: One or more

Page 22: a/an
1. Is that <u>a</u> pear?
2. No, it's <u>an</u> apple.
3. We don't have <u>an</u> air conditioner.

4. Do you have <u>a</u> TV?
5. She's <u>a</u> doctor.
6. I'm <u>a</u> waiter.
7. He eats <u>an</u> egg every day.
8. You're <u>an</u> interesting person.

Page 23: adding *s* to nouns
1. I have two <u>sisters</u>.
2. Can I have <u>a hot dog</u> please.
3. They're <u>pilots</u>.
4. I play <u>video games</u>. (not just one game)
5. I eat three <u>bananas</u> every morning.
6. <u>A mechanic</u> fixes cars.*
7. <u>Bus drivers</u> drive buses.*
8. A lot of <u>men</u> like sport.

* The *s* in *fixes* shows us the sentence is about one other person: a typical mechanic. (He/She fixes...)
Drive (no *s*) shows the sentence is about many people: bus drivers. (They drive...)

Page 25: things we sometimes don't count
1. We usually say "**eggs**". We have many we can count. In some situations we say "egg", for example: if it is mixed up in a bowl.
2. We usually say "**milk**". We could say "milks", for example: if there are many small bottles/cartons of milk for kids.
3. We usually say "**juice**". We can sometimes say "juices" (similar to *milks* above). We may also say "juices" if there is more than one kind of juice.
4. We usually say "**grapes**".
5. We usually say "**strawberries**".
6. We usually say "**cheese**". We say "cheeses" if there is more than one kind of cheese or individually wrapped cheeses.
7. We say "**lamb**". *Lambs* would mean the animals, not the meat—I've never seen them in a fridge!

1. We have **a sofa** in our living room. We can count sofas.
2. I read **books**. We can count books.
3. Do you need **medicine**? We speak about medicine generally. We can't count it, all medicines are different.
4. There is **sand** in my shoe. Sand is made up of many tiny grains—we can't count it.
5. Rainbow Beach is in Australia. People commonly say "Rainbow Beach has colored **sands**." We can count the different colored sands (Some say there are 72!) However, saying "Rainbow Beach has colored **sand**," is also correct. We can think of the sand on the beach as something we can't count. It is colored.
6. I like **avocado** on toast. I cut the avocado and put some on my toast.
7. I buy **avocados** at the market. I buy whole avocados.
8. I have some **cake** with my tea. I cut the cake and eat some. But we could say I have some <u>cakes</u> with my tea if I eat more than one cake (maybe they're small cakes) or more than one variety of cake.
9. I like **beans**. This refers to the vegetable. "I like <u>bean</u>," could refer to something we can't count, for example the flavor.
10. I like **pumpkin**. I like the vegetable: we don't usually eat the whole thing. If we say "I like <u>pumpkins</u>" we are thinking about whole pumpkins, we might be carving them for Halloween or something.

Page 26: things we don't count
1. I have some <u>headphones</u>. (2)
2. Scientists do <u>research</u>. (abstract)*
3. I need more <u>information</u>. (abstract)*
4. She wears <u>earrings</u>. (2)
5. He wears <u>jewelry</u>. (group)
6. The <u>electricity is</u> on. (abstract)*
7. Do you have any <u>news</u>? (abstract)*
8. Take out the <u>trash</u>. (group)
9. I'm thirsty. Where <u>is my glass</u>? (1)
10. I can't see! Where <u>are my glasses</u>? (2)

*The things marked *abstract* are things we can't see or hear. They are groups of many small pieces, too many to count

Page 27: some and any
1. Do you have <u>any</u> sisters?
2. I have <u>a</u> car.
3. Is there <u>a</u> restroom near here?
4. Are there <u>any</u> restrooms near here?
5. There's <u>a</u> computer on the desk.
6. There are <u>some</u> pens in the drawer.
7. We don't have <u>any</u> children.
8. There's <u>some</u> ice in the glass..

Page 29: the
1. A: I have <u>a</u> new job. (one of many)
   B: Great! What's <u>the</u> job? (your job)
   A: I'm <u>an</u> office worker. (one of many)
   B: Where's <u>the</u> office? (your office)
   A: It's in <u>the</u> city. (this city)
2. A: Do you play <u>the</u> piano? (known instrument)
   B: I have <u>a</u> piano but I don't play it. (one of many)
3. Can you turn off <u>the</u> TV please? (in this room)
4. I go to <u>a</u> park in <u>the</u> morning. (one of many parks, known time of day)
   or I go to <u>the</u> park in <u>the</u> morning. The listener knows what kind of place a park is. it doesn't matter which one.
5. I work on <u>a</u> boat. (one of many)
6. I swim in <u>the</u> sea. (known place)
7. <u>The</u> restaurant opens at 6. (known place)
8. Can I have <u>a</u> drink, please? (one of many)
9. My company has <u>a</u> boat and <u>a</u> hotel. I work on <u>the</u> boat. Anne works in <u>the</u> hotel. (one of many boats, one of many hotels, my company's boat, my company's hotel)

Page 30: names
1. <u>the</u> Great Sphinx,
2. ____ Angel Falls,
3. <u>the</u> Great Wall of China,
4. ____ Machu Picchu,
5. <u>the</u> Grand Canyon,
6. ____ Mt Fuji,
7. ____ Uluru,
8. ____ Stonehenge,
9. <u>the</u> Forbidden City and
10. <u>the</u> Empire State Building.

4: Other basic words

Page 32: 's
1. Mike is <u>Kelly's</u> husband.
2. Kelly is <u>Mike's</u> wife.
3. <u>Ruby's</u> brother is Joshua.
4. <u>Joshua's</u> sister is Ruby.
5. Joshua and Ruby's mother is <u>Kelly</u>.
6. <u>Mike</u> is Ruby and Joshua's father.
7. <u>Joshua</u> and <u>Ruby</u> are Mike and Kelly's children.
   or <u>Ruby</u> and <u>Joshua</u> are Mike and Kelly's children.

Page 33: her, his, its, my, our, their, your
1. She is <u>my</u> sister.
2. Fred is <u>her</u> husband.
3. Emily and Johnny are <u>their</u> children.
4. We all like music. <u>Our</u> favorite singer is Taylor Swift.
5. Is this <u>your</u> cat?
6. What is <u>its</u> name?

Page 34: hers, his, its, mine, ours, theirs, yours
1. Whose bag is that? It's <u>hers</u>.
2. Your house is tidier than <u>mine</u>.
3. Here are our dinners. <u>Yours</u> is on the white plate.
4. My clothes are dirty but <u>theirs</u> are clean.
5. Is this my drink? No, it's <u>his</u>.
6. Whose jackets are these? They're <u>ours</u>.

Page 35: one
1. Where is my key? I can't find <u>it</u>.
2. The tomatoes are growing well. Look at that <u>one</u>. It's huge!
3. A: Is there an ATM near here?
   B: Yes, there's <u>one</u> in the convenience store.
4. These dresses are nice. How much is this <u>one</u>?
5. These pants are nice. How much are these <u>ones</u>?
6. Those grapes look good. Can I have <u>one</u>?
7. A: Excuse me, can I use your phone?
   B: Sorry, I don't have <u>one</u>. (one = a phone) This means I don't have a phone. In some situations we might say "Sorry, I don't have <u>it</u>." (it = my phone) I left it somewhere or someone else has it at the moment.

Page 36: simplifying sentences
My name is Isabella.
1. <u>I</u> live in Florida.
2. <u>I</u> have one brother and one sister.
3. <u>My</u> brother's name is William.
4. <u>My</u> sister's name is Ava. Ava likes sport.
5. <u>Her</u> favorite sport is soccer.
6. <u>She</u> is very good at <u>it</u>.
7. <u>I</u> like <u>it</u> too.
8. <u>We</u> play <u>it</u> together on Saturdays.
9. These are <u>our</u> soccer balls.
10. This one is <u>hers</u>.
11. This one is <u>mine</u>.

Page 37: and
1. Abigail writes and records music.
2. Abigail plays the keyboard and I play the drums.
3. Noah studies French and English.
4. Jackson trains on Mondays and Wednesdays.
5. I work on Fridays and go to a restaurant on Saturdays.

Page 39: or
1. We usually say "I like dancing **and** singing." I like both.
   We could say "I like dancing <u>or</u> singing." I am happy doing either one.
2. We usually say "I don't watch TV **or** read books." We could say "I don't watch TV <u>and</u> read books" if we are thinking about doing these things at the same time or one after the other.
3. We usually say "I don't like running **or** swimming." In some situations we could say "I don't like running <u>and</u> swimming." if we think about doing them one after the other.
4. We usually say "I don't know what to get for dinner... pasta **or** rice" I'm thinking and will choose one.
   We could say "...pasta <u>and</u> rice..." if we were thinking of having both.
5. "Can I have a hamburger **and** fries, please?" This is my decision. I want both. I don't want the staff to choose one.
6. We say "Do you play tennis **or** baseball?" to ask which one?
   We say "Do you play tennis <u>and</u> baseball?" to ask if someone plays both sports.
7. "I have two brothers **and** a sister." Using or sounds like I can't remember.

Page 41: but
1. I study English <u>and</u> I practice speaking it with my friends.
2. I can drive <u>but</u> I don't have a car.
3. Madison plays tennis <u>but</u> Chloe doesn't.
4. We live near the lake <u>and</u> we love it.
5. We usually say "This restaurant is good **but** expensive." We think good is positive and expensive is negative.
   We could say "This restaurant is good <u>and</u> expensive," if we generally think good things are expensive (same thought).
6. We usually say "I live in the city **and** I enjoy it." We think positively about both things. However, some people may think negatively about living in the city and positively about enjoying life. So we could also say "I live in the city <u>but</u> I enjoy it."
7. We usually say "I live in the city **but** I want to move to the country." We are talking about different things: city life and country life. We could say "I live in the city <u>and</u> I want to move to the country." These things are about the same topic—me!

5: Review of basic building blocks

Page 46-48: quiz
1. (c) I play baseball. (See page 2.)
2. (b) I don't watch TV. (See page 3.)
3. (a) Do you drink juice? (See page 3.)
4. (a) I'm at the hotel. (See page 4.)
5. (a) I'm at the beach.
   (c) I'm on the beach.
   (d) (a) or (c) (See page 4.)
   We say "I'm at the beach" to generally say where we are.
   We say "I'm on the beach" if the listener is at or near the beach. This extra little bit of information helps them find us. (I am not near the beach, but on it)
6. (b) I'm in the living room. A room has clear boundaries (walls). (See page 4.)
7. (c) It's on Saturday. Days do not have clear starts and ends. (See page 6.)
8. (a) It starts at 8PM. (a point in time)(See page 6.)
9. (b) I was born in January. Months have clear starts and ends. (See page 6.)
10. (b) I was born in 1992. Years have clear starts and ends. (See page 6.)
11. (b) I have black hair. My hair is part of me. (See page 13.)
12. (a) I'm home at 6. (See page 12.)
    (c) I go home at 6. (See page 19.)
    (d) I get home at 6. (See page 20.)
    (e) (a), (c) or (d)
    These sentences have different meanings and are all very useful.
13. (d) Do you live in Germany? We use do because we are asking about the verb: live, and asking about you: the person we are talking to. (See page 15.)
14. (c) Are you hungry? We use are because we are asking about the description: hungry, and asking about you: the person we are talking to. (See page 15.)
15. (b) Is she from Korea? We use is because we are asking about where she is from: Korea, and asking about she: one other person (female). (See page 15.)
16. (e) Does he read books? We use does because we are asking about the verb: read, and asking about he: one other person (male). (See page 15.)
17. (d) Do they read books? We use do because we are asking about the verb: read, and asking about they: more than one other person. (See page 15.)
18. (d) Do you have a brother? We use do because we are asking about the verb: have, and asking about you: the person we are talking to. (See page 15.)
19. (b) I don't have a sister. We use a. Many people have sisters, but I don't have one. (See page 22.)
20. (b) He helps me. We use me as an object. (See page 36.)
21. (a) We speak English. We use we as a subject. (See page 36.)
22. (c) Which one do you want?
    (d) Which ones do you want?
    (f) (c) and (d) (See page 35.)
    We use one for one thing and ones for more than one. We know what the thing

is or things are.
23. (b) Do you eat pumpkin? We cut the pumpkin and eat some of it. (See page 24.)
24. (a) Do you eat grapes? We eat whole grapes. (See page 24.)
25. (b) I like your furniture. Furniture describes a group of things. (See page 26.)
26. (a) I eat an egg every morning.
    (b) I eat eggs every morning.
    (c) I eat egg every morning.
    (d) all of the above. (See page 24.)
    We can think of one egg, more than one egg or just "egg".
27. (c) He plays the trumpet. (known instrument) (See page 28.)
28. (a) She drinks water. (In general)(See page 24.)
29. (c) Can you pass the pepper please? The listener knows which pepper you want. (See page 28.)
30. (d) Her name is Lucy.
    In most situations the simplest sentence is best. Her is the simplest word. We know who it refers to (Connor's sister). "His sister's name..." and "The sister's name..." may also be used. (See page 36.)

Verb forms

6: Tenses

Page 53: present form
1. We eat at work. **(a)** many times
2. They live in Sweden. **(b)** generally permanent
3. She works on Wednesdays. **(a)** many times
4. I'm hungry. **(c)** true now
5. She arrives at 3PM tomorrow. **(d)** future
   He eats breakfast at 7:30.
   This usually means **(a)** many times
   It could mean **(b)** if we are talking about someones schedule for the day.
6. She wins the race. **(e)** as it happens
7. You like swimming. **(b)** generally permanent
8. I play soccer on Sundays. **(a)** many times

Page 55: past form
1. I <u>went</u> to school yesterday.
2. I <u>didn't eat</u> breakfast this morning.
3. <u>Did you play</u> golf last week?
4. <u>Did he go</u> to work this morning?
5. They <u>didn't go</u> on vacation in July.
6. She <u>didn't live</u> in South Africa last year.
7. We <u>had</u> a good day on Sunday.

Page 56: Compare the past form and the present form.
   A: Where do you work?
1. B: I <u>work</u> in a restaurant, but I <u>didn't work</u> yesterday.
2. A: What <u>did you do</u> yesterday?
3. B: I <u>played</u> golf.
4. A: Where <u>did you play</u>? (thinking about yesterday)
   or Where <u>do you play</u>? (thinking about where you usually play)
5. B: What sport <u>do you like</u>?

6. A: I <u>don't like sport</u>. I <u>played</u> tennis last week, but I <u>didn't like</u> it. (last week) or ...but I <u>don't like</u> it .(generally)

7: Unfinished actions

Page 59: -ing form
1. I<u>'m not eating</u> breakfast this morning.
2. <u>Are you playing</u> golf next week?
3. <u>Is he working</u> this morning?
4. They <u>aren't going</u> on vacation in July.
5. She <u>isn't living</u> in South Africa.
6. We<u>'re swimming</u> in the lake on Sunday.
7. A: Where <u>are you going</u>?
   B: I<u>'m going</u> to school.
4, 5: using They're not and She's not is also fine.

Page 60: Compare the past form and am/are/is + -ing form.
1. A: What <u>are you doing</u> next weekend?
   B: Nothing. Why?
2. A: I<u>'m having</u> a barbecue. Do you want to come?
3. B: Yeah maybe. What <u>are you cooking</u>?
4. A: I <u>cooked</u> sausages and steak last time.
5. The steak <u>was</u> very popular,
6. so I<u>'m doing</u> that again.
7. B: Yeah, it <u>was</u> very tasty.
8. I <u>liked</u> the sausages last time too.
9. A: I<u>'m trying</u> something new this time.
10. I<u>'m making</u> hamburgers.
    B: Sounds good.
11. A: What <u>are you doing</u> now?
12. B: I<u>'m watching</u> TV.
13. A: Me too. I<u>'m watching</u> the rugby.
14. B: Who<u>'s winning</u>?
15. A: The All Blacks... They <u>won</u> last week too.

Page 61: Compare the present form and am/are/is + -ing form.
A: Hello.
B: Hi. How are you doing?
1. A: Great. I<u>'m walking</u> in the mountains.
2. I<u>'m not working</u> this week!
3. B: Sounds good. You usually <u>work</u> really hard. Are you on vacation?
4. A: Yeah. I<u>'m really enjoying</u> myself. How are you?
5. B: Not great, I <u>have</u> a headache. How's the weather?
6. A: It <u>doesn't usually snow</u> much at this time of year,
7. but it<u>'s snowing</u> a lot today,
8. so I<u>'m going</u> skiing tomorrow.
9. B: I'm envious. I <u>love</u> the mountains.
10. A: Sorry, I have to go. The bus <u>is coming</u>.
5: I have a headache. Person B is describing how they feel in the present. It is not an action they are doing.

Page 63: unfinished in the past
1. A: I tried to call you yesterday but you didn't answer your phone.
   B: Sorry, I didn't hear it. I <u>was watching</u> the football.
2. We packed our bags because we <u>were leaving</u> the next day.
3. I found my wallet when I <u>was cleaning</u>

my room.
4. We <u>were waiting</u> all day but the package didn't come.
5. Did you see Steve at the party? He <u>was wearing</u> a cowboy hat.
6. Did I tell you about the time I rescued a koala? I <u>was living</u> in Byron Bay and....
7. We <u>were listening</u> to music so we didn't hear the doorbell.
8. We renewed our passports because we <u>were going</u> abroad.

Page 64: Compare am/are/is + -ing form and was/were + -ing form.
1. A: What <u>are</u> you <u>doing</u> tomorrow?
2. B: I<u>'m applying</u> for a driver's license.
3. I <u>was going</u> to do it yesterday but
4. I <u>was studying</u> English and I lost track of the time.
5. A: I<u>'m living</u> in America now but
   or I <u>live</u> in America now.
6. I <u>was living</u> in Canada last year.
   or I <u>lived</u> in Canada last year.
7. B: What <u>were</u> you <u>doing</u> in Canada?
8. A: I <u>was working</u> at a ski field.
9. I <u>was saving</u> money because
10. I <u>was starting</u> college later in the year.
    A: How is college?
11. B: Boring. I<u>'m quitting</u> and
12. <u>moving</u> back to Canada next month.

Page 65: Compare the past form and was/were + -ing form.
1. A man <u>was sitting</u> next to me and
2. he <u>was talking</u> on the phone.
   These things were happening at the same time. We can also say "A man sat next to me and talked on the phone" if I was there reading first. (I was reading a book, then he sat.)
3. We <u>went</u> to the pet shop last week to buy a dog. *It finished. The next sentence is about what happened at the pet shop.*
4. There <u>were</u> so many cute dogs. *Describing the shop at that time in the past.*
5. Some of them <u>were scratching</u>. *Not finished. They probably kept doing this after we left. If we are only thinking about what they did at the time we could say "Some of them scratched".*
6. Some of them <u>were sniffing</u> each other. *Similar to 5.*
7. Then one dog caught my eye. *Finished. Happened at a point in time in the past.*
8. She <u>looked</u> at me. *(finished)* or She was looking at me. *(emphasizing a longer action.)*
9. I <u>knew</u> from the minute I saw her that *(describing the time in the past. What I knew at that point in time. We think of knowing as permanent, it never finishes.)*
10. She <u>was</u> the dog for me. *Describing what I knew at a time in the past.*
11. I <u>was driving</u> home from work yesterday and *(not finished)*
12. it <u>started</u> snowing. *The start is only a point in time, after that it was snowing.*

13. It <u>was snowing</u> so heavily that *(not finished)* or It <u>snowed</u> so heavily *(at the time)*
14. I <u>had</u> to stop the car because *(Finished. I stopped it then didn't have to do it anymore.)*
15. I <u>couldn't</u> see. *It was not possible at the time. (Can and could are covered in more detail in Options and possibilities 1)*

Page 66: -ing form: as a subject
1. <u>Cooking pasta</u> is easy.
2. <u>Smoking</u> causes health problems.
3. <u>Helping people</u> feels good.
4. Is <u>snowboarding</u> your favorite winter sport?
5. <u>Learning English</u> is fun.

Page 67: -ing form: as an object
1. I like <u>swimming</u>.
2. They love <u>eating</u> oysters.
3. He likes <u>playing darts</u>.
4. We love <u>running</u>.
5. She enjoys <u>watching sport</u>.

Page 68: go + -ing form
A: Hi.
B: Hi. How are you doing?
A: Good. How was your day?
1. B: Good. I <u>went shopping</u> this morning.
2. <u>Did</u> you <u>go shopping</u> this morning too?
3. A: No. I <u>went swimming</u> instead.
4. B: <u>Do</u> you <u>go swimming</u> every week?
   A: Yes, most weeks. Are you doing anything tonight?
5. A:. I<u>'m going clubbing</u>. Do you want to come?

8: Results of actions

Page 72: -en form
1. <u>Have you played</u> golf?
2. I<u>'ve sent</u> you a letter.
3. <u>Have you been</u> to Europe?
4. <u>Have you heard</u> the news?
5. She <u>hasn't lived</u> in South Africa.
6. I watched The Shawshank Redemption last night. <u>Have you seen</u> it?

Page 73: adding a length of time
1. A: Nice house! How long <u>have</u> you <u>lived</u> here?
2. B: I<u>'ve lived</u> here <u>for</u> about three years.
   A: You have a piano! Do you play it?
3. B: Yes, I<u>'ve played</u> it <u>since</u> I was a child. I love it.

Page 74: ever and never
A: I'm hungry. I <u>haven't eaten</u> since breakfast.
1. B: I <u>haven't eaten</u> either.
   A: Do you want to get something to eat?
2. B: Sure. <u>Have</u> you <u>ever had</u> Mexican food?
3. A: Yes. I<u>'ve had</u> tacos.
4. B: Have you <u>ever had</u> a burrito?
5. A: No. I<u>'ve never had</u> one.

Page 75: already and yet
1. Have you renewed your passport <u>yet</u>?
2. B: Yes, I have and I've <u>already</u> got a visa.

3. A: You got the visa <u>already</u>? That was quick.
4. B: Yeah. Have you booked the flights and the hotel <u>yet</u>?
5. A: Well, I've booked the flights but I haven't booked the hotel <u>yet</u>.
6. B: The flights were easy because they <u>already</u> had our details from when we booked last time.

Page 76: Compare have/has + -en form and the past form.
1. A: Have you ever been to South America?
   B: Yes, I have. Once.
2. A: When <u>did you go</u> there?
3. B: I <u>went</u> there last year with my family.

4. A: <u>Have you ever saved</u> someone's life?
5. B: No, I haven't, but I'<u>ve saved</u> a dog's life.
6. A: What <u>did you do</u>?
7. B: I <u>pulled</u> it out of the path of a moving car.

Page 77: Compare have/has + -en form and the present form.
1. A: What music <u>do you like</u>?
2. B: I <u>like</u> Muse.
3. A: <u>Have you heard</u> their new album?
   B: No, I haven't.
4. A: <u>Have you ever played</u> futsal?
   B: Yes, I have.
5. A: I <u>play</u> on Sundays. Come along.
6. A: Guess what? I'<u>ve got</u> a new car! There is a result in the present. I have it now. We can also say "I <u>got</u> a new car!" This happened in the recent past.
7. I <u>love</u> it.
8. I <u>drive</u> it every day, so
9. my husband <u>hasn't driven</u> it yet.
10. <u>Do you want</u> my old car?
11. No thanks, I'<u>ve just bought</u> a new car too. or I <u>just bought</u> a new car too. (recent past)

Page 78: Compare have/has + -en form and am/are/is and the -ing form.
1. A: <u>Have you ever been</u> to Alaska?
2. B: No, but I'<u>m going</u> there next month.
3. The oven <u>is heating up</u> so don't put the potatoes in yet.
4. Wait until it <u>has heated up</u>.
5. A: How long <u>have you been</u> here?
6. B: I'<u>ve been</u> here since Monday.
7. A: How long <u>are you staying</u>?
8. B: I'<u>m staying</u> for three weeks.
9. A: <u>Have you ever studied</u> English?
10. B: Yes! I'<u>m studying</u> English now.

9: Results of actions 2

Page 80: have got / have
1. I <u>have</u> a car.
2. My brother <u>has</u> a boat.
3. We <u>don't have</u> a jet ski.
4. We <u>have</u> a daughter.
5. <u>Do</u> you <u>have</u> a sister?

1. I'<u>ve got</u> a car.
2. My brother'<u>s got</u> a boat.
3. We <u>haven't got</u> a jet ski.

4. We'<u>ve got</u> a daughter.
5. <u>Have</u> you <u>got</u> a sister?

Page 81: have done / have to do
A: How are the preparations for our Asia trip coming along?
1. B: Good. How about you? <u>Have</u> you <u>got</u> your passport?
2. A: Not yet. <u>Do</u> I <u>have to get</u> a visa too? or <u>Have</u> I <u>got to get</u> a visa too?
3. B: Yes. You <u>have to get</u> a visa for China. or You'<u>ve got to get</u> a visa for China.
4. A: Ok. <u>Have</u> you <u>booked</u> the flights and the hotel?
5. B: I'<u>ve booked</u> the flights but I <u>still have to book</u> the hotel. or I'<u>ve still got to book</u> the hotel.

Page 82: adding to
1. He ___ has <u>**to**</u> go home.
2. She ___ wants ___ a rabbit.
3. They ___ jog <u>**to**</u> keep fit.
4. We ___ want <u>**to**</u> learn <u>**to**</u> speak English.

Page 83: adding to
1. He eats vegetables to lose weight.
2. I'm trying to find a solution.
3. They've gone to get some milk.
4. We're about to go home.
5. I have to work tomorrow.

Page 85: to or -ing?
1. I promise <u>to help</u> you.
2. I recommend <u>going</u> to the museum.
3. Sorry, I forgot <u>to get</u> a cake.
4. I don't like <u>running</u>. or I don't like <u>to run</u>.
5. Keep <u>going</u>.
6. What will they choose <u>to do</u>?
7. We're planning <u>to go</u> to the theater.
8. Stop <u>writing</u> and hand in your exam!

Page 87: results in the past
1. Everyone got lost except Andrea because she'<u>d been</u> there when she was a child.
2. I was late to work because I'<u>d been</u> stuck in traffic for two hours.
3. When I got home, I realized I'<u>d forgotten</u> my bag.
4. After the rain <u>had stopped</u>, the children went out to play.
5. She got good grades because she'<u>d worked</u> so hard on all her assignments.
6. I tried papaya the other day. I <u>hadn't had</u> it before. or I'<u>d never had</u> it before.
Note: It is common to use the past form in many situations that we can use had + -en form. We are thinking about a time in the past, then another time in the past. We don't need to make it clear that something happened before something else. The order they happened is obvious.
1. Everyone got lost except Andrea because she <u>went</u> there when she was a child.
2. I was late to work because I <u>was</u> stuck in traffic for two hours.
3. When I got home, I realized I <u>forgot</u> my bag.
4. After the rain <u>stopped</u>, the children went out to play.
5. She got good grades because she <u>worked</u> so hard on all her assignments.

6. The past form doesn't fit this situation because we aren't talking about two things that happened in the past. We are talking one time: when I ate papaya, and my experience at the time.

Page 88 : Compare had + -en form and the past form.
1. I <u>finished</u> work late and
2. <u>rushed</u> to the train station, hoping to catch the last train.
3. Luckily, the train <u>hadn't left</u>.
4. I <u>put</u> my hand in my pocket but
5. <u>couldn't</u> find my wallet.
6. I <u>had left</u> it in the office. or I <u>left</u> it in the office.
7. Then I <u>realized</u>.
8. I <u>had left</u> my phone in the office too. or I <u>left</u> my phone in the office too.
9. This is a real problem, I <u>had done</u> the same thing the week before too. or I <u>did</u> the same thing the week before too.

10: Shifting focus

Page 91: be + -en form
1. My guitar <u>was made</u> in Indonesia.
2. Christmas <u>is celebrated</u> in December.
3. The Starry Night <u>was painted</u> by Vincent Van Gogh.
4. The lost dog <u>was returned</u> to his owner.
5. Her music <u>is enjoyed</u> by people all over the world. (or *was enjoyed* if she is no longer popular)
6. The telephone <u>was invented</u> by Alexander Graham Bell.
7. The winner <u>was announced</u> last night.

Page 92: with other sentence patterns
1. A meeting has been arranged for Thursday.
2. The incident is going to be investigated.
3. Your application hasn't been received.
4. A new shopping center is being built.
5. Your credit card has been declined.
6. Successful applicants are being notified by email.
7. Other options are not being considered.

Page 93: get + -en form
1. My car is getting fixed next week.
2. When are we getting paid?
3. The dog didn't get hit by a car.
4. There was an accident, but nobody got hurt.
5. The sheets didn't get washed.
6. The pizza got delivered to the wrong address.
7. I got accepted for an interview.
Note: We can use *be* instead of *get* in these situations. Using *be* usually sounds softer and more formal.
1. My car is being fixed next week.
2. When are we being paid?
3. The dog wasn't hit by a car.
4. There was an accident, but nobody was hurt.
5. The sheets weren't washed.
6. The pizza was delivered to the wrong address.

7. I was accepted for an interview.

Page 94: feelings
1. They had so many chances but they couldn't score. It was really <u>disappointing</u>.
2. The news was very <u>shocking</u>.
3. This drink is really <u>refreshing</u>.
4. The new album comes out tomorrow. I'm really <u>excited</u>.
5. I was <u>shocked</u> when I read what happened.
6. I just had a massage. I feel <u>relaxed</u>.
7. I watched a movie on Saturday. It was <u>inspiring</u>.

11: Putting it all together

Page 98: Compare have + been + -ing and have + -en form
1. A: Hi. What <u>have</u> you been doing this week?
2. B: I<u>'ve been playing</u> a lot of guitar.
3. A: <u>Have</u> you <u>written</u> any new songs? (Do you have anything new **now**?)
    or <u>Did</u> you <u>write</u> any new songs? (Did you write anything **earlier this week**?)
    or <u>Have</u> you <u>been writing</u> any new songs? (recent activity, result in the present)
4. B: I<u>'ve been working</u> on a new one but it isn't finished yet. (recent activity, result in the present, but not finished)
    or I<u>'m working</u> on a new one but it isn't finished yet. (not finished)
5. <u>Have</u> you <u>heard</u> the song I wrote last week? (Do you know it **now**)
    <u>Did</u> you <u>hear</u> the song I wrote last week? (I expect that you listened to it in the **past**)
6. A: Yeah, I listened to it this morning. It's so catchy. I<u>'ve been humming</u> the melody all day.
7. How about you? What <u>have</u> you <u>been doing</u>?
8. A: I<u>'ve been</u> sick for the last few days.
9. So, I<u>'ve been lying</u> around the house, <u>sleeping</u> and <u>watching</u> TV.
10. B: How long <u>have</u> you <u>been feeling</u> sick?
    A: Since Tuesday.

Page 99: Compare have + been + -ing and am/are/is + -ing form
1. A: Hi. It's been a while. What <u>have</u> you <u>been doing</u> recently?
2. B: Lots. We<u>'re moving</u> to Ireland next week. (not finished - happening in the future)
3. So we<u>'ve been packing</u> and <u>getting</u> ready to move. (recent activity, not finished)
    or So we<u>'re packing</u> and <u>getting</u> ready to move. (not finished)
4. A: Great! I<u>'m living</u> in Ireland now! (not finished - temporary)
    or I <u>live</u> in Ireland now! (generally permanent)
5. Which part of Ireland <u>are</u> you <u>moving</u> to? (not finished - happening in the future)
    B: Dublin.
6. A: I<u>'m living</u> in Dublin!
    or I <u>live</u> in Dublin.
7. B: How long <u>have</u> you <u>been living</u> there?

(result in the present, not finished)
or How long <u>have</u> you <u>lived</u> there? (result in the present)
8. A: About six months. I<u>'ve been working</u> at a hotel but I don't really like it. (result in the present, not finished)
    or I<u>'m working</u> at a hotel. (not finished)
9. So, I<u>'ve been looking</u> for a new job for the last few weeks. (result in the present, not finished)
10. B: How long <u>have you been working</u> at the hotel? (result in the present, not finished)
    or How long <u>have you worked</u> at the hotel? (result in the present)

Page 101: Compare had + been + -ing...
1. A: Last time I saw you you said you<u>'d been studying</u> Spanish, how is that coming along? (Not finished with a result in the past: last time I saw you you had something to talk about.)
    or Last time I saw you you said you <u>were studying</u> Spanish... (not finished at a time in the past)
    or Last time I saw you you said you <u>studied</u> Spanish... (general truth at a time in the past. This sounds like I don't know you well. I only know some basics like the fact that you studied Spanish.)
2. B: It's going really well. I had a test last month so I<u>'d been reading</u> books in Spanish and <u>practicing</u> with my tutor every day leading up to that.
    or I <u>was reading</u> books in Spanish and <u>practicing</u> with my tutor...
    or I <u>read</u> books in Spanish and <u>practiced</u> with my tutor...
    A: So how did the test go?
3. B: I think I'll pass. How's it all going with you? Last time you said you <u>were looking</u> for a new job. (not finished in the past)
    or ...you<u>'d been looking</u> for a new job.
4. A: Yeah, I<u>'d been looking</u> for about five months. (result in the past: five months of looking, not finished)
    or I <u>was looking</u> for about five months. (not finished at the point of time in my story)
    or I <u>looked</u> for about five months. (finished now)
5. I<u>'d been taking</u> interview after interview and was getting nowhere, but then I got a call back for a job in a warehouse.
    or I <u>was taking</u> interview after interview...
    or I<u>'d taken</u> interview after interview...
    or I <u>took</u> interview after interview...

12: Review of verb forms

Page 106-108: quiz
1. *have.*   (a) (See page 13.)
2. *be.*   (b) (See page 12.)
3. I play tennis on Mondays.
    (a) last Monday
    (b) next Monday
    (c) probably both (a) and (b) and others (See page 52.)
4. We went shopping on Wednesday.

(a) last Wednesday (See page 54.)
5. She's going cycling on Saturday.
    (b) next Saturday (See page 58.)
6. He's worked on Sunday.
    (d) we don't know which Sunday
    It could be any Sunday in the past. (See page 70.)
7. (b) <u>Do</u> you live in Malaysia now? (See page 52.)
8. (d) <u>Did</u> you watch TV yesterday? (See page 54.)
9. (c) <u>Have</u> you lived in Brazil? (See page 70.)
10. (a) <u>Are</u> you watching TV? (See page 58.)
11. (c) <u>Have</u> you eaten lunch? (See page 70.)
12. (d) <u>Did</u> you sleep well last night? (See page 54.)
13. Which of these sentences can be used to talk about tomorrow?
    (b) He's walking home. (See page 58.)
14. Which of these sentences can be used to talk about yesterday?
    (b) He walked home. (See page 54.)
15. Which of these sentences can be used to talk about today?
    (a) He walked home.
    (b) He's walking home.
    (c) He's walked home.
    (d) all of the above (See page 104.)
16. Which of these sentences can be used to talk about every day?
    (a) He walks home. (See page 52.)
17. She's cooking dinner. (b) is (See page 58.)
18. She's cooked dinner. (a) has (See page 70.)
19. Which of these refers to the future?
    (a) The show starts at 10:00.
    (c) The show is starting at 10:00.
    (d) both (a) and (c). (See page 104.)
20. What are you doing tomorrow?
    (c) I'm going fishing. (See page 58.)
21. What did you do yesterday?
    (b) I went fishing. (See page 54.)
22. Do you have any brothers or sisters?
    (a) Yes, I have one sister.
    (b) Yes, I've got one sister.
    (d) (a) and (b) (See page 80.)
    Note: (c) isn't very good in this situation because the question isn't about you, it's about your brothers and sisters.
23. What do you drink with breakfast?
    (a) I have a cup of coffee. (generally: every day)(See page 80.)
24. Do you have a bicycle?
    (c) Yes, I do. (See page 3.) (See page 80.)
    We could also answer with a full sentence using have got. 'Yes, I've got one'. We need an object (one).
25. Do you like Taiwan?
    (a) I don't know, I haven't been there. (See page 70.)
    (b) I don't know, I've never been there. (See page 74.)
    (c) Yes, I do. I went there last year. (See page 54.)
    (d) all of the above.
26. am
    (a) I <u>am</u> a child. (See page 14.)
    (b) I <u>am</u> hungry. (See page 14.)

27. have
(a) I <u>have</u> a child. (See page 13.)
28. jogging
(a) I'm <u>jogging</u>. (See page 58.)
(b) <u>Jogging</u> is fun. (See page 66.)
(c) I like <u>jogging</u>. (See page 67.)
(d) all of the above.
29. jogged
(a) I've <u>jogged</u>. (See page 70.)
30. (b) Do you <u>like</u> pizza? (See page 16.)
31. (d) Have you <u>seen</u> my keys? (See page 70.)
32. (a) Did you <u>eat</u> my pasta? (See page 54.)

(c) I am talking. (See page 58.)
(d) all of the above.

Options and Possibilities

13: Options and possibilities 1

Page 113: can/could

1. <u>Can</u> you drive a car? (asking about ability) In some situations we might say "<u>Could</u> you drive a car?" We are thinking hypothetically; I'm making a request. I want you to drive one. "<u>Can</u> you drive a car?" can also be used in these situations.
2. A: Where are they?
   B: I don't know. They <u>could</u> be stuck in traffic or something. (hypothetically)
3. He <u>could</u> play the piano when he was six. (past)
4. I <u>can</u> come to see you tomorrow. It is possible for me.
   I <u>could</u> come to see you tomorrow. It is hypothetically possible, I don't know what is possible for you.

Page 114: real or hypothetical?

1. Hi, <u>can</u> I help you? (in the real future) <u>Could</u> I help you? (in the hypothetical future.) We often use can in this situation because we refer to the real future. I can really help you.
2. Yes, <u>could</u> I have a coffee please.
   or Yes, <u>can</u> I have a coffee please.
3. <u>Could</u> you please make it extra strong?
   or <u>Can</u> you please make it extra strong?
4. Ok. <u>Can</u> I get you anything else?
   or <u>Could</u> I get you anything else? (as in 1)
5. Yes, <u>could</u> I have some cake, please.
   or Yes, <u>can</u> I have some cake, please.

Page 115: Could have done

1. A: Why? What <u>could</u> you <u>have done</u> differently?
2. B: I <u>could have answered</u> the questions faster and I <u>could have been</u> more direct.
   A: Do you think you'll get the job?
3. B: I <u>could get</u> it, but I'm not very confident. (future)
   or I <u>could have got</u> it... (the decision was made in the past but I don't know what they decided.)
4. A: Yeah, you don't look very well presented. You <u>could have worn</u> a tie.

14: Options and possibilities 2

Page 119: will/would

1. I<u>'ll</u> cook dinner tomorrow. (real)
2. I<u>'d</u> cook dinner tomorrow but I can't because I have to work. (hypothetical)
3. When I was young we<u>'d</u> often go swimming in summer. (past)
4. A: Imagine winning the lottery. What <u>would</u> you do? (hypothetical)
   B: I<u>'d</u> buy a new car for my mother. I<u>'d</u> also give money to charity.
5. A: What time <u>will</u> Alex get here? (real)
   B: He<u>'ll</u> be here in about an hour.
6. I<u>'ll</u> have the pasta, please. (real)

Page 120: will be doing

1. Don't come next month, we<u>'ll be traveling</u> Asia then.
2. We have to go now. Fred <u>will be waiting</u>.
3. You<u>'ll be working</u> hard in the office tomorrow, I<u>'ll be sitting</u> on the beach.
4. The next time you see me, I<u>'ll be wearing</u> a new uniform.

Note: Using *will* in questions 1 and 2 shows us we are thinking about options or possibilities. If we know for certain, we might not think about options and possibilities and not use *will*. "We're traveling Asia..." "Fred is waiting".

Sentence 3 works better with *will* because we want the listener to think about the possibility of sitting on a beach instead of working. We can also form this sentence without *will* but it simply says what is happening: "You're working hard in the office tomorrow but I'm sitting on the beach."

We use *will* with sentence 4 because we don't know exactly when you will see me. There are possibilities. If we know the exact time we can simply say what is happening without *will*. "On Monday, I'm wearing a new uniform."

Page 121: will have done

1. Come in September, we<u>'ll have been</u> back for a while then. We use *will* because we are thinking about possibilities and saying when is good for you to come.
2. We have to go now. Fred's flight <u>will have landed</u>. If we know that Fred's flight has already landed, we can also say "Fred's flight has landed" without *will*.
3. I'm reading a book now, but I<u>'ll have finished</u> it by the time you get here. There are possibilities. We don't know exactly when I'll finish it.
4. They<u>'ll have fixed</u> the problem by now. There are possibilities. We aren't certain that they have fixed it. We don't know exactly when they fixed it. *By* means it could be any time before now. If we are certain, we can simply say what has happened without *will* and *by* "They <u>have fixed</u> the problem."

Note: When we talk about what happens before something else in the future (as in 1 and 3), there are usually options and possibilities relating to how the events might unfold. So we generally use *will*.

Page 122: would like

Waiter: The house red is very good.
1. Customer A: We<u>'ll</u> have a bottle of that, please.
2. Waiter: What <u>would</u> you like to eat?
3. Customer A: I<u>'d</u> like the steak.
4. Customer B: I<u>'ll</u> have the chicken curry.
5. Waiter: <u>Would</u> you like any salads? Customer B: No, thank you.
6. Waiter: Ok, so a bottle of house red, the steak and the chicken curry. Your meals <u>will</u> be ready soon.
   Customer A: Thank you.

Page 123: would have done

A: I didn't see you at the barbecue yesterday.
1. B: I didn't go. I <u>would have gone</u> but I didn't have enough money.
   A: I could have lent you some.
2. B: I <u>wouldn't have enjoyed</u> myself anyway. I had a bad headache.
3. A: <u>Would</u> you like to go out for a drink tonight?
4. B: I <u>would</u>, but I already have plans. How about tomorrow night?

Page 125: shall/should

1. I went into someone's house with my shoes on. I <u>should have taken</u> them off at the door. (a better option in the past, a better result in the present)
2. A: Haha, really? You wore your shoes inside? Everyone knows you <u>shouldn't do</u> that! (hypothetically the right thing)
3. B: I know. I just forgot. You <u>should bow</u> to people too. (hypothetically the right thing)
4. You <u>shouldn't try</u> to shake hands. (hypothetically the right thing)
5. A: Yeah ok. Anyway, <u>shall</u> we get a coffee? (the right thing in the real present-future) or Anyway, <u>should</u> we get a coffee? (hypothetically the right thing)
6. B: You <u>should have asked</u> me earlier. I've just had one. (a better option in the past, a better result in the present)

15: Options and possibilities 3

Page 129: may/might

1. I knocked but there is no answer. They <u>might be</u> asleep or they <u>might have gone</u> out.
   or They <u>may be</u> asleep or they <u>may have gone</u> out.
2. I found $50. I <u>might go</u> out for lunch today.
   or I <u>may go</u> out for lunch today.
3. I'm not feeling well so I <u>might not be</u> able to make it to dinner.
   or I'm not feeling well so I <u>may not be</u> able to make it to dinner.
4. I can't find my phone. I <u>might have left</u> it at the restaurant.
   or I <u>may have left</u> it at the restaurant.
5. They didn't put the dishes away. They <u>might not know</u> where they go.

or They <u>may not know</u> where they go.
6. Olivia isn't at work. She <u>might have quit</u>.
   or She <u>may have quit</u>.
7. I <u>might take</u> a break.
   or I <u>may take</u> a break.

Page 131: permission- can, could and may

1. A: Do you have any plans this evening?
   B: Maybe. Levi and I <u>might</u> go to a restaurant.
   or Levi and I <u>may</u> go to a restaurant.
   We use may or might. We have more than one option.
2. Hey Amy, <u>can</u> I borrow your car?
   or Hey Amy, <u>could</u> I borrow your car?
   or Hey Amy, <u>may</u> I borrow your car?
   We use can/could to ask if this one thing is an option. We use may to ask if it is one of our options (we have more than one option). Might is too formal for this situation.
3. <u>Can</u> I take your order?
   or <u>Could</u> I take your order?
   or <u>May</u> I take your order?
   Can is very common in this situation; we ask if it is a real option.
   We can also use could (hypothetical) or may (referring to more than one option) to be less direct and a little more polite
4. <u>Can</u> you do me a favor?
   or <u>Could</u> you do me a favor?
   We use can/could. We are asking if it is an option. There is only one option we are thinking about. We want it done.
5. It looks like it <u>might</u> rain.
   or It looks like it <u>could</u> rain.
   or It looks like it <u>may</u> rain.
   We say there is more than one possibility and this is one of them (may/might). We say that hypothetically, it is a possibility—in reality something else may happen (could). We don't use can because we are thinking about more than one possibility, (rain, sunshine, cloudy: these things are all possible).
6. <u>Can</u> I help you with your bags?
   or <u>Could</u> I help you with your bags?
   or <u>May</u> I help you with your bags?
   We use can/could to ask if this one thing is an option. We use may to ask if it is one of our options (we have more than one option). In a very formal situation someone might use might. "Pardon me sir, might I assist you with your bags?"
7. <u>Can</u> I please have some dessert?
   or <u>Could</u> I please have some dessert?
   or <u>May</u> I please have some dessert?
   (as with 6)

Page 133: must/must have done

1. A: I lived in downtown New York in 2010.
   B: Sounds good. It <u>must have been</u> convenient. (past)
2. We've been traveling all day. We <u>must be</u> almost home. (present)
3. We <u>mustn't leave</u> the door open.
   (generally: present-future)
4. Your hands are dirty. You <u>must wash</u> your hands. (present)
5. His hands are clean. He <u>must have washed</u> his hands. (past)

6. I knocked but there's no answer. They <u>must be</u> out. (present)
7. I knocked but there's no answer. They <u>must have gone</u> out. (past)

Page 135: must, have to, have got to, mustn't or don't have to

1. You <u>must be</u> here on time tomorrow.
   or You <u>have to be</u> here on time tomorrow.
   or You<u>'ve got to be</u> here on time tomorrow.
2. A: I'll see you tomorrow. What should I bring?
   B: You <u>don't have to bring</u> anything. We've got it covered.
   It is ok if you do it or if you don't.
3. I <u>have to get</u> a present for my nephew.
   or I<u>'ve got to get</u> a present for my nephew.
   or I <u>must get</u> a present for my nephew.
4. We <u>mustn't forget</u> to call Jane. *If it doesn't happen, there will be negative consequences.*
5. You <u>don't have to wash</u> everything by hand. We have a dishwasher. *It is ok if you do it or if you don't.*
6. I <u>have to go</u> shopping this afternoon.
   or I<u>'ve got to go</u> shopping this afternoon.
   or I <u>must go</u> shopping this afternoon.

Page 138: must, may, can't, might, maybe or could

1. A: I can't find my shoes.
   B: You always leave them by the front door. They <u>must</u> be there somewhere.
   or (if we are less certain): They <u>might</u> be there somewhere. or They <u>may</u> be there somewhere. or They <u>could</u> be there somewhere.
2. A: I can't find my laptop.
   B: It <u>might</u> be in the bedroom, you sometimes use it there.
   or It <u>may</u> be in the bedroom...
   or It <u>could</u> be in the bedroom...
3. A: I can't find my pen.
   B: You just had it so it <u>can't</u> be far away.
   or You just had it so it <u>mustn't</u> be far away.
4. Wow! What an amazing house. They <u>must</u> be rich.
5. A: Can we meet up tomorrow?
   It <u>could</u> be ok. Let me check with my husband.
   or It <u>might</u> be ok.
   or It <u>may</u> be ok.
6. A: Can we meet up tomorrow?
   <u>Maybe</u>. Let me check with my husband.
7. A: The air conditioner is making strange noises.
   B: That <u>can't</u> be good. We should get it repaired.

Page 138: must, had better or should

1. Come and look at this bird. It'll probably go soon, you<u>'d better</u> come quick!
   You can also use must but it is strong for this situation. It's not really about what is right so should doesn't fit well either. Had better is good because hypothetically if you want to see the bird, your only option is to come quick.

2. He got me a present for my birthday so I<u>'d better</u> get him something. *Hypothetically my only option. Not getting something is not an option.*
   or I <u>should</u> get him something. *The right thing to do.*
   or I <u>must</u> get him something. *My only option.*
3. All staff <u>must</u> wear suits. Anyone who doesn't wear a suit will be fired.
   Must is the best word for this situation. Must is strong. One option. If you don't do it there are negative consequences.
4. He was so sick, he <u>should</u> have died but he recovered and now he's healthy again.
   If everything went as expected, he would have died.
5. We're getting busier all the time. We <u>should</u> hire some more staff.
   Hypothetically, the right thing to do.
   or We<u>'d better</u> hire some more staff.
   Hypothetically our only option.
   or We <u>must</u> hire some more staff.
   Realistically our only option. (strong)
6. We'll leave at 5:00 sharp. You<u>'d better not</u> be late. *Hypothetically your only option.*
   or You <u>mustn't</u> be late. *Realistically your only option. (strong)*

16: if

Page 141: if

1. I'm not rich, but if <u>I was</u> rich, I'<u>d buy</u> a big house. (past forms: hypothetical)
2. If <u>I were</u> you, I'<u>d get</u> a new job.
   (past forms: hypothetical)
3. <u>We'll go</u> shopping if it <u>rains</u> tomorrow. If it <u>doesn't rain</u>, <u>we'll go</u> fishing.
   (present forms: real)
4. A: Shall we do something tonight?
   B: Maybe, but I might have to work late. If I <u>finish</u> on time, I'<u>ll call</u> you.
   (present forms: real)
5. If you <u>could have</u> any super power, what power <u>would</u> you have?
   What <u>would</u> you do if you <u>had</u> super powers? *(past forms: hypothetical)*
6. A: Are you going out tonight?
   B: I'd like to, but I'm feeling a bit sick. I <u>won't</u> go out if <u>I'm</u> still feeling sick.
   (present forms: real)
7. A: It's great to see you out. Are you still feeling sick?
   B: I'm feeling great! I <u>wouldn't</u> be out if <u>I was</u> feeling sick.
   (past forms: hypothetical)

Page 143: would have... if...

1. We <u>would have gone</u> shopping if it <u>had rained</u> yesterday.
   or We <u>would have gone</u> shopping if it <u>rained</u> yesterday.
2. If it <u>hadn't rained</u> we <u>would have gone</u> fishing.
   or If it <u>didn't rain</u> we<u>'d have gone</u> fishing.
3. Sorry I didn't call you. I had to work overtime. If I <u>had finished</u> on time, I <u>would have called</u> you.
   or If I <u>finished</u> on time, I'<u>d have called</u> you.
4. A: Did you go out last night?

B: No, but I <u>would have gone</u> out if I <u>hadn't been</u> feeling sick.
or I'd <u>have gone</u> out if I <u>wasn't</u> feeling sick.
or I'd have gone out if I <u>weren't</u> feeling sick.

5. A: You went out last night? Were you still feeling sick?
B: I felt great! I <u>wouldn't have gone</u> out if I <u>had been</u> feeling sick.
or I <u>wouldn't have gone</u> out if I <u>was</u> feeling sick.
or I <u>wouldn't have gone</u> out if I <u>were</u> feeling sick.

Page 144: if polite expressions

There are many possible answers to these questions. Any of the polite expressions can be used. Check your use of *could* and *if*.

1. If it's not too much trouble, <u>could</u> you help me with something.
2. Do you mind <u>if</u> I use your phone?
or If you don't mind, <u>could</u> I use your phone?
3. If you have time, <u>could</u> you buy some milk.
4. If it's not to much trouble, <u>could</u> you do me a favor?
5. If it's ok, <u>could</u> I take the day off tomorrow?
or Is it ok if <u>if</u> I take the day off tomorrow?
6. Do you mind <u>if</u> we meet at 10 tomorrow instead of 9?
or If it's ok with you, <u>could</u> we meet at 10 tomorrow instead of 9?
7. If it's not too much trouble, <u>could</u> you cook dinner tonight?
or Would it be ok <u>if</u> you cook dinner tonight?

17: Review of options and possibilities

Page 148-149: quiz

1. I am unsure.
(c) I may see you tomorrow. (See page 128.)
2. I have decided.
(b) I will see you tomorrow. (See page 118.)
3. It is possible.
(a) I can see you tomorrow. (See page 112.)
4. It is the only option.
(d) I must see you tomorrow. (See page 132.)
5. What is the right thing to do?
(I want your opinion)
(c) Shall we leave soon? (See page 124.)
6. Are you hot? _____ I open the window?
(a) Shall (See page 124.)
(b) Should (See page 124.)
(c) Can (See page 114.)
(d) Could (See page 114.)
(e) Any of the above.
We ask if it is right (*shall/should*) or if it is an option (*can/could*). *May* is also used in this situation.
7. (d) If you <u>could</u> have any car in the world,

what car would you have? (if it is possible, hypothetically) (See page 113.)

8. If you can't move your car...
(b) I'll call a tow truck. (See page 112.)
If it is **not possible** I'll get the tow truck to move it for you.
9. If you won't move your car...
(a) I'll call the police. (See page 118.)
If you **refuse** (strongly decide not to) to move it I'll get the police involved.
10. Can I get you anything to drink?
(b) I'd like a cup of coffee. (See page 122.)
11. Are you ready to order?
(a) I'll have a chicken sandwich. (See page 122.)
12. Would you like anything else?
(c) Could I have some fries, please?
(asking if it is possible) (See page 122.))
13. Would you like a dessert?
(a) Can I have some ice cream, please?
(b) May I have some ice cream, please?
(c) Could I have some ice cream, please?
(d) Any of the above. (See page 122.)
(See page 130.)
14. What will you be doing in 10 years?
(a) I'll be living in the mountains. (See page 118.)
(c) I may be living in the mountains. (See page 128.)
(d) I might be living in the mountains. (See page 128.)
(e) (a), (c) or (d)
(depending on how certain we are)
15. What would you be doing if you didn't have to work?
(b) I'd be living in the mountains.
(a hypothetical decision)(See page 119.)
16. I lost my job last week. I don't have much money,...
(a) I have to find another job soon. (See page 134.)
(b) I must find another job soon. (See page 134.)
(c) I'll find another job soon. (See page 118.)
(d) Any of the above.
I can say it is required (*have to* or *must*) or make the decision to do it (*will*)
17. Can I see you tomorrow?
(c) Sorry, I'll be on vacation. (See page 118.) We consider possibilities and say what we think. However, we don't need to consider possibilities in this situation. We can also say "Sorry, I'm on vacation (then)", without *will*.
18. A: Where are my glasses?
B: You just had them, they _____ be far away.
(a) can't (See page 136.)
19. The bus will be late...
(a) if there is a lot of traffic. (See page 140.) It is possible that the bus is late: The bus will be late. We describe this situation in the present-future: there is a lot of traffic.
20. I'd tell them the truth...
(c) if I was you. (See page 140.)
We use the past form, this is hypothetical. Note: if I were you. is also possible. (See page 143.)

21. I would have got you lunch...
(a) if you'd asked me earlier
(b) if you asked me earlier.
(d) (a) or (b) (See page 142.)

Page 150: can/could, shall/should or will/would

The answers given below are what I would say but there are many options. Think about the different words and the subtle differences in meaning.

1. A: Where <u>shall</u> we go? (what do you think is right?)
or should or can or could or will
2. B: We <u>could</u> go to Italy. (hypothetically possible)
or should (suggestion: hypothetical)
or will (strong: decision)
3. A: That <u>could</u> be good.
or would (hypothetical: what I think)
4. I'd like to go to Rome.
5. My aunt lives there and I really <u>should</u> visit her. (I haven't been for a long time) We could also say, "I really <u>want to</u> visit her." It's what I want.
6. We <u>could</u> probably stay with her for a few days.
or can
7. B: We <u>can</u> go to Rome first, then other parts of Italy? (This is more real, the plan is developing.)
or will or could or should or would
8. How long <u>can</u> we travel for? (what is possible) or **will** (what has been decided) or shall (what do you think is right?)
A: One week.
9. So, we <u>could</u> stay in Rome for a few days, then go to Milan or Venice?
or can (possible) or will (decided) or should (right for the aunt) or would (hypothetical: if that is the plan...)
10. B: I'd like to go to another country for a few days, maybe Sweden?
11. A: I think we <u>should</u> go somewhere closer to Italy. How about Spain? (hypothetically right)
12. B: Yes, I'd like to go to Spain.
13. I <u>can</u> speak some Spanish.
or could (hypothetical, if we go) or should (right: I need to practice it) or will (decided)
14. A: Great, you <u>can</u> speak with the locals.
or could or should
15. It <u>would</u> be good practice for you. (hypothetically what I think)
or could or should
16. B: I <u>could</u> translate for you.
or can (possible, real) or will (decided) or should (right)
17. A: When <u>shall</u> we go? How about summer? or should or can or will
18. B: That'd be good. or will (prediction) or could (hypothetically possible) or should (if all goes right)
19. We <u>can</u> go to the beach. or could or will or should
20. A: Ok great, so we'll go to Rome for a few days, then we'll have a few days in Spain. (what we have decided)
21. B: Sounds great. I <u>can't</u> wait. I really want to go, it seems like waiting is not possible.

313

1. B: We <u>might</u> go to the cinema. I'm not sure. or may or could
2. I'<u>d</u> like to see a good action movie.
3. <u>Would</u> you like to come?
   A: Sure, why not.
   later...
4. A: I'm just finishing work and I'<u>ll</u> leave the office in five minutes. or can or should
5. <u>Can</u> you meet me outside? or could or would or will (strong)
6. B: Ok, where <u>should</u> I wait? or shall or can
7. A: <u>Can</u> you meet me in front of the office? It's number 37, Main St. or could or will (strong)

   later...
8. B: (to self) Main St... It <u>should</u> be around here... or must or will
9. Number 37, this <u>must</u> be the place. or should or will

   later...
10. A: Sorry, I'<u>ll</u> be a bit late.(clear) or might (soft) or may (soft)
11. <u>Can</u> you go to the cinema and get the tickets? or could
12. I'<u>ll</u> be there in the next ten minutes. or should (if all goes right)
13. <u>Would</u> you be able to buy some drinks and snacks? (hypothetical)
14. B: Ok. <u>should</u> I get some chips?
    A: Yes, that sounds good. or shall

Future and past

18: Ways of talking about the future

Page 152: ways of talking about the future
1. A: What time does the show start?
   B: It <u>starts</u> at 7:30.
   or It'<u>s starting</u> at 7:30.
2. We'<u>re having</u> a surprise party for Julia.
3. A: <u>Are</u> you <u>coming</u> running tomorrow?
   B: Sorry, I can't. I <u>have</u> an appointment.
4. The flight <u>departs</u> at 11:54.
   or The flight <u>is departing</u> at 11:54.
5. A: I'<u>m going</u> on vacation next week.
   B: Great. Where <u>are</u> you <u>going</u>?
6. Billy and Sandra have changed their plans. They <u>aren't coming</u> tomorrow.
   or They'<u>re not coming</u> tomorrow.

Page 156: will/be going to
1. A: Can you please wash the car?
   B: Yes, I'<u>ll</u> do it this afternoon. (thinking about options and deciding)
   or I'<u>m going</u> to do it this afternoon. (already decided)
2. A: Where do you want to go for our summer vacation?
   B: I want to go to the Netherlands.
   A: Me too. We'<u>ll</u> go to the Netherlands then. (thinking about options and deciding)
3. A: What are your plans for the summer?
   B: We'<u>re going to</u> go to the Netherlands.

(saying what has already been decided)
   or We'<u>ll</u> go to the Netherlands. (quickly thinking about other options and saying what we previously decided)
4. Excuse me, do you know how to use the photocopier?
   B: Yes, I'<u>ll</u> show you. (thinking about options and deciding)
5. A: Can you help me with the computer?
   B: I'<u>m going to</u> show Lily how to use the photocopier now, so I'<u>ll</u> help you after that.
6. A: Why is she so happy?
   B: She just found out she's pregnant. She'<u>s going to</u> have a baby.
7. It's my birthday so my wife <u>is going to</u> take me to a concert tonight.
   or It's my birthday so my wife <u>will</u> take me to a concert tonight. (my wife thought about options and decided)
8. A: Are you free on Sunday afternoon?
   B: No, sorry. I'<u>m going to</u> go hiking. (plan)
   Note: We use *will* in this situation with *be* "I'll be hiking (at the time)."
9. A: Robert has an allergy so we can't have seafood tonight.
   B: Ok, I'<u>ll</u> cook chicken instead. (thinking about options and deciding)
10. A: Why is he looking for his gloves?
    B: He'<u>s going to</u> go skiing. (already decided)

Page 157: Which do you think is the best answer?
1. There's nothing for dinner... I know!
   (a) I order a pizza. (not scheduled)
   (b) I'll order a pizza. (thinking about options and deciding)
   (c) I'm ordering a pizza. (not a future unfinished action until we think of it)
   (d) I'm going to order a pizza. (not decided)
2. Do you have any plans for tomorrow?
   (a) Yes, I go running.(if it's a scheduled thing- for example, same day every week)
   (b) Yes, I'll go running. (thinking about other options)
   (c) Yes, I'm going running. (unfinished future action)
   (d) Yes, I'm going to go running. (plan)
3. What time does the game start?
   (a) It starts at 6. (scheduled)
   (b) It'll start at 6. (thinking)
   (c) It's starting at 6. (future action)
   (d) It's going to start at 6. (plan)
4. What do you think about the future?
   (a) We have more robots. (not fixed)
   (b) We'll have more robots. (prediction: thinking about possibilities)
   (c) We're having more robots. (not an unfinished action)
   (d) We're going to have more robots. (already decided)
5. Are you coming to pick me up?
   (a) Yes, I'm there in 5 minutes. (fixed, scheduled)
   (b) Yes, I'll be there in 5 minutes. (thinking about possibilities: predicting)
   (c) Yes, I'm being there in 5 minutes. (not an unfinished action)
   (d) Yes, I'm going to be there in 5

minutes. (plan)
6. What are you doing next week?
   (a) I go to New Orleans. (scheduled - we would often say when: on Tuesday)
   (b) I'll go to New Orleans. (thinking about options)
   (c) I'm going to New Orleans. (unfinished action)
   (d) I'm going to go to New Orleans. (plan)
   Note: It's more natural to answer with -ing because the question is in that form.
7. When do you arrive?
   (a) I arrive at 11.
   (b) I'll arrive at 11.
   (c) I'm arriving at 11.
   (d) I'm going to arrive at 11. (same as 3)
8. We have some news...
   (a) We get married! (not referring to a scheduled event) We can talk about it as a scheduled event if we add a time "We get married on Saturday."
   (b) We'll get married!
   We thought about our options.
   (c) We're getting married! (unfinished action, decided)
   (d) We're going to get married! (plan, decided)
9. Oh no, you broke my watch!
   (a) Sorry, I buy you a new one. (not scheduled)
   (b) Sorry, I'll buy you a new one. (thinking about options and deciding what to do)
   (c) Sorry, I'm buying you a new one. (unfinished action)
   (d) Sorry, I'm going to buy you a new one. (plan) This is what I always do when I break things
10. (a) Do you come to the party? This sounds like a repeated action - it's not.
    (b) Will you come to the party? (think about it and decide)
    (c) Are you coming to the party? (unfinished action in the future) Is it happening or not?
    (d) Are you going to come to the party? Is this your plan?

19: Ways of talking about the past

Page 163: which one should I use?
1. A: Hi... Sorry I didn't reply to your email.
   I'<u>ve been</u> traveling around America.
   or I <u>was</u> traveling around America.
   B: Awesome. Did you have a good time?
2. A: Yeah. I <u>used to live</u> there so I <u>went</u> out for drinks with some old friends.
   B: How are they all doing?
3. A: They're good. They've all got families so they don't go out as much as they <u>used to</u>.
4. In the old days we <u>used to go</u> out for dinner,
   (or we'<u>d go</u> out for dinner,)
   then we'<u>d go</u> to a concert and party all night. (or we <u>used to go</u> to a concert and party all night.)

Page 164: which one should I use?

1. I <u>live</u> in Australia now but I <u>used to live</u> in Japan. It was great.
2. We <u>used to go</u> skiing a lot.
   or We <u>went</u> skiing a lot.
3. I <u>used to live</u> there too.
4. I <u>used to go</u> snowboarding in the winter.
   or I<u>'d go</u> snowboarding in the winter.
   or I <u>went</u> snowboarding in the winter.
5. We <u>used to go</u> on weekdays and there <u>was</u> no one there.
   or We<u>'d</u> go on weekdays and there <u>used to be</u> no one there.
   or We <u>went</u> on weekdays and there<u>'d be</u> no one there. (other combinations of *used to*, *would* and the past form are possible too)
6. What <u>did</u> you <u>use to do</u> in the summer?
   or What <u>did</u> you <u>do</u> in the summer?
7. We <u>used to have</u> barbecues.
   or We<u>'d have</u> barbecues.
   or We <u>had</u> barbecues.

Page 164: Which do you think is the best answer?

1. What did you have for dinner yesterday?
   (a) We had tacos. (one time, yesterday)
   (b) We'd have tacos. (not during a period of time in the past)
   (c) We used to have tacos. (not during a period of time in the past)
2. When I was a child,...
   (a) we had tacos for dinner on Fridays. (happened in the past)
   (b) we'd have tacos for dinner on Fridays. (during a period in the past)
   (c) we used to have tacos for dinner on Fridays. (during a period in the past)
3. I live in Scotland now.
   (a) Really? I lived in Scotland!
   (b) Really? I'd live in Scotland!
   I would sounds hypothetical.
   (c) Really? I used to live in Scotland! (during a period in the past)
4. When I lived in Bangladesh,...
   (a) we often played cricket.
   (b) we'd often play cricket.
   (c) we used to often play cricket. (same as 2)
5. When I was young,...
   (a) I didn't eat mushrooms. (basic) It didn't happen in the past.
   (b) I wouldn't eat mushrooms. (strong) I refused.
   (c) I didn't used to eat mushrooms. It didn't happen during a period in the past.
6. (a) I played the piano.
   (b) I'd play the piano.
   I would sounds hypothetical.
   (c) I used to play the piano. (during a period in the past)
7. **(a) I was good at playing the piano.** (in the past)
   (b) I'd be good at playing the piano.
   I would sounds hypothetical.
   (c) I used to be good at playing the piano. (during a period in the past)
8. These have different meanings:
   (a) Did you like coffee?
   If we had just drunk coffee we would use *the*, "Did you like the coffee?" We know

which coffee and when.
   (b) Would you like coffee? Do you want one? (hypothetical)
   (c) Did you use to like coffee? (during a period in the past)
9. Where did you use to go for holidays?
   (a) We always went to the lake.
   (b) We'd always go to the lake.
   (c) We used to always go to the lake.
   (same as 2)

Page 165: used/be used

1. The new job is tough, but I<u>'m used to</u> it now.
2. My old job was good, I <u>used to</u> take long breaks.
3. He <u>used to</u> drink too much soda.
4. She<u>'s used to</u> working in a noisy place.
5. I <u>didn't use to</u> like olives.
   or I <u>didn't used to</u> like olives.
   Note: Both of these sentences sound the same, but there are two ways to write it. In negative sentences, some people use *didn't use to*. *Use* is thought of as a **verb** followed by *to*. The first verb (*did*) is in the past form:
   *wanted to / didn't **want** to*
   *used to / didn't **use** to*
   Other people write *didn't used to*. *Used to* is thought of as an **expression** (with a different meaning to the verb *use*). it can be made negative simply by putting *didn't* first:
   *used to / didn't **used** to*
   Both ways are common.
6. They <u>aren't used to</u> shoveling snow.

20: Review of future and past

Page 170: quiz

1. Which of the following sentences is about the future?
   (d) I'm going soon. (See page 152.)
2. Which of the following sentences is about the past?
   (b) I felt good. (See page 160.)
3. What are you doing tomorrow?
   (c) I'm going to school. (See page 152.)
4. What did you do yesterday?
   (a) I went to school. (See page 160.)
5. I want to watch the game...
   (a) It starts at 6. (See page 152.)
   (b) It's starting at 6. (See page 152.)
   (c) It'll start at 6. (See page 153.)
   (d) It'll be starting at 6. (See page 158.)
   (e) any of the above.
6. Choose the best sentence.
   (a) I'll have time to help you next week. Thinking about options. (See page 153.)
7. Choose the best sentence.
   (d) Next time I see you we'll be living in Asia.(See page 158.)(See page 120.)
8. A: Have you sent the invitations?
   B: Sorry, I forgot!...
   (b) I'll do it this afternoon.(See page 153.)
9. When I was a teenager...
   (a) I worked in a shop.
   (c) I used to work in a shop.

(d) (a) or (c) (See page 160.)
   Note: (b) is strange because we think about this as a period of time that we had the job, not the many times we worked. If we talk about the past we talk about it as a period: I worked in a shop for two years.
10. When I was a student I used to study every day...
   (a) I did my homework every evening.
   (b) I'd do my homework every evening.
   (c) I used to do my homework every evening.
   (e) (a), (b) or (c) (See page 160.)

Think and say

21: Think and say 1

Page 173: say

1. She says (that) her name is Yuki.
   or She said (that) her name is Yuki.
2. She says (that) she lives in Tokyo.
   or She said (that) she lives in Tokyo.
3. She says (that) she's studying science.
   or She said (that) she's studying science.
4. She says (that) she's been to America before.
   or She said (that) she's been to America before.
5. She says (that) she went to North Carolina last year.
   or She said (that) she went to North Carolina last year.
6. She says (that) her brother lives in Greensboro.
   or She said (that) her brother lives in Greensboro.

1. Stephanie said (that) sales were down.
2. Raymond said (that) we needed to get more customers.
3. Justin said (that) some customers were having trouble ordering.
4. Stephanie said (that) delivery had been taking too long.
5. Raymond said (that) customers had asked for cheaper products.
6. Brenda said (that) we had to hire new staff.
7. Justin said (that) he had a headache.

Page 174: said about the past

1. Kate said (that) they went away on vacation in December.
   or Kate said (that) they'd been away on vacation in December.
2. Daniel said (that) they went away for two weeks.
   or Daniel said (that) they'd been away for two weeks.
3. Daniel said (that) they had a great time.
   or Daniel said (that) they'd had a great time.
4. Kate said (that) she got a new job last week.
   or Kate said (that) she'd gotten a new job last week. (or *she'd got*)
5. Kate said (that) she got a haircut on Tuesday.

315

or Kate said (that) she'd gotten a haircut on Tuesday. (or *she'd got*)
6. Daniel said (that) he ate a big sandwich for lunch on Sunday.
   or Daniel said (that) he'd eaten a big sandwich for lunch on Sunday.
7. Kate said (that) they saw a good movie on Wednesday night.
   or Kate said (that) they'd seen a good movie on Wednesday night.

Page 175: said about the future
1. Kate said (that) they were going away on vacation in July.
   or Kate said (that) they're going away on vacation in July.
2. Daniel said (that) they leave on the 6th.
   or Daniel said (that) they are leaving on the 6th.
   or Daniel said (that) they left on the 6th. (but this may be confusing)
3. Kate said (that) she was starting her new job yesterday.
4. Daniel said (that) he was going to eat a big sandwich for lunch.

Page 177: said about options and possibilities
1. He said (that) he could play the drums.
   or He said (that) he can play the drums. (still possible now)
2. She said (that) she might watch the football.
3. I said (that) I'd buy him a present.
   or I said (that) I'll buy him a present. (if it is still in the future)
4. She said (that) we could have rice for dinner.
   or She said that we could have had rice for dinner. (if dinner was in the past and we didn't have rice)
5. He said (that) he'd be late.
   or He said (that) he'll be late. (if it is still in the future)
6. He didn't go. He said (that) he might have gone if he had the money."
7. She said (that) she'd like a sandwich. (She'd still like it now.)
   or She said (that) she would have liked a sandwich. (if this happened in the past and she wouldn't like one now)

Page 179: time and place
1. Dianne said (that) they'd been away on vacation the month before.
   or Dianne said (that) they went away on vacation the month before.
2. Eric said (that) they had come back the week before.
   or Eric said (that) they came back the week before.
3. Dianne said (that) she could help me plan my trip the next month. (or could help us plan our trip) (or the following month)
4. Dianne said (that) she'd gotten a new job the year before. (or *she'd got*)
   or Dianne said (that) she got a new job the year before.
5. Dianne said (that) she'd gotten a haircut the day before. (or *she'd got*)
   or Dianne said (that) she got a haircut the

day before.
6. Eric said (that) he'd eaten a big sandwich for lunch that day.
   or Eric said (that) he ate a big sandwich for lunch that day.
7. Dianne said (that) they were going to the cinema that Friday.
   or Dianne said (that) they'd go to the cinema that Friday.
   or Dianne said (that) they'd be going to the cinema that Friday.
   or Dianne said (that) they were going to go to the cinema that Friday.
8. Eric said (that) he'd be really busy at work the next week. (or the following week)
   or Eric said (that) he was going to be really busy at work the next week. (or the following week)

Page 180: think and know
1. James thinks (that) Germany will win.
2. I think (that) I'll be late.
3. Joan thought (that) the beef was very good.
   or Joan thinks (that) the beef was very good. (she still thinks it now)
4. James thought (that) Germany would win. They lost. (past) James thought this sometime before the game ended.
   or James thought (that) Germany would have won. They lost. James thought this until he heard the result that Germany had lost.
5. I thought (that) I'd be late. I thought this sometime in the past I may have arrived or not arrived yet.
   or I thought (that) I would have been late. I thought this until something happened, for example: "The buses weren't running so I thought that I would have been late but a friend offered to drive." (*I'd be late* fits this situation too)

22: Think and say 2

Page 182: ask
1. Lola asked if you're from America.
   or Lola asked if you were from America.
2. Chloé asked if you like France.
   or Chloé asked if you liked France.
3. Hugo asked if you're hungry.
   or Hugo asked if you were hungry.
4. Pierre asked if you can teach him English.
   or Pierre asked if you could teach him English.
5. Chloé asked if you've seen the Eiffel Tower.
   or Chloé asked if you'd seen the Eiffel Tower.
6. Lola asked if you're coming shopping tomorrow.
   or Lola asked if you were coming shopping tomorrow.
7. Hugo asked if you'd like to have some coffee.

Page 183: ask
1. Lola asked (you) what food you like.
   or Lola asked (you) what food you liked.
2. Chloé asked (you) where you're from.

or Chloé asked (you) where you were from.
3. Hugo asked (you) what your name is.
   or Hugo asked (you) what your name was.
4. Pierre asked (you) when you arrived.
5. Chloé asked (you) how your flight was.
6. Lola asked (you) who you're traveling with.
   or Lola asked (you) who you were traveling with.
7. Hugo asked (you) how long you'll be in France.
   or Hugo asked (you) how long you'd be in France.

Page 185: the meaning
There are other ways you can say what people said. The answers given here are some common ways we might say it. The words we use depend on how we view the situation. We get the meaning from the words and the context.
1. "May I have a drink of water, please?"
   He asked if he could have a drink of water.
   or He asked if he can have a drink of water. (if we think he still wants it now)
   or He asked if he could have some water.
   or He asked for a drink of water.
   or He asked for some water.
2. "Would you mind taking the dog outside?"
   She asked (me) if I could take the dog outside.
   or She asked me to take the dog outside.
3. "I must buy her a present."
   He said (that) he had to buy her a present.
   or He said (that) he needed to buy her a present.
   or He said (that) he had to get her a present.
   or He said (that) he needed to get her a present.
   or He said (that) he wanted to buy her a present.
   or He said (that) he should buy her a present.
4. "Can we go soon?"
   Sienna asked if we could go soon.
   or Sienna asked if we could go.
   or Sienna asked if we could leave soon.
   or Sienna asked if we could leave.
5. "Shall we go soon?"
   He asked (me) if I wanted to go soon.
   or He asked (me) if I wanted to go.
   or He asked (me) if I wanted to leave.
6. "You must wear a tie."
   She said (that) you had to wear a tie.
   or She said (that) you have to wear a tie.
   or She said (that) you needed to wear a tie.
   or She said (that) you needed a tie.
7. "I'm going to the park on Friday."
   You said (that) you were going to the park on Friday.
   or You said (that) you were going to go to the park on Friday.
   or You said (that) you'd go to the park on Friday.
   or You said (that) you'd be going to the park on Friday.
   If it is still in the future:
   You said (that) you're going to the park

on Friday.
or You said (that) you're going to go to the park on Friday.
or You said (that) you'll go to the park on Friday.
or You said (that) you'll be going to the park on Friday.

8. "If it's not too much trouble, could I take the day off?"
She asked if she could take the day off.
or She asked to take the day off.
or She asked for the day off.

Page 186: telling people what do to

1. "Please open your textbooks to page 128".
The teacher told us to open our textbooks to page 128.
2. "Could you call Hannah?"
Sienna said to call Hannah.
3. "Don't be late."
He said not to be late.
4. "Please don't leave the door open"
Leo told me not to leave the door open.
5. "Could you please carry my bags?"
She asked me to carry her bags.

Page 187: about

1. Tell me **about** your new job.
2. Could you tell me _____ the time?
3. We asked _____ how hot it was.
4. We asked **about** the weather.
5. She gave a presentation **about** the environment.
6. He always thinks **about** other people.
7. Hey, stop! What are you doing here? Who are you? Tell me _____ your name.

Page 188: hopes and wishes

1. I <u>wish</u> I could fly.
2. I <u>hope</u> they compromise.
3. Amanda <u>wishes</u> she was famous.
4. She <u>hopes</u> to be a singer.
5. They <u>hope</u> they can afford it.
6. They <u>wish</u> they could afford it.
7. Martin <u>wishes</u> he was young again.

23: Review of think and say

Page 192: quiz

1. Jackson said he wanted something to eat. Did Jackson say "I want something to eat"?
(c) maybe
He might have said "I'd like something to eat" or something similar. (See page 184.)
2. A: (Tuesday) "We're having pasta for dinner."
B: (Thursday)
(c) He said they were having pasta for dinner. (dinner was in the past) (See page 175.)
3. A: (1:00PM) "We're having curry for dinner."
B: (2:00PM)
(a) He says they are having curry for dinner.
(b) He said they are having curry for dinner.
(c) He said they were having curry for

dinner.
(d) any of the above (said in the past, but still true in the present) (See page 172.)
4. A: (1:00PM) "I'll be home at 6PM."
B: (4:00PM)
(b) She said she'd be home at 6PM.
(c) She said she'll be home at 6PM.
(d) either (b) or (c) (said in the past, but still true in the present) (See page 176.)
5. A: (1:00PM) "I'll be home at 6PM."
B: (7:00PM) She's still not home, but...
(b) She said she'd be home at 6PM. (6PM is in the past)(See page 176.)
6. (b) I wish I had more time. (hypothetical) (See page 188.)
7. (a) I hope you have a great day.
(b) I hope you had a great day.
(c) (a) for future or (b) for past. (See page 188.)
8. (c) You're on time! I heard you'd be late. (past: you have arrived on time so you can't be late in the present-future.) (See page 176.)
9. A: (May)"I went shopping yesterday."
B: (November)
(b) She said she went shopping the day before.
(c) She said that she'd been shopping the day before.
(e) either (b) or (c) (See page 174.)
10. A: (3:07PM) "I live in Moscow."
B: (3:08PM)
(a) He says that he lives in Moscow.
(b) He said that he lives in Moscow.
(c) He said that he lived in Moscow.
(d) any of the above (See page 172.)
11. A: Don't take the garbage out today. It's Tuesday.
B:
(c) My mistake, I thought it was Wednesday. (I thought it in the past; I don't think it is Wednesday now.) (See page 180.)
12. A: (1:00PM)"Are you cooking dinner tonight?"
B: (2:00PM)
(a) She asked if I was cooking dinner tonight.
(b) She asked if I was going to cook dinner.
(c) either (a) or (b) (See page 184.)
13. A: (Monday) "You must wear leather shoes tomorrow."
B: (Thursday)
(a) She said that we must wear leather shoes on Tuesday.
(b) She said that we had to wear leather shoes on Tuesday.
(c) She said that we needed to wear leather shoes on Tuesday.
(d) any of the above (using had to or needed to makes it clear we are talking about the past.)(See page 184.)

Adding information

24: Where and when

Page 195: adding a place

1. Hannah is sitting <u>near</u> the door.

or Hannah is sitting <u>by</u> the door.
or Hannah is sitting <u>next to</u> the door.
or Hannah is sitting <u>close to</u> the door.
or Hannah is sitting <u>in front of</u> the door.
or Hannah is sitting <u>at</u> the door.
2. Patrick is sitting <u>in front of</u> the window.
or Patrick is sitting <u>near</u> the window.
or Patrick is sitting <u>by</u> the window.
or Patrick is sitting <u>close to</u> the window.
3. Phil is sitting <u>next to</u> Patrick.
or Phil is sitting <u>beside</u> Patrick.
4. Courtney is sitting <u>opposite</u> Hannah.
or Courtney is sitting <u>across from</u> Hannah.
5. ...check the calendar <u>above</u> Courtney.
or ...check the calendar <u>behind</u> Courtney.
or ...check the calendar <u>near</u> Courtney.
6. Have you seen my keys?
7. That could be them <u>under</u> the table, <u>between</u> Patrick and Phil.

Page 197: adding a place

1. A: Where is my wallet?
B: It's <u>behind</u> your bag.
2. A: Where's Cheryl?
She's gone <u>into</u> the supermarket.
3. A: Where does Roger eat lunch?
B: He eats lunch <u>at</u> a park <u>between</u> the office and the train station.
4. A: Where are you studying tomorrow?
B: I'm studying <u>in</u> the library.
5. A: Where did you go yesterday?
B: I went on a tour <u>through</u> Zurich.
6. A: Where is the bathroom?
B: Go <u>down</u> the hall, <u>past</u> the bedrooms. It's <u>at</u> the end of the hall.

Page 199: adding a time

1. I'm at home. I'll be here <u>until</u> 3PM.
2. She's moving to the city in January. I'm moving two months <u>before</u>.
3. I'm still at work, but I'll be home <u>after</u> 7 o'clock.
4. I played baseball <u>two days ago</u>.
5. I've played baseball <u>since</u> I was three.
6. He played professional football <u>until</u> he was 35. (He's retired now.)

Page 200: adding a time

1. A: When's the meeting?
B: It's <u>at</u> 11:00.
2. A: When does the bus leave?
B: It leaves <u>in</u> 10 minutes.
3. A: How long have you played tennis?
B: I've played tennis <u>since</u> I was five.
4. A: When does Roger eat lunch?
B: He eats lunch <u>after</u> 12:30.
5. A: When is the best weather?
B: The best weather is <u>in</u> August.
6. A: When did you go to Zurich?
B: I went to Zurich <u>two weeks ago</u>.

25: Who, what, why and how

Page 203: adding a recipient / to: adding a destination

1. The boss gave <u>me</u> a raise. (I got it)
or The boss gave a raise <u>to me</u>. (where the raises went/who they went to)
2. He sent the package <u>to Africa</u>. (where it

went)

~~He sent Africa the package.~~ (unless Africa is someone or something's name)

3. She threw the ball to the catcher. (where the ball went)
    or She threw the catcher the ball. (the catcher got it)

4. She announced her decision to the committee. (information relating to her decision went to the committee.)

5. The meal cost him $100. He got the check (which was $100) and paid for it. The $100 didn't go to him.

6. A: Where is your skateboard? B: I sold it to Wendy. (where the skateboard went)

Page 204: adding a recipient / to: adding a destination

1. A: Where did you go on your vacation?
    B: We went to Florida.

2. A: Who did she pass the ball to?
    B: She passed it to Sophia.

3. A: Where are you from?
    B: I'm from Ireland.

4. A: What address should I sent it to?
    B: Send it to 14 Main Rd, Franklin.

5. A: Where do you go on Mondays?
    B: I go to school.

Page 205: for: making connections

1. They cooked us dinner. We got dinner.
    or They cooked dinner for us. (reason)

2. I wrote you a song. You receive it.
    or I wrote a song for you. (reason)

3. This is really heavy, could you take my bag for me, please? (reason)

4. Could you take my bag to the car please? (destination)

5. They opened the door for me. (reason)

6. I gave her a hug. She received it.

7. I send my friends messages on their birthdays. They receive the messages.
    or I send messages to my friends on their birthdays. (destination)

Page 206: another reason for using to and for.

1. We gave the cake to the guests who attended our wedding. (where it went, clearer with the long part at the end)

2. I ordered him a coffee. He got it.
    or I ordered a coffee for him. (reason)

3. We ordered a pizza for the people at the party. (reason, clearer with the long part at the end)

4. I cooked dinner for my brothers, sisters, aunts and uncles. (reason, clearer with the long part at the end)

5. I tell my secrets to only my closest friends. Where my secrets go. This is clearer with the long part at the end.

6. I'm baking you a cake. You get it.
    or I'm baking a cake for you. (reason)

7. I've left you some pizza in the fridge. You get it.
    or I've left some pizza for you in the fridge. (reason)

8. That awesome shot won them the game. They got the win.
    or That awesome shot won the game for them. (reason: they wanted to win)

Page 207: other ways to add a reason

1. A: Why are you going running?
    B: I go running because I like staying fit.

2. A: What are you preparing for?
    B: I'm preparing for the festival. (what thing: an event)

3. A: Why does Anthony work overtime?
    B: He works overtime to get more money.

4. A: Why didn't you go out yesterday?
    B: It rained a lot so we didn't go out.

5. A: Why have you opened a savings account?
    B: I've opened a savings account to save money for college.

Page 209: by: adding a method / with: adding a part

1. He goes to work by train.
2. They played soccer with Shirley last week.
3. I paid by credit card. (method)
4. I paid with a credit card. (thing)
5. I grabbed him by his arm. (method: grabbing his arm)
6. Sally is busy. I'm going swimming without her.
7. She played with her hair.
8. She plays the guitar by ear. (her method: just listening and playing)
9. She plays the guitar with a pick.
10. He's fixing the chair with glue. (thing)
11. I picked up the mouse with my fingers. I + my fingers picked up the mouse.
12. I picked up the mouse by its tail. The method I used: I grabbed its tail, then picked up the mouse.

Page 210: how, who or what

1. A: How does Melissa pay for her groceries?
    B: She pays by credit card.

2. A: What did you cut the bread with?
    B: I couldn't find the bread knife so I used my pocket knife.

3. A: Who was it written by?
    B: Shakespeare.

4. A: How are you getting home tonight?
    B: Mum is picking me up.

5. A: Who did you have dinner with?
    B: Natalie.

26: Describing nouns

Page 213: of

1. Could I have a slice of cheese, please?
2. Who is the president of the United States?
3. Who is Maria's sister?

Page 215: adding information after nouns

1. The president of the company has decided to retire.
2. I bought a cup of coffee with the change from lunch.
3. Some of my coworkers go home at 4:20.
4. The keys are in the bag under the table near the window.
5. The meat for dinner is in the fridge.

Page 217: adjectives

The most common orders are given below, we may use a different order if we want to emphasize something.

1. I want to buy a large black leather sofa.
2. They live in a big expensive house.
3. Can I have another thick slice of cake please? (another always comes first, it has an attached to it. A and an come before adjectives)
4. They cooked us a delicious 7-course Vietnamese banquet. (what kind of Vietnamese banquet)
    or They cooked us a delicious Vietnamese 7-course banquet. (what kind of 7-course banquet)
5. She seems like an intelligent young woman.
6. The group has just released an amazing new album.
7. That little boy took the other little boy's toy car.

Page 219: how or which

1. A: How old do you have to be to vote?
    B: 18.

2. A: How many centimeters are in a foot?
    B: About 30 I think.

3. A: How was the concert?
    B: It was great. (See page 210.)

4. A: How much are these shoes?
    B: They're $50.

5. A: How deep is Lake Baikal?
    B: It's 1642m deep.

6. A: Which one should I buy?
    B: That one.

7. A: How much water does Dominick drink?
    B: Eight glasses a day.

8. A: How long is a game of cricket?
    B: Five days.

9. A: How many dollars can I get for £100?

Page 221: other ways to describe nouns

1. This looks like Oliver's bag.
2. They wrote a picture book for kids.
3. I'm thirsty. Could I have a glass of water, please?
4. They swam to the end of the pool.
5. She's president of the company.
    or She's the company president.
6. Would you like to see my photo album?

27: Adverbs

Page 225: adding information to verbs

1. We sleep here. (where)
2. He quickly picked up his bag. (what happened)
    or He picked up his bag quickly. (how)
3. I went running yesterday. (when)
4. They worked late. (when)
5. The team played poorly. (how)
6. We've nearly finished the page. (what has happened)
7. I can definitely help you. (what I can do)

Page 226: linking and emphasis

1. Yesterday morning I was half asleep. The doorbell rang.
    or I was half asleep yesterday morning.

2. I <u>slowly</u> crawled out of bed and went to the door. It was the postman.
   or I crawled out of bed <u>slowly</u>.
   or <u>Slowly</u>, I crawled out of bed.
3. While I was talking to him, the door <u>suddenly</u> blew closed behind me. (what happened while I was talking to him) Putting *suddenly* before *blew* fits well in this situation, but putting *suddenly* in another position is ok too.
4. <u>Unfortunately</u>, I was locked out of the house, in my pajamas. (perspective)
   or I was <u>unfortunately</u> locked out of the house, in my pajamas. (what: a fact, it was unlikely, but it happened)
   or I was locked out of the house, <u>unfortunately</u>, in my pajamas. We use a comma, this is an added perspective at the end.
5. I went around the back and, <u>luckily</u>, a window was left open. (perspective)
   or I went around the back and a window was <u>luckily</u> left open. (what: a fact, it was unlikely, but it happened)
   or I went around the back and a window was left open, <u>luckily</u>. We use a comma, this is an added perspective at the end.

Page 227: start, middle or end?
1. She didn't have a c-section, she gave birth <u>naturally</u>. (how: a natural birth)
2. She was at the end of the pregnancy, so <u>naturally</u> she gave birth. (perspective: as expected)
3. Please speak up. We can't hear you <u>clearly</u> at the back. (how: we can hear you, but not clearly)
4. Tap him on his shoulder to get his attention. He <u>clearly</u> can't hear you. (what: a fact - he obviously can't hear you)
5. We didn't know they were famous so we treated them <u>normally</u>. (how)
6. People <u>normally</u> treat them special. (what usually happens)
7. We <u>simply</u> told them what we needed and they gave it to us. (what we did)
8. What a great solution, how did you do it so <u>simply</u>? (how)

Page 229: saying how often
   A: What do you do on the weekend?
1. B: Lots of things. I <u>usually</u> go to the park. (how often)
   or <u>Usually</u>, I go to the park. (perspective)
   or I go to the park <u>usually</u>. (when)
2. I <u>often</u> go to a local restaurant.
   or <u>Often</u>, I go to a local restaurant.
   or I go to a local restaurant <u>often</u>.
3. They <u>always</u> have good food. (how often)
4. I <u>never</u> have to pay for it. (how often)
5. My girlfriend <u>always</u> pays.
6. <u>Sometimes</u> we get ice cream for dessert.
   or We <u>sometimes</u> get ice cream for dessert.
   or We get ice cream for dessert <u>sometimes</u>.

Page 231: negative sentences
1. I work really long hours. I <u>usually</u> don't get home in time for dinner.
2. I <u>often</u> don't get home until 11PM.

3. We don't <u>often</u> have visitors, but my cousin is staying with us this week.
4. We are really busy with her so I <u>sometimes</u> don't have time to check my email before work.
5. We don't <u>always</u> have our meals together, but we're having dinner together on Friday.
6. I don't <u>usually</u> go out on Fridays but it's a special occasion. (not usually = rarely)
   or I <u>usually</u> don't go out on Fridays but it's a special occasion. (I usually make the decision not to)

Page 232: more than one verb
   A: Do you think you'll come to the barbecue on Sunday?
1. B: I've been thinking about it, but I <u>probably</u> won't go.
2. A: Just come. You'll <u>definitely</u> enjoy it.
   or You <u>definitely</u> will enjoy it.
3. B: Sorry, I <u>honestly</u> can't make it this time. A: That's ok. How have you been anyway?
4. B: Good. I've been <u>quickly</u> going through all my notes to revise for the exam tomorrow. It is pretty difficult.
   or I've <u>quickly</u> been going through all my notes to revise for the exam tomorrow.
5. I <u>probably</u> should have started earlier.
   or I should <u>probably</u> have started earlier.
   or I should have <u>probably</u> started earlier.

Page 233: one verb: be
1. A: Steve's <u>always</u> late.
   B: He might be stuck in traffic.
2. C: He <u>probably</u> **is** stuck in traffic. (emphasis on *is* - that's where he **is**)
   or He **is** <u>probably</u> stuck in traffic.
3. The traffic's <u>often</u> really bad around here.
   or The traffic <u>often</u> **is** really bad around here.
   or The traffic **is** <u>often</u> really bad around here.
4. D: He messaged me earlier. He'll <u>definitely</u> be here soon.
   or He <u>definitely</u> **will** be here soon.
   or He **will** <u>definitely</u> be here soon.
5. Steve: Hi everyone! Nice to hear you all talking about me. I <u>actually</u> **was** stuck in traffic. There was an accident. (emphasis)
   or I **was** <u>actually</u> stuck in traffic.
6. By the way, I'm <u>usually</u> on time.
   or I usually **am** on time.
   or I **am** usually on time.

Page 234: adverbs and adjectives
1. It went really <u>fast</u>. (It was fast)
2. Please play <u>safe</u>. (be safe)
   or Please play <u>safely</u>. (how)
3. Come <u>quick</u>! Help! (be quick)
   or Come <u>quickly</u>! Help! (how)
4. We <u>hardly</u> ever work. (adding information to *ever*)
5. We're working <u>hard</u>. We are hard workers.
6. We've <u>nearly</u> finished. (what we have done - well almost)
7. We'll stay home and take it <u>easy</u>. (It will be easy)
8. I passed the test <u>easily</u>. (how)
9. Seafood should be eaten <u>fresh</u>. It should be fresh.

10. Add some <u>freshly</u> ground pepper. (adding information to *ground*)
   or Add some <u>fresh</u> ground pepper. (using *fresh* and *ground* as adjectives, adding information to *pepper*)

Page 235: a lot / any more
1. I've been vacuuming all morning. Please try to keep the house clean. I don't want to do <u>any more</u> vacuuming.
2. What do you think about candidate A? I like <u>a lot of</u> his policies, but I don't agree with all of them.
3. How about candidate B? I like her <u>a lot</u>. I'll definitely vote for her.
4. I'm so tired. I can't keep my eyes open <u>anymore</u>. (when: from now on)
5. The door is fully open. It can't be <u>any more</u> open.
6. We love hiking. We go to the mountains <u>a lot</u>—every month.
7. We love hiking. We go to <u>a lot of</u> the mountains—different ones.

28: Stronger descriptions

Page 239: very / really
1. The movie was <u>really</u> fantastic.
2. It's <u>very</u> hot today.
   or It's <u>really</u> hot today.
3. I don't <u>really</u> like dogs.
4. We <u>really</u> had a great time.
5. Yesterday morning was cold, but it wasn't <u>very</u> cold this morning.
   or Yesterday morning was cold, but it wasn't <u>really</u> cold this morning.
6. He drives <u>very</u> slowly.
   or He drives <u>really</u> slowly.

Page 242: so / such
1. You're lucky to have <u>such</u> good friends.
2. He is <u>so</u> generous.
3. I've been waiting <u>so</u> long.
4. My grandfather is <u>so</u> old.
5. She is <u>such</u> a comedian.
6. Have you ever heard <u>such</u> an amazing singer?
7. We have <u>so</u> much to talk about.

Page 243: enough / too
1. I have to be back at work at 2:00, so we have <u>enough</u> time for lunch.
2. I wanted to buy some coffee, but the line was <u>too long</u> so I went home.
3. He can't stand up. He's had <u>too much</u> to drink.
4. It's 40°C. It's <u>too hot</u> to go out.
5. My bag is really heavy, I brought <u>too much</u> stuff.
   (If we are talking about someone else we might sarcastically say "You brought enough stuff!")
6. We <u>didn't bring enough</u> food. We're all still very hungry.

29: Comparing

Page 247: -er than
1. She's <u>taller</u> than me.
2. I have <u>longer</u> hair than her.

3. Watching grass grow is <u>more exciting</u> than the movie I just watched.
4. Baseball is <u>more popular</u> in America than Europe.
5. We are <u>busier</u> this month than we were last month.
6. Is that the price? It's much <u>more expensive</u> than it was yesterday.
7. A: Can I have some more coffee, please?
   B: Ok.
   (person A pours a small amount)
   B: Have <u>more</u> than that if you like.
   (Have more coffee than that)
8. A: What do you think?
   B: That looks much <u>better</u>. (than before)

Page 249: as... as...
1. That's so expensive! It costs <u>twice as much as</u> it did yesterday!
2. A: Can I have some more coffee, please?
   B: Sure. Have <u>as much as</u> you like.
3. A: Can I stay here for another week?
   B: Sure. Stay <u>as long as</u> you like.
4. A: Can you turn on the air conditioner? It's <u>as hot as</u> a sauna in here!
5. A: What does 'travel light' mean?
   B: It means you take <u>as little as</u> possible.
6. A: Mom, can I go to my friends house this afternoon?
   B: Ok, <u>as long as</u> you do your homework first.
7. A: How many tomatoes can I have?
   B: <u>As many as</u> you can carry.

Page 251: the -est / not as... as...
1. The Nile is <u>the longest</u> river in the world.
2. The Amazon River is<u>n't as long as</u> the Nile, but it is <u>the largest</u> river in the world, in terms of water flow.
3. My wife is <u>the most amazing</u> woman I've ever met.
4. This is <u>the best</u> restaurant in the city.
5. It was<u>n't as good as</u> I thought it would be.
6. I scored <u>the most</u> points. Daniel did<u>n't</u> score <u>as many points as</u> I did.
7. Horses are<u>n't as fast as</u> cheetahs. Cheetahs are <u>the fastest</u> animals on land.

Page 253: like
1. A: Would you like to get a coffee?
   B: That <u>sounds like</u> a good idea.
2. Those clouds are really dark. It <u>looks like</u> it'll rain.
3. A: What is your favorite food?
   B: I <u>like</u> noodles.
4. A: What would you like to eat?
   B: I <u>feel like</u> noodles.

Page 254: like / as
1. It looks <u>like</u> you've had a great day.
   or It looks <u>as if</u> you've had a great day.
   or It looks <u>as though</u> you've had a great day.
2. We often eat seafood <u>like</u> shellfish, crab and shrimp.
   or We often eat seafood <u>such as</u> shellfish, crab and shrimp.
3. It's a hot day today, <u>like</u> the weather report said.
   or It's a hot day today, <u>as</u> the weather report said.

4. Take as much time <u>as</u> you like.

30: Review of adding information

Page 258: quiz
1. (a) I bought it for you. (See page 205.)
2. (b) I sent the letter to Russia. (See page 202.)
3. (a) Alex gave me this bag.
   (b) Alex gave this bag to me.
   (c) either (a) or (b) (See page 202.)
4. (a) Her story gave me courage. (See page 202.)
5. (a) We went by car. (See page 208.)
6. Would you like a drink?
   (b) Could I have a glass of juice please? (See page 212.)
7. (a) It's an old story. (See page 216.)
8. (c) It works well. (See page 225.)
   (We can say "Well, it works" but in needs a comma (,) after *well* or a pause when speaking. This has a different meaning.)
9. (b) It'll probably rain. (See page 231.)
10. (a) Sometimes I go hiking.
    (b) I sometimes go hiking.
    (c) I go hiking sometimes.
    (d) any of the above (See page 228.)
11. Which sentence is more natural?
    (b) We don't always work on Saturdays. (See page 230.)
12. Which sentence is more natural?
    (a) I sometimes don't get home until 8. (See page 230.)
13. (a) I'm very hungry.
    (b) I'm really hungry.
    (c) either (a) or (b) (See page 238.)
14. (b) I really like it. (See page 238.)
15. (a) I don't really like it. (See page 239.)
    (b) I really don't like it.(See page 239.)
    (d) both are good, (b) is stronger
16. (b) This one is more expensive than that one. (See page 246.)
17. (a) It's fairly good.
    (b) It's pretty good.
    (c) It's quite good.
    (d) It's rather good.
    (e) any of the above (See page 240.)
18. (a) A is bigger than B. (See page 246.)
19. (c) A isn't as big as B. (See page 251.)
20. (b) A is as big as B. (See page 248.)

Adding more

31: Talking about time

Page 261: when
Note: You can also put the *when* part first.
(1. When I was 23, I lived in London.)
1. I lived in London <u>when</u> I was 23.
2. I went skiing a lot <u>when</u> I was on vacation.
3. I'll go out for dinner every night <u>when</u> I'm in Spain.
4. I can call you <u>when</u> I arrive.
5. I saw Joe <u>when</u> I was playing tennis.
6. I'll be working <u>when</u> the game is on.

Page 263: while
1. I read a magazine <u>while</u> I waited to see

the doctor. (between the start and end of waiting)
2. We made a lot of friends <u>while</u> we were on holiday. (between the start and end of the holiday)
   or We made a lot of friends <u>when</u> we were on holiday. (at the time we were on holiday)
3. I liked video games <u>when</u> I was a child. (general information about that point in time)

Page 265: as
Note: You can also put the *as* part first.
(1. As I left work (yesterday), I saw Joe.)
1. I saw Joe as I left work (yesterday).
2. Islands will go underwater as sea levels rise.
3. Put the clothes in the basket as you take them off the washing line.

1. You arrive at 6:00. I leave at 6:00. I won't really see you because I'll leave <u>as</u> you arrive.
   (at the same time)
   If we use *when* in this situation it has a very different meaning: 1. You arrive. 2. I leave. You arriving may be the reason I leave.
2. We're waiting for you in the parking lot. We'll give you more information <u>when</u> you get here.
   (1. You get here. 2. You get more information)
3. I fell asleep <u>while</u> they were talking about politics. (between the start and end of their talk)
   or I fell asleep <u>when</u> they were talking about politics. (at the time)
4. Leo ran <u>when</u> he saw the dog.
   (1. Leo sees a dog. 2. He runs)
5. We sat and looked out to sea <u>as</u> the sun went down. (at the same time)
   or We sat and looked out to sea <u>while</u> the sun went down. (between the start and end of the sun going down)
6. Grace liked drawing <u>when</u> she was a child. (general information about the time)
7. It's sunny now. Let's go out <u>while</u> the weather is good. (before the end of the good weather)

32: A sentence in a sentence

Page 270: explaining which one
1. My friend <u>that</u> plays the drums plays in a band.
2. This is the ring (that) I gave to my wife.
3. Russia is the country (that) I was in in June. (in in: in the country and in Russia)
4. The team <u>that</u> won yesterday played really well.

Page 271: when, where, which, who
1. Which park do you want to go to?
   The park (that) we went to last time.
   The park <u>where</u> we went last time.
2. Which team won?
   The team <u>that</u> wears red.

The team <u>who</u> wears red. (people)
The team <u>which</u> wears red. (a team is a thing)

3. Which person got the job?
   The one <u>that</u> came to the interview on time.
   The one <u>who</u> came to the interview on time.

Page 273: describing things in two ways / simplifying

1. The cheetah, (an animal) which can reach speeds of up to 120Km/h, is the fastest animal on land.
   or The cheetah, (an animal) that can reach speeds of up to 120Km/h, is the fastest animal on land.
2. Soda, (a drink) which is high in sugar, is unhealthy.
   or Soda, (a drink) that is high in sugar, is unhealthy.
3. My brother, (the one) who is a dentist, lives in Sydney.
   My brother, (the one) that is a dentist, lives in Sydney.
4. Elizabeth, (the woman) who I met this morning, likes skiing.
   or Elizabeth, (the woman) that I met this morning, likes skiing.
   or Elizabeth, the woman I met this morning, likes skiing.

Page 274: -ing and -en

1. The woman playing the piano is very good.
2. The person elected president will have a lot of responsibility.
3. I gave them a letter written by my boss.
4. My friends living in the city really enjoy it.

Page 275: what

1. I remember <u>who</u> you are.
2. I don't know <u>where</u> she went.
3. He told me <u>why</u> he was late.
4. I remember <u>when</u> the rain started.
5. They explained <u>how</u> it works.

Page 276: polite questions

Note: We can use either expression in these sentences: *do you know...* or *could you tell me...*

1. Do you know <u>where he lives</u>?
2. Do you know <u>when the meeting is</u>?
3. Do you know <u>how old she is</u>?
4. Could you tell me <u>what the time is</u>?
5. Do you know <u>if there's an ATM near here</u>?
6. Could you tell me <u>how you get to the supermarket</u>?
   or Could you tell me <u>how to get to the supermarket</u>?
7. Could you tell me <u>who that bag belongs to</u>?

33: Other sentence patterns

Page 279: make it happen

1. He asked me <u>to</u> buy milk.
2. He was made <u>to</u> feel like he didn't matter.
3. I helped them ____ clean the house.
   or I helped them <u>to</u> clean the house.
4. My boss makes me ____ work overtime.

5. I told her <u>to</u> be here on time.
6. Let's ____ go home.

Page 281: experience it

1. I look <u>at</u> the tide times before I go ____ fishing.
   We could say 'I go to fishing' if it is a regular event we go to, like a fishing club, but this is unusual)
2. I listen <u>to</u> the news <u>to</u> keep up to date with current events. (reason I listen: to keep up to date)
3. I watched ____ my daughter ____ open her birthday presents.
4. I watched ____ a documentary <u>to</u> learn about history. (the reason I watched)
5. I heard ____ you ____ got a new car.
   Note: We are talking about two times (the time I heard about it and the time it happened). We use the past from (*got*) to make it clear we are talking about another time in the past. This is the same sentence pattern as with *say*. (See page 172.)
   We saw her rescue a dog. One time: We experienced it.
   We saw (that) she rescued a dog. Two times: I saw this somewhere (on TV, in a newspaper, on the Internet, etc.), she rescued a dog sometime before that.
6. Look <u>at</u> him ____ dance!
7. I saw ____ her ____ give him a present.

Page 283: here you are / here comes the end

1. I'm looking for my shoes. <u>There they are</u>.
   or <u>They're there</u>.
2. Can I borrow your car? Sure, <u>here are the keys</u>. (giving the person the keys)
   or Sure, <u>The keys are here</u>. (pointing)
3. Can I borrow your car? Sure, <u>the keys are in the drawer</u>.
4. The beat in this song is awesome! <u>Here it comes</u>!
5. This song is awesome! <u>Here comes the best part</u>!
6. We're ready for our journey. And <u>away we go</u>!

34: Review of adding more

Page 288: quiz

1. (a) We went home when it started raining. (See page 260.)
2. (a) I did the shopping when she was at work.
   (b) I did the shopping while she was at work.
   (c) either (a) or (b) (See page 262.)
3. (a) As I got in the car, the sun came out.
   (b) When I got in the car, the sun came out.
   (c) either (a) or (b) (See page 264.)(See page 260.)
4. (a) We left before the rain started. (See page 266.)
5. (a) I'll be here until 6. (See page 199.)
6. (a) The lady that works here is my aunt. (we need *that*) (See page 268.)
7. (a) The lady that I live with is my aunt.
   (b) The lady I live with is my aunt.

(c) either (a) or (b) (See page 268.)
8. (a) The man that I live with is my uncle.
   (b) The man who I live with is my uncle.
   (c) either (a) or (b) (See page 268.)
9. (a) This is the place where we saw the bear.
   (c) This is the place we saw the bear.
   (d) either (a) or (c) (See page 268.)
10. (a) The ostrich, which is the largest bird in the world, is found in Africa. (talking about the species) (See page 272.) However, in (b) "The ostrich which is the largest bird in the world..." (without commas) implies one particular ostrich is the largest bird in the world.
11. (a) Matt, the friend who lives in the city, is having a party tonight.
    (b) Matt, who lives in the city, is having a party tonight.
    (c) either (a) or (b) (See page 272.)
12. Which is more natural?
    (a) Did you hear what happened? (See page 275.)
13. (a) She helped save the injured koala.
    (b) She helped to save the injured koala.
    (c) either (a) or (b) (See page 278.)
14. (a) The teacher made her do it again. (See page 278.)
15. (a) We had the carpet cleaned.
    (b) We got the carpet cleaned.
    (c) either (a) or (b) (See page 280.)
16. (a) They had him perform for the class. We could say "They got him to perform for the class." (See page 280.)
17. The train should be here soon...
    (b) here it comes! (See page 283.)
18. We're finished. Let's celebrate!
    (b) Let's = Let us (See page 278.)

index

final thoughts

We all learn by understanding core concepts and connecting new information to what we know. This book explains connections I have found while exploring English to find what different parts of the language mean and how they work together. Languages are ever-changing systems and there is always more to be discovered. This book was written to help others discover basic truths of English and the beauty of how languages combine simple components to achieve so much.

The English language is constantly changing and evolving. This book shows how international English works based on the experiences of a 35 year old Australian in 2016 who has spent many years abroad interacting with a variety of English speakers from different backgrounds. We all have different experiences with our language and there will be some differences in how people use English, largely due to their age and where they are from. This book aims to address the core concepts of the language that we all share in common.

I wrote this book to move away from the rules and exceptions that are currently used to teach grammar. I see no evidence of exceptions within a language. Everything happens for a reason. In my view, if there is an exception to a rule, the rule simply doesn't fit and should be refined or discarded. While researching for this book I have reworked and dismissed many rules and explanations that work most of the time but don't fit every situation. This has pushed me to go deeper to find the core meanings that always hold true.

> "Virtually everything in language falls into systematic patterns, even the seeming exceptions, if only you bother to look for them."
> - Steven Pinker,
> The Language Instinct

The explanations in this book are based on my experiences interacting in English and in-depth grammar research to make sure my explanations fit with all uses of each word or structure. However, learning is an ongoing process. I have learned a lot while researching for this book but I am continuing to find out new interesting things about the language and how it is used all the time.

This book was written to provide you with the initial framework you need to get started. I hope that by reading this book, you have a deeper understanding of how the English language really works.

I wish you all the best with your studies,

Carl

Stay up to date at www.realgrammar.com.

Made in the USA
Las Vegas, NV
27 June 2024